PENGUIN BOOKS

THE HOMINID GANG

Delta Willis is a writer and photographer whose work has appeared in many magazines, including *Omni, Connoisseur,* and *People.* For seven years she worked with the producer of the *Survival* wildlife documentaries, featured on PBS. She lives on a boat in New York City.

To Norman Tomdin
With thanks for your
help and friendship over
the years! and may your
bones always rattle!

Delta Willis

1 June 1991 New York

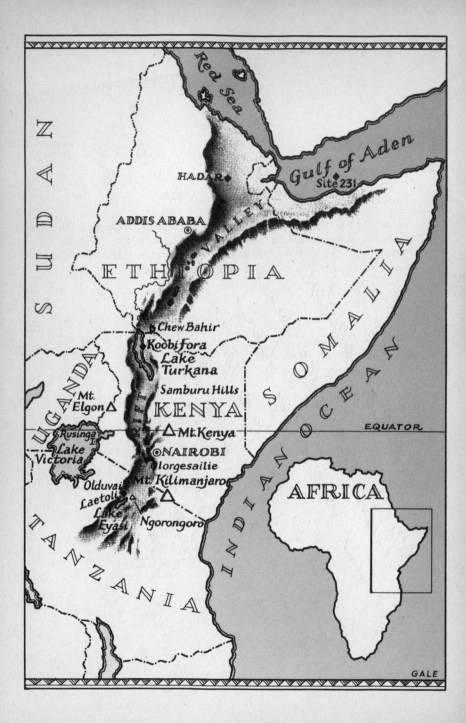

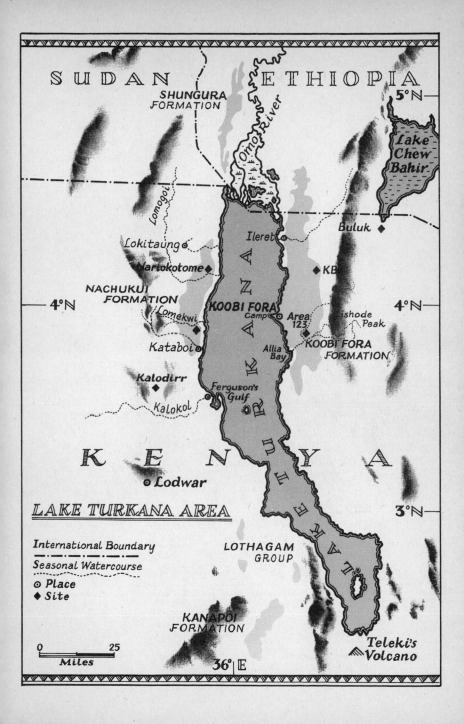

LAKE TURKANA AREA

International Boundary
Seasonal Watercourse
⊙ Place
◆ Site

0   25
Miles

DELTA
WILLIS

The
Hominid
Gang

Behind the
Scenes in
the Search
for Human
Origins

INTRODUCTION BY
STEPHEN JAY GOULD

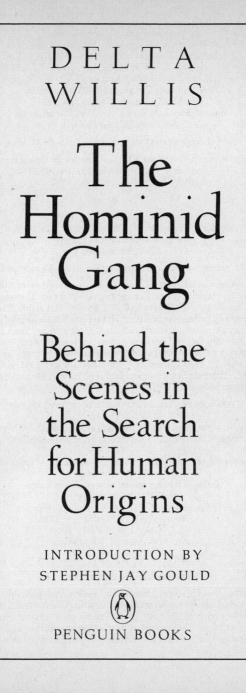

PENGUIN BOOKS

PENGUIN BOOKS
Published by the Penguin Group
Viking Penguin, a division of Penguin Books USA Inc.,
375 Hudson Street, New York, New York 10014, U.S.A.
Penguin Books Ltd, 27 Wrights Lane, London W8 5TZ, England
Penguin Books Australia Ltd, Ringwood, Victoria, Australia
Penguin Books Canada Ltd, 2801 John Street,
Markham, Ontario, Canada L3R 1B4
Penguin Books (N.Z.) Ltd, 182–190 Wairau Road,
Auckland 10, New Zealand

Penguin Books Ltd, Registered Offices: Harmondsworth, Middlesex, England

First published in the Unted States of America by Viking Penguin,
a division of Penguin Books USA Inc., 1989
Published in Penguin Books 1991

1 3 5 7 9 10 8 6 4 2

All photographs by the author unless otherwise indicated.

Grateful acknowledgment is made for permission to reprint the following copyrighted works: Excerpt from script for the Universe program hosted by Walter Cronkite. © CBS, Inc. All rights reserved. Reprinted by permission of CBS, Inc. Excerpts from letters by Glynn Isaac. By permission of Barbara Isaac. Excerpts from "The Clock of Evolution" by Stephen Jay Gould, *Natural History*, April 1985. By permission of *Natural History*. Material from *Nature*, issues of November 20, 1980, December 4, 1980, January 1–8, 1981, February 26, 1981, December 16, 1982, and January 24, 1985. By permission of Macmillan Magazines Ltd.

LIBRARY OF CONGRESS CATALOGING IN PUBLICATION DATA
Willis, Delta.
The Hominid Gang: behind the scenes in the search for human
origins/Delta Willis; introduction by Stephen Jay Gould.
p.   cm.
"First published in the United States of America by Viking Penguin
. . . 1989"—T. p. verso.
Includes bibliographical references and index.
ISBN 0 14 01.4732 2
1. Fossil man—Africa, East.   2. Human evolution.
3. Anthropology, Prehistoric.   I. Title.
[GN282.W55 1991]
573.3—dc20   90–44964

Printed in the United States of America

Maps and line drawings by Bob Gale

To my most
recent ancestors,
my mother
and father

Contents

Color photographs follow p. 208.

Introduction

No subject in the evolutionary sciences could possibly be more important than paleoanthropology—the study of human fossils—in our attempt to fulfill the Socratic injunction: know thyself. Unfortunately, no subject is more encumbered by bias and mythology arising from our extreme reluctance to treat such a close and emotive issue with dispassion.

In our unwillingness to think clearly, we often follow one or the other extreme of unreason. Either we try to separate humans from the rest of nature as something uniquely unanalyzable by science, or, with even greater hubris, we try to interpret all nature in our inappropriate terms. (I call the first strategy "the picket fence," and recall A. R. Wallace's claim that natural selection could not account for the human brain, which must represent a direct and divine effusion. I call the second strategy the "encompassing wave," and think of so many natural phenomena—"slavery" in ants, for example—that we mischaracterize in our tendency to anthropomorphize.)

Humans are such pathetically fallible creatures, yet all the more worthy of compassion for our weaknesses. Even if we break through these conceptual barriers and recognize humans as part of nature, but endowed with some wonderful specializations, including consciousness, we must still face another set of myths about the procedures of science. For even if we get the conclusions right, we will not understand science until we grasp the methods for reaching these conclusions.

Mythology about methods also clusters at two extremes—the romanticism of solitary intuition in the field, and the stereotype of disciplined research teams twirling dials and reading numbers in a laboratory. The reality of paleoanthropology explodes both these myths: fieldwork must be intensely organized and systematic; how else do you avoid tsetse flies, keep the trucks running, and maintain adequate supplies of water in deserts? Lab work can be a solitary, seat-of-the-pants, gum-and-shoestring operation.

Chronicles of actual practice, written by people who know the work in an intimate day-by-day manner, are our best sources of insight into the actual practice *and* content of science—and therefore our best antidote to all these mythologies. Fine works of this genre are among the rarest commodities of good writing in science. Some have been done by practicing scientists themselves, most notably (in recent years) Jim Watson's *The Double Helix*. Others have been composed by writers who make the rare step of immersing themselves so deeply into the daily lives of scientists that they develop the requisite, but nearly indefinable, "feel" of professional understanding. (John McPhee's several books about geology, notably *Basin and Range*, are the best recent examples.)

The Hominid Gang lies firmly in this second and rarest genre of books by good writers who truly understand by dint of penetrating intelligence and extraordinary effort. Delta Willis did not grow up with the advantages of museums on the next block, or fossils in her backyard. She hails from Arkansas where, in her words, "the teaching of evolution was legally banned when I attended high school, and I developed crow's feet before I could spell 'australopithecine.' " An interest in African travel and wildlife prompted her fascination with human origins. For several years now, she has traveled to field sites with leading paleontologists, hiked all over East Africa, haunted libraries, laboratories, museums, and university corridors—all to understand science as daily practice, replete with drudgery, tedium, boredom, inefficiency, and failure.

The Hominid Gang gives ample space to names in the news, for these people are leaders in research. But Delta Willis also shows us the true complexity and camaraderie of science as a collective enterprise. She has followed and questioned the people who do not make daily news, but who form the backbone of our industry. The book's title honors the greatest of all fossil finders and keepers—the corps of African professionals who work with Richard Leakey through the National Museums of Kenya: The Hominid Gang. ("Leakey's luck" is euphonious mythology. Speak rather of Leakey's skill in training so many keen observers. Fossils in the Rift Valley are needles in haystacks; you find them by patience and manpower, not serendipity.) We meet Kamoya Kimeu, greatest of all observers and discoverers; Emma Mbua, curator of the Hominid Vault; Joseph Mutaba, dean of preparators. Also the Western scientists who join in this international effort: Shirley Strum and her studies of baboon behavior; Alan Walker and his uncanny skill in reconstructing fossils; Peter Jones the toolmaker; Rick Potts the taphonomist; Frank Brown, geologist extraordinaire (and subject of Willis's most impressive chapter on a crucial subject left out of almost every popular account until this book). Paleoanthropology is not a battle between Leakey and Johanson, but a focus for a hundred skills and professionalisms, each backed by people of excellence.

In 1872, Charles Darwin correctly surmised from very little evidence (and no fossils at all) that humans had evolved in Africa. The evidence of fossils, now combined with impressive data from the human family tree as reconstructed by genetic distances among modern groups, has affirmed and extended Darwin's insight. Africa is the mother continent of us all—not only for the basic split of ape and human lineages some six to eight million years ago, but also for the origin of every single species on the hominid tree thereafter—all the australopithecines, *Homo habilis, Homo erectus*, and *Homo sapiens*, otherwise known as us. Thus, the greatest and most ample stories of human history are told by the fossil record of Africa—subject of *The Hominid Gang*.

We care about all this because we are human. We can't help it; primates are curious animals—and paleoanthropology holds the key to some of the greatest riddles of existence, insofar as science can address such subjects at all: who are we? where do we come from? what does life mean anyway? Knowledge has sometimes been downgraded or even feared for misuse (based on unethical practices that cannot be part of science). In this year of the two-hundredth anniversary of the French Revolution, we must strive to recover that fundamental faith of the Enlightenment—that knowledge is liberating, and that the pursuit of knowledge is our most sublime task.

—STEPHEN JAY GOULD

THE

HOMINID

GANG

Prologue

Ex Africa semper aliquid novi:
Africa is always producing some novelty.
—Pliny the Elder

The term "Hominid Gang" was coined in the late sixties to describe a team of Africans trained in the fine art of fossil finding. Fossilized bones, as such, are relatively abundant in the terrain they survey, for the geological faults and eroding winds of Africa's Great Rift Valley reveal a virtual bestiary of the former world, from massive elephant to the delicate cocoon of a locust. Their weekly bounty might include the skull of a saber tooth cat, giraffe more curious than the present form, or antelope of a prodigious nature, with horns spanning six feet. Theirs are revelations of unimaginable change and occasionally the unthinkable, for they seek with special dedication the remains of ancient hominids, of Hominidae, the family of "Man."

The term "hominid" includes us as well as our ancestors; by this scientists denote an upright primate, an ape that found advantage in surveying its world by means of a bipedal gait. A hominoid, on the other hand, is a quadrupedal ape, and one of the most intriguing questions is when and how this transition occurred, and whether the missing link was a knuckle-walker. It's hardly an item of daily discussion, though the consequences of such adaptations as bipedalism and a large brain certainly are.

I had no particular interest in the subject when I began to visit Africa twelve years ago, and less than visceral responses to discoveries that literally surrounded me, frequently explaining that I was more interested in endangered species—a stance I now see as ironic.

Eight species of hominids are known, seven of these based only on the earth's fossil record and therefore extinct. The only one surviving chose to name itself *Homo sapiens sapiens*, or "wise Man," with the emphasis on our wisdom. Wise is the creature who knows its history and knows that time is no intruder, but the passage of nature, without units divided arbitrarily. Yet the mind of the modern hominid prefers some order, a sense of resolution, and often as not a terrible simplicity, which will become familiar in these pages as a tyranny of dichotomies.

As is the habit of humans to create order by dichotomies, hominid species are grouped under two genera: *Homo*, often deemed "true Man," and the australopithecines, or "Southern Ape," so named because the first specimen was found in South Africa. Knowing an australopithecine when you see one depends on the eye of the beholder. Experts disagree on the older hominid specimens, which may reflect less on their expertise than on the puzzle nature has presented them.

Characteristics of both *Homo* and *Australopithecus* feature in the bones in question, which ought to happen in a search for intermediary forms. Nevertheless, such led to a widely publicized "rivalry" between paleoanthropologists Richard Leakey and Don Johanson, which created a sort of dust devil around hominids, obscuring what is known.

These fossils from Africa suggest our older ancestors were not so neatly distinguished from the chimpanzee, that for well over three million years intermediate forms lived. As I was uneducated in the matter of missing links, and therefore somewhat unconvinced, the work of the Hominid Gang attracted my attention.

In the beginning, they numbered only half a dozen men, and their survey was largely confined to a 500-square-mile region east of Lake Turkana, just below the Kenya/Ethiopia border. Their numbers have since grown and the team has dispersed to new sites in Kenya, to Baragoi in the Samburu Hills, to a place called Buluk, at the southern tip of Lake Chew Bahir, and in Tanzania, at Laetoli, thirty miles south of Olduvai Gorge. They frequently work in tandem with scientists—paleoanthropologists who interpret the hominids they find, geologists who determine the age of the fossils, and paleontologists who delight in their bounty. Occasionally they return to an old site, like Rusinga Island on Lake Victoria, where one of the most famous "missing links"—of great antiquity, the sixteen-million-year-old *Proconsul*—was found. Twenty-eight new sites along the western shores of Lake Turkana now compete for their attention.

The monsoons inspired by the Indian Ocean dictate their schedule. Surveys are concentrated during the dry seasons in East Africa, from mid-June until September, and from December until the rains begin in March or April. Their eyes seek a subtle hint of bone against a horizon both hostile and breathtaking, a landscape kindly described as parched grandeur, where the outpourings of volcanoes reflect the heat of the equatorial sun, where collisions and upheavals of the earth's crust have pushed old sediments up, reporting the past to the present. The final exposure of fossils usually relies on the winds, though "final" is misleading. This search belongs in a file marked Unfinished Business.

The odds of finding a hominid bone have been put at one in a billion, and (subsequently) one in ten million. A discovery made in August 1984 by the leader of this team, Kamoya Kimeu (Kah-'moy-yah Kah-'meo), mocked the odds in a comprehensive fashion. To find a more complete ancient skeleton, one would need to exhume the European burial sites of the Neandertal—a figure of relative recency in the chronology of human origins, around seventy thousand years ago.

Yet this skeleton was found in African soil, in sediments dated at 1.6 million years old. In a search where controversy often greets discoveries, where (according to Yale paleoanthropologist Andrew Hill) participants "commonly stab each other in the front" over the naming of fossils, the designation of these bones as a *Homo erectus* met no challenge. And in a search notoriously long on assertions and short of evidence, where fragmentary finds are reconstructed toward fiction, here was evidence in irrefutable detail.

It has a skull and plenty of teeth, it has arm bones and leg bones and even delicate shoulder blades that when held to the sun admit light. The teeth revealed it was a teenager, the pelvis suggested it was a male, the leg bones confirmed that it walked upright—the stance for which *erectus* is named. The full forehead and a round smooth cranium indicate this skull embraced a brain substantially larger than the australopithecines'—a large brain being the paramount characteristic for *Homo*. Its name is so apt that even a cynic should smile, which in this instance might be the result of a contagious reaction: because of the extraordinary complement of teeth (and now, an inability to frown) the skeleton boasts an everlasting smile. It is known as the Turkana Boy, honoring both the name of the vast lake in northern Kenya and the nomadic people who still live along the western shores where it was found.

The skeleton of the Turkana Boy was reassembled to near perfection. There are 206 bones in a skeleton such as mine and yours; the count on ancient hominids is the same—the bones differ only in form.

The differences on the Turkana Boy are slight, but every detail was solicited.

Several members of the Hominid Gang, research scientists from the National Museums of Kenya, and a writer who'd expressed a desire to see exactly how fossils were found, took the hands-and-knees approach to digging for a few missing toes and finger bones. We inched away at soil aptly denoted as sandstone; our tools were steel picks of a less relentless nature than the sun. Occasionally I joined the sieving team, washing excavated soil at the lakeshore, pinching tiny clods in search of a toebone, a fingertip. There were days, and weeks, when nothing was found. They had been digging for two field seasons before I arrived and they continued two seasons after I'd gone. That the Turkana Boy might become a hundred percent says something for human determination, that in a terrain where time is sovereign and the earth does not impart such secrets easily, the exception inspires, as if a phoenix might arise from ashes.

The Turkana Boy is only one of the discoveries featured in this account, a single episode in what insiders often refer to as "an explosion of evidence." The phrase accommodates both a surge in fossil discoveries and a little time bomb set off by the biochemical community in Berkeley, drawing up the family tree by means of molecules. New technology dictated that the minute would figure in the abysmal. Of course it always figured, but it took vision to make this connection between contemporary forms and the primordial soup. From within the strands of the double helix and the amazingly individual complaints of the immune system, the order of descent leapt across a notorious fossil gap, a curious absence of bones between four and fourteen million years old. There are many fossil gaps in the earth's record of all sorts of creatures, but this one is particularly confounding because it covers a time frame when hominids presumably made the big break from apes. This entry by a seemingly disparate discipline lent the search a certain momentum. The discrepancies could be viewed as horrible mistakes, they could inspire new rivalries and great headlines, like the "Bones vs. Blood War." They could also inspire a new direction of inquiry. Such discrepancies were the place to look.

The value of dialogue between disciplines is a central theme of this book. (The odds against finding it were said to be a million to one.) It surfaced with all the regularity of a hominid fossil, because in many instances such dialogue is curtailed by egos, or off the record. In the days of Darwin, you could read of doubts and surprises in correspondence; today, such exchanges occur on the telephone or in the laboratory—which in many cases is the field. The second theme is context, particularly time; consequently I tread lightly on the third theme, that of extinction. The fossil record may suggest that our own extinction is inevitable, but for every law of nature, there is an outlaw, and of all the novelties that Africa produced, there is still no reasonable explanation as to what initially inspired an African ape to set out on the long road to become, say, a composer of crossword puzzles, or for that matter, "A Fanfare for the Common Man." What might seem hyperbole dazzles when you consider the relative brevity of such a path, what Stephen Jay Gould refers to as a geological millisecond.

Geology is central to this inquiry, for the earth's strata provide context for these bones. For this reason alone the work of geologist Frank Brown should figure. As it happens, the African terrain was a personal interest, and the clarity of geological terms appealed to me—in inverse proportion to the cumbersome and confounding nomenclature for hominids. The bias of a writer figures here, for I sought the clear expression of geology as an inroad to understanding the rest.

Within these pages you will find names not commonly associated with the search for human origins. The focus shifts from fossil finders to those who seek their clues in laboratories far afield—and in many instances this involves the minute. There are people who study evidence as diminutive as fossil pollen, others microscopic scratches on hominid teeth, the shape of snails, the ooze of an ocean bog. The ancient environment of Africa is being reconstructed in stunning detail.

Charles Darwin reasoned that missing links should surface in Africa, simply because this was the provenance of the great apes— the hominoids. Darwin's suggestion occurred well over a century ago, but until the 1950s a form of apartheid prevailed among most researchers, an "apartness" that preferred our origins anywhere but in Africa—in China and Mongolia, in the Piltdown gravels of the United Kingdom, along the banks of France's Dordogne, in Java. The first missing link found in African soil was denied its legitimacy for three decades.

Ironically, the phrase that once disparaged the first australopithecine discovered in 1924—that of "an odd African ape"—now finds favor among scientists describing modern humans: "We are apes," some put it bluntly. Both the beauty and the bane of this search lie in the human view of it. Paleontologist J. T. Robinson, noticing more humanlike characteristics in fossils he'd previously described as "those brutes," promptly began to refer to them as "these chaps."

During the late fifties to the mid-seventies, the search seemed to be a contest to find the oldest ancestor. Hominid discoveries, whatever their antiquity, continued to be held aloft in certain exaltation from the rest of creatures on the landscape. But as anatomist Alan Walker says, "If you really wanted to learn about evolution, the last thing you'd be looking for is hominid bones." It's akin to writing the history of China by reading fortune cookies—a recent invention of American-based restaurants. Walker, it should be said, is unusually successful at discovering hominids, unearthing the so-called black skull in 1985. But he is also representative of a new bent in the search that prefers to refine data before resolving ideas.

From Nairobi to Berkeley, evidence is being analyzed, debunked, and reconsidered with a new intensity. Much of this required a big eraser. The veracity of the Turkana Boy is exceptional in that it did not require a new name or a revision in the branches of our family tree. Other discoveries did.

The time frame for this inquiry (1982–88) is fortuitous. In addition to the Turkana Boy and the "black skull" (an australopithecine), other new sites on the west side of Kenya's Lake Turkana delivered. Three unknown skulls surfaced at a Miocene site called Kalodirr. And the oldest stone tools ever found in Kenya—2.3 million years old—lay strewn across a West Turkana site that remains unnamed. More ancient tools were found in Zaire; and in Tanzania, Olduvai Gorge proved that good sites never die, they just erode away—revealing more fossils. New evidence from DNA suggested a single female source for all modern hominids, a concept promptly dubbed the Theory of Eve. From deep-sea core drillings there arose an extraordinary record of climatic changes. From the ashes of volcanoes another sort of missing link emerged, a comprehensive tie between hominid sites.

Now the search for our roots seems to be hung up on trees. A story that once began with a fig leaf and forbidden fruit now features branches and twigs. Branching order based on bones is inferred; even the most recent and abundant fossil evidence is confounding. Where, for example, does the Neandertal belong? There are three proposed drawings: Neandertals as an extinct species; Neandertals as an extinct subspecies; and Neandertals as ancestral to us. It all depends on how the evidence is viewed, and this depends on both the personal history of those doing the viewing, and the order in which discoveries surface. Africa imparts what the history of science confirms, that with inquiry, facts change. The Kikuyu tribe have a saying for this: The truth is like a lizard's tail. You might seize it in your hand; meanwhile, the lizard moves on, creating a whole new tail.

This is a biased book about biased scientists. I raise this early on to dispense with the myth of objectivity. It should come as no surprise that scientists might view the past based on present inclinations, as we too assume the ahistorical view, like the tourist in San Antonio who complained, "Why on earth did they decide to put the Alamo downtown?"

We tune in to science as if it were the weather report, favoring the forecaster with a sunny disposition. But when they cite the odds for extinction, assigning our very existence to the random and higgledy-piggledy, or lead us into time frames we can scarcely fathom, suggesting there were many in which we do not even appear, time frames in which the dinosaur prevailed and our ancestors were— let's face it—mammals contained in a stature akin to that of the bandicoot, we wish to seek a second opinion. They have dared to put us on the edge of a mystery that features our favorite subject, our identity. Many people thought there ought to be a law against our knowing this identity.

The teaching of evolution was legally banned when I attended high school, and I developed crow's feet before I could spell "australopithecine." The substantial gaps in my knowledge were bridged by exceptional tutors.

I am especially grateful to the many scientists who allowed me the privilege of accompanying them at work, often sharing the results of unpublished data and private doubts. Their scrutiny was invited on this manuscript; any errors are mine alone. The acknowledgments due various institutions and individuals appear on pages 325–28.

The Hominid Gang are symbolic of many unknown players—a virtual fleet of scientific sleuths who at first glance appeared to be strange scientific bedfellows. There are those who rarely set foot in Africa and those who know little else. Yet success in the search depends on the same elements that make the Hominid Gang so extraordinary—vision and elasticity: to ask, at the end of the day, what the others had seen, to doubt their own eyes, to go back over familiar terrain and grant a double-take to something they did not mark the first time, something that caught their eye because it was . . . odd.

A number of things struck me as odd during my first venture into the field, among them a hominid skull that has no name.

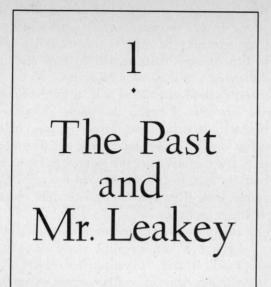

1.
The Past and Mr. Leakey

At six o'clock in the evening the shadows along the eastern shores of Kenya's Lake Turkana extend the details on this landscape, and every creature is followed by a long dark form of itself. Impartially, Africa extends my own shadow, but like most who come to this country, the novelty of the human form was never a matter of preponderance, or has worn thin, even dissipated in downtown Nairobi, capital city of the fastest-growing nation in the world, and you are drawn away by the promise of space. The Cradle of Mankind is not commonly listed on the visitor's itinerary, though safari guides often describe the elephant and rhino that you see in the game parks as "prehistoric." In this ancestral zone the prehistoric is genuinely antiquated and generally buried, for these vast horizons include layers of the earth that geologists also call horizons, revealing ancient histories of the creatures that roam the surface.

Their longest shadows are offered in haste by the equatorial sun. The distorted silhouette of a zebra that grazes along the small bay to the north quickly stretches some forty feet across golden grasses; the delicate legs of a plover are reproduced to a quarter the length of my own. A few minutes later the plover itself is barely visible, a luminescent dot against dark waters, and the zebra known only by its occasional bark. Throughout this, crocodiles imitate logs on a sandy spit known as Koobi Fora.

Kenya's Northern Frontier is not everyone's idea of a magical place. It would hold a certain appeal for stockholders in sunscreen lotions, insect repellent, and anti-venom, but readers of *The Green Hills of Africa* might demand reimbursement. Manufacturers of windmills would sense great potential. Yet there are moments when it is serene, and serenely beautiful. These occur regularly at six o'clock in the evening. I was introduced to this phenomenon in September of 1982, when the world about me became exceptionally still. Even the plover paused.

At dusk the winds tend to die, as if to announce the changes made on the landscape during the day. After midnight they begin to howl again, and the sediments to the east of the escarpment behind me were once again rearranged, as if engaged in a bitter property settlement: Erosion says, This is mine; Deposition, No, it's mine. Volcanoes cast great influence over these claims: these sediments are marked by huge formations of volcanic rock, and the lake before me is thick with alkaline as a result of hundreds of eruptions. The water is about as drinkable as the soil is arable. Such conditions make the formidable area known as East Turkana ideal for the harvest of fossils.

Other conditions make it relatively ideal. Should a fossil surface near a ravine, where they often do, it is apt to be carried downstream in the sudden rivers that form during the rainy seasons, to be smashed into bits during its journey. This is especially true of the most sought-after prize on this landscape, a fossilized skull. On very rare occasions, a fossilized brain, or endocast, is recovered, but most of our ancestors are by this time empty-headed and vulnerable. Heavy downpours can send a skull headlong toward oblivion, smashing bone against boulder, dispersing teeth. Teeth, stronger than fossilized bone, are the only likely survivors; molars rolled on the bottom of a river for long periods of time emerge in the form and luster of large brown pearls.

Occasionally these winds render a triumph of excavation. That they might take so long to do so, and that additional clues might refine ideas as they surface, was the inspiration for this book. The delivery itself was a gentle reminder of the limits of our knowledge, that so much remains buried and unknown. The first demonstration of a hominid being enhanced by a footnote occurred at Koobi Fora, at Area 123.

Only a week earlier I had explored an archeological site known as Olorgesailie (Ol-'or-ga-'sal-lee), just south of Nairobi, where hundreds of stone tools still litter the landscape. Initially these "assemblages" of tools were described as former campsites of *Homo erectus*. But no *erectus* bones have been found; some of the tools may have been delivered to their current location by floodwaters, and the age of the site has doubled. This doesn't mean the stone tools are illegitimate; and the idea of a campsite was natural, since unnaturally broken bones of baboons accompanied the tools. But the scenario surrounding the tools and the behavior of their makers is undergoing substantial revision. A few years earlier a detailed portrait of camp life would have been drawn up (indeed, such was illustrated). Now scientists describe the site with considerable caution.

While Richard Leakey is regarded as the world's foremost spokesman on human origins, he is not renowned for his caution. In his early twenties, when he first found fossils at East Turkana (then East Rudolf), he forgot to make a notation of exactly where they came from, crucial to dating the finds. In his early thirties, amid continuing challenges to the age of one of the most famous discoveries, a skull known as "1470," Leakey stubbornly defended the older date. He also preferred to designate 1470 as *Homo*, even though one of his most respected colleagues, anatomist Alan Walker, finding many characteristics of an australopithecine, urged caution.

So I had been surprised to find myself transcribing the following remarks, made by Leakey, aged thirty-eight: "When I say we don't know about the common ancestor, I really mean we don't know. And we may never know. We need more evidence. . . . We're not sure about issues like behavior or language—words don't fossilize. . . . I could speculate, but it's meaningless. . . . You've got to always be careful to indicate to your reader or your viewer the transition from what you know to what you think." Such caution emerged during an interview in Leakey's Nairobi office only a few months after I'd screened a videotape of a nationally televised program. Pressed for his version of our family tree, he abruptly drew in a huge question mark. I nearly fell off my chair. Leakey's response was admittedly extreme. It was also a reaction to passionate facts, which was sweet irony; a few years earlier he could have argued with the mirror. Somewhere in between these two dichotomies, there was promise of reasonable answers. I had long thought that the world of stones and bones deserved to remain as remote as it seemed, that the inquiry was plagued by considerable fecklessness. Now I was interested, and made plans for what had become a familiar commute to Nairobi, this time to cover unfamiliar terrain.

I first met Leakey in 1974, when I worked with the British producer of the wildlife documentaries known as the "Survival" series. "Bones of Contention," featuring his work, was broadcast on PBS that same year. There were dramatic sequences of fossil finders astride their camels, finding a complete skull perched on the landscape, as obvious as a Halloween pumpkin. Richard's wife Meave, herself a paleontologist, instantly identified the skull as an australopithecine. Even the authoritative voice of narrator John Huston didn't convince me that this was profoundly unusual.

My impression of Leakey off camera was equally shallow. At the time I felt no need to inquire further about his discoveries. Upon the heels of our introduction, he requested that I bring him a cup of coffee; I was in my dressed-for-success stage, and had my secretary deliver.

The 1982 interview in Nairobi began with Leakey pouring tea. It ended by his saying that he planned to fly up to Koobi Fora; I was welcome to come along. Since I was on an assignment for *Omni* magazine, I saw this as a photo opportunity: fossil-finder in field.

A few day later, shortly after dawn, I found Leakey waiting by his Cessna 206 at Nairobi's Wilson Airport. His large hands folded a necktie which he stuffed into the pocket of a navy blazer. It was the beginning of a metamorphosis; later, wearing safari shorts and desert boots, he would carry the standard canvas pouch of paleontologists—the briefcase of bonebrokers. In it are dental picks and brushes, a roll of toilet tissue for wrapping around fossils to protect them, and a tiny bottle of Bedacryl, a preservative used on brittle bones.

Searching for hominid fossils was not part of Leakey's carefully planned agenda for September 1982. Research at East Turkana had been officially curtailed the previous season; after over a decade of surveying the 500-square-mile region for six days a week, six months a year, other sites, some boasting older hominids, had begun to compete. Leakey's visit to Koobi Fora was a regularly scheduled bimonthly shuttle, carrying a couple of the camp staff back and forth, checking on supplies and conditions at the camp.

He prepares for takeoff with all the familiarity of driving a car. Over the past two decades Leakey has enhanced the legacy engendered by his parents, Louis and Mary Leakey, by making frequent commutes to Kenya's Northern Frontier. "Kilo–November–Mike" requests clearance; the registration numbers on the fuselage are 5Y-KNM for Kenya National Museums. Leakey is the director of the largest museum in Africa.

Every morning that he goes to work at his office, he must walk past the figure of his father, cast in bronze. Authentically decked in safari jumpsuit and desert boots, Louis Seymour Bassett Leakey holds a stone tool and challenges one's gait with an intent gaze. This statue marks the entrance to the Louis Leakey Memorial, a building that houses the museum's departments of prehistory: archeology, and paleontology. The statue has none of the remoteness of the giant Roosevelt atop his horse on the steps of the American Museum of Natural History, or of the grandiose, chiseled Lincoln overlooking the sensational antics that occur in the pond before him. It is, instead, life-sized and lifelike, with the presence of character that was

The Koobi Fora research camp figures as small dark specks pointing toward the sand spit, where crocodiles and hippos share the lake with scientists who welcome a return to Lake Turkana from the volcanic badlands.

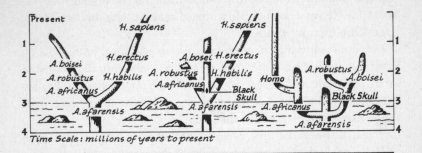

Three renderings of the hominid family tree (Bob Gale). The first (left) was proposed by Johanson and White in 1979. The second is the minimum restructuring of branches imposed by the 1985 discovery of the black skull. The third, proposed by Eric Delson, features the black skull as ancestral to A. boisei and A. robustus (Bob Gale).

"lionized" by Robert Ardrey in *African Genesis*. Richard Leakey slips by with surefootedness and a few inches to spare.

Richard was (of four) the son least favored by Louis, and challenged his father as soon as he was capable of speech. Once, at the Rusinga camp, when Louis imposed a breakfast of sardines, eggs, and rice, Richard ate the meal as ordered, then forced his finger down his throat "with predictable results," as Mary Leakey tactfully wrote in her autobiography. The offering was struck from the menu.

Formal education held equal appeal; he displayed the same enthusiasm for the classroom demonstrated by his mother a few decades earlier. Both Mary and Richard Leakey's doctorates are bestowed; Richard's are begrudged. "He's not a scientist, you know," a Nairobi journalist warned. "It's not Dr. Leakey, it's Mr. Leakey," a distinction repeated by academics in the United States when citing "the deficiencies of his education."

Yet his matriculation in this world without walls could not have been more perfectly suited. The most practical tutelage available anywhere was endowed by his parents, who demonstrated on location with visual aids, debating in the evening with learned visitors to whom new fossil evidence was served as dessert. Louis would pull fossils out of his pocket, or from a shelf, dramatically lifting the lid off a tin container normally resigned to tea or flour. Late at night in camps at Olduvai and Rusinga, a lone Coleman's lantern seemed to emit a new language, sending strange words across the still night, words like *Australopithecus africanus* and *Zinjanthropus boisei*, *Homo habilis* and *erectus*, words that confront college students, like the rest of us, in cold text, with none of the tangible hands-on reference, none of the uncovering *in situ* that made them the familiar objects of Leakey's boyhood treasure hunts—words that rolled off his tongue before he was big enough for his own pony. He unearthed his first major discovery at the age of six.

Now he subscribes to his mother's discipline and his father's interdisciplinary approach. All were stoic when confronting serious health problems; even close colleagues were unaware of Richard's debilitating renal failure, diagnosed in 1968. Ten years later he underwent a kidney transplant, courtesy of his younger brother Philip. A rejection episode followed, creating a condition described by one newspaper as "the late Richard Leakey." Leakey does not contest this, and wrote of being "reborn" in an autobiography entitled *One Life*.

Now he enjoys eating, which he didn't before, and has become an accomplished chef, like his father, with visible results. To close associates, the edges have literally smoothed. There was a time when he "never" wanted to do what his father did, and for a while he served as a safari guide. Planning research expeditions appealed to him, and once he was in the field with other scientists, the obvious potential struck—as it might one named Rothschild who happened to gaze over a vineyard the size of a small sea. Once, in a New York restaurant, Leakey greeted the maitre d' by saying, "I'm from Kenya!" the way you or I might say, "I won first prize!" He did indeed, and wasted no further time in claiming it.

"In 1967, I made a definite decision that if I was to make a career of paleontology, without a university degree, I needed to have an institutional base of my own." Leakey managed, "through unfair means, I think," to be appointed the administrative director of the Kenya Museum at the age of twenty-three. The British director was asked to resign in favor of Africanization. Leakey, Kenya-born, stepped in.

At the time, the staff numbered twenty-two; now there are over six hundred employees and annex museums dot the country. What began as a small natural history museum had no official role in archeology or anthropology, but through a series of bills submitted to the Kenya Parliament, the museums now control all research, antiquities, and archeological sites. "When I first began, sites such as Olorgesailie were under the National Parks. But I got them back." He adds: "It's all part of the game plan." The protection of antiquities in most Third World countries is perilously slack, with research of little benefit to the host country. The new Kenya laws allow prosecution in the case of theft, and visiting scientists must include a Kenya student in their field research team.

Some of his plans were contrary to his father's. "He wanted to send fossils to England for casting," Richard says, recalling an example; "I suggested we bring in some English technicians and teach our own people how to do it. He'd made some commitments and tried to push me. I said, 'Look, I'm the director.' It was a question of who could persuade the minister. I persuaded the minister; he didn't.'' As director, Richard Leakey reviews and counsels the government minister on the approval of research permits; critics view this as his way of controlling which scientists are allowed to research in Kenya.

Territorial battles lace the history of the search. In the 1920s, Americans in search of the "Dawn Man" were confined to finding dinosaur eggs in the Gobi Desert, because all research in China (rich in hominid fossils) was granted to Swedish investigators. In 1985, American paleoanthropologist Donald Johanson announced an "exclusive" agreement for the Institute of Human Origins at Berkeley, which he directs, to research in Tanzania.

Paleoanthropologists in the active stage of field research number less than a dozen. The majority spend the better part of their year teaching at universities or serving as curators to museum collections, their field research, at best, confined to six weeks a year. No one else has command of a territory more clearly marked or aggressively surveyed than the one Leakey traverses in his Cessna. Consequently, there is no shortage of opinion on Leakey, or the fossils he holds aloft at a press conference.

Beyond limited access to fossils, this is not a scientific discipline that attracts grants easily, nor are there many Americans willing to write a check to a foundation so that our kinship with apes might be more vividly demonstrated. A substantial number prefer the stance of the wife of the Bishop of Worcester, who is said to have exclaimed upon hearing of Darwin's suggestion of our kinship with apes, "Let us hope it is not true, but if it is, let us pray that it will not become generally known." Proof of kinship has been demonstrated by biochemical evidence; the complex structure of proteins in chimpanzees differs less than 1 percent from ours; experiments with DNA suggest a similar tie. The anatomical similarities are visible despite large gaps in the fossil record; you don't have to be an anatomist to recognize an ancestor. Yet paleontology, unlike biochemistry, remains a low-profile science. Should some paleoanthropologist actually find the Common Ancestor, the missing link between hominids and apes, the feat would not be eligible for the Nobel Prize.

Public interest in the subject was largely inspired by the extraordinary charm and energy of Louis Leakey. Tall, robust, with a quick clip to his voice and a twinkle in his eye, Louis Leakey might easily have persuaded the Bishop of Worcester's wife to become his publicity agent. He was the first to obtain funding from the National Geographic Society, and set the pace for promotion by publishing popular books. (In addition to various scientific publications, the elder Leakey wrote two autobiographies and was writing a third when he died in 1972.) He attracted large audiences and he lectured often, for a fee. His son expanded the public forum with a BBC television series and a companion book, *The Making of Mankind*. Richard Leakey undertakes two lecture tours in the United States every year, averaging two weeks long. Podium to podium, he is not so much a frequent flyer as a connecting passenger; another night, another campus; his London/New York leg employs the Concorde.

The wheels of the single-engined Cessna clear the fence designed to keep zebra and antelope in neighboring Nairobi National Park from delaying flights. We climb toward the southwest, over the Ngong Hills. As we clear the crest of these hills—like "blue waves against the sky," wrote Karen Blixen—the altimeter, relying on a barometric reading, stays relatively steady, but the landscape suddenly changes like a jumpcut in a film—from green, near, and lush, to hazy, distant, and arid—the latter inching its way toward sea level. Just last week I had driven around these hills on the road to Olorgesailie, descending by hairpin curves down into the eastern branch of the Great Rift Valley.

The Great Rift Valley is a huge ragged scar in the face of the earth that stretches through seven countries, from the southernmost tip of Turkey to Mozambique. The Rift is nothing if not great; on a clear day it is visible from the moon. It began around fourteen million years ago when the earth's crust started to pull apart from east to west, creating what geologists refer to as a zone of divergence. General chaos ensued, with volcanoes erupting, blasting boulders, spewing red pyroclastics. The greatest activity occurred in what is known today as Ethiopia's Afar Triangle, where the African and Arabian plates of the earth's crust collided in a geological "hotspot."

The ashes and boulders from one hundred and twenty-five volcanic eruptions are used to date the fossils found by the Hominid Gang.

All this complementary data originated from heat deep within the earth, a planet yet to cool from its own origins. Stretched thin, the crust of the earth domed, buckled and dropped to form the floor of the Rift Valley, leaving tall escarpments on the side. The scenario was complex; a rift valley, by definition, features two parallel fault lines marking collisions and upheavals. At various points these faults are less parallel than at others, so different pressures came to bear at different times. Leakey explains: "In some cases it's not the floor that has dropped, but the shoulder of the Rift that has been pushed up." He describes what I had difficulty perceiving on the road. "When you left Nairobi, which is at 5,500 feet, you dropped down because Olorgesailie is at about 4,000 feet. Those 1,500 feet represent strata that were laid down by volcanoes." The Ngong Hills, for example, are volcanic, as is Mount Olorgesailie. "But if you drove north, to Lake Naivasha, even though you appear to drop down en route, you're actually climbing up to about 8,000 feet before you begin to drop into the Great Rift Valley. That's the shoulder being pushed up. Lake Naivasha, at 6,000 feet, is higher than Nairobi." But Naivasha, at 6,000, is in the floor of the Rift; Nairobi, at 5,500, is on the shoulder.

Naivasha was one of the lakes formed when the floor of the Rift settled, creating basins that collected the rains. These lakes—in their current names of Baringo, Chew Bahir, Nakuru, Natron, Turkana, Olduvai, and Olorgesailie—each reveal evidence of ancient hominids along their former shorelines.

The land far beneath our wings represents an engraved invitation to salt water. The Rift expands more rapidly in the north than it does here; the Red Sea is an ocean in a youthful stage. If the expansion of the Rift continues, someday the sharks of the Red Sea may glide where now a shadow of wings traces our wide bank to the north. Koobi Fora lies two hours and forty minutes away.

The Koobi Fora research camp wasn't even on the map a couple of decades earlier, yet today it is a name that marks indelibly the provenance of ancient hominids. Like Olduvai Gorge in Tanzania, Hadar in Ethiopia's Afar Triangle, and various sites in South Africa,

Koobi Fora has become a bold star on the maps featured in *National Geographic*. Distant constellations appear in China, in Europe and Asia, but Africa's Great Rift Valley offers hominid fossils of the greatest antiquity, so it is known as the Cradle of Mankind—the source. The Neandertal of Germany and the Cro-Magnon from France appeared in later chapters in human origins, after the migration of hominids out of Africa, and both are associated with *Homo sapiens*, which became extinct forty thousand years ago. Older finds in China, Asia, and Europe are largely *Homo erectus*. In addition to being the most complete hominid skeleton ever found, the Turkana Boy unearthed on the west side of Lake Turkana is also the oldest *Homo erectus*, at 1.6 million years.

The rock-strewn sediments east of the Koobi Fora camp have produced hominid fossils nearly two million years old. Older hominid fossils have been found at other sites in Kenya, and in Ethiopia and Tanzania. Substantial gaps appear in the fossil record between two million and three million. Substantial gaps appear after four million. But the most confounding gap is any fossil evidence of the penultimate missing link, the common ancestor between hominids and apes, thought to exist around six million years ago. The ancient fossil record picks up again at fourteen million years ago, and does so with increasing abundance back to twenty million years ago. The older fossils are generally considered hominoid, though one fifteen-million-year-old find, known as *Ramapithecus*, was suggested as the oldest *hominid* until very recently, when new discoveries indicated that the split between apes and hominids occurred much later, and that these bones were ancestral to today's orangutan.

The discovery of the Neandertal Man in 1857 inspired a science of contests and controversy, long frustrated and some would say illegitimate. The bold brow ridges of the Neandertal were initially thought to be the result of brows furrowed in pain. A tooth found in North America in 1922 was proclaimed the Nebraska Man; additional discoveries proved the molar was that of a pig. There were numerous gaffes, the clues enigmatic because they were elusive. The rules of science require comprehensiveness: rich data, population surveys, documented patterns.

The gaps in the hominid fossil record are sufficiently elastic to embrace almost any theory. This, along with the fragmentary nature of most finds, makes it relatively easy to say, Oh, sure, I know what this is, and how it relates to that. And there is little to refute such arguments.

This deficit is being addressed nowhere with more intensity than in the area known broadly as the Turkana basin, which extends its topographical features north just across the Ethiopian border, west to the volcanic mountains on the other side of the lake, and just below Teleki's volcano at the southern tip of the lake. Fossils buried for one or two or even seventeen million years emerge at a pace assigned by the winds. For the humans who chance upon these clues to former worlds and former selves, the experience qualifies as a terrestrial first contact. Yet these bones are just as likely to confirm the limits of our knowledge. At least now nature appears to be the Joker in the deck.

There are many theories as to the source of the famous Piltdown hoax; some favor Sir Arthur Conan Doyle. The creator of Sherlock Holmes not only lived near the Piltdown gravels but was apt to confound scientific sleuths. In any case, the discovery of a large skull and primitive jaw of the Piltdown Man in England in 1912 confirmed the expectations of the day, and considerable pride was attached to the notion of humanity arising in the British Empire. With this "evidence" in hand, the first hominid discovered in Africa in 1924 was rejected, an orphan of reason. It could not be a hominid: there was no evidence of a large brain; the skull was that of a child's.

Big-headedness, in hindsight, should not have influenced the interpretation; the principal distinction of a hominid is a bipedal gait. Evidence of bipedalism requires neither leg bones nor pelvis as testimony. A central clue figures in the bottom of every hominid skull, where a round gap allows attachment to the spine. This is known as the *foramen magnum*—literally, "big hole." In hominids, the *foramen magnum* appears at the very bottom of the skull; in apes, it is more to the rear of the skull. Because a hominid stands upright, its skull rests atop the vertical spine.

The *foramen magnum* at the base of the skull was one of the clues noted on the discovery from South Africa by anatomist Raymond Dart. Although it is known informally as the Taung child, after the Taung limestone quarries where it was found, Dart assigned it the scientific name *Australopithecus*, or "Southern Ape," for its classification of genus, and *africanus* as the species: Southern Ape from Africa. (Dart called it an ape based on the precedent *Hesperopithecus*, or "Western Ape," honoring the complex rules of official nomenclature. But he argued rightly though unsuccessfully that *Australopithecus* was a hominid.) Dart created the new name because several characteristics distinguished the Taung child from the Neandertal and Java Man, both forms of *Homo*. Incredibly, the Taung child was accompanied by an endocast, or fossilized brain; equally incredible, Dart was an expert on neurological form, and found furrows and grooves on this fossilized brain that distinguish hominids from apes. It was hominid.

But very few scientists were familiar with this new line of neurological evidence, and other diagnostic clues were obscured by Dart's sensational writing. Among much of the scientific community, who preferred human origins anywhere but Africa, the Taung child was perceived as "an odd African ape." The legitimacy of the australopithecines was eventually enhanced by further finds from South Africa at the same time that the illegitimacy of the Piltdown Man was exposed, triggered by the observations of a geologist named Kenneth Oakley. The hoax ended in 1953—forty-one years after the "discovery" at Piltdown gravels.

A historian of the episode, Frank Spencer, allowed that Piltdown was presented to "an unsuspecting scientific community." Normally this qualifies as oxymoron, yet there was subsequent misinterpretation of real evidence, like *Ramapithecus*. In the case of the Piltdown Man, a bony hinge linking the skull to the jaw was curiously absent. In the case of *Ramapithecus*, the composition was based on authentic fossils, a lower jaw broken into two pieces. In hominids, the tooth row is U-shaped; in hominoids, it was V-shaped. The lower jaw of the *Ramapithecus* was broken down the center. If you put it together one way, it was a hominid. If you put it together another, it was a hominoid. In each case, the context of time proved key to the true interpretation of the bones. In the search for human origins, a relatively small group of scientists work backward in reconstructing a story that extends deep into the Miocene era, twenty million years ago.

Flying to Lake Turkana from the capital city of Nairobi requires taking leave of the present. There are visual cues en route, a remarkable and endlessly satisfying in-flight movie.

Before the Rift began, much of this area was covered in rain forests, like those that still exist to the western side of the Valley, in Uganda, Zaire, and Rwanda. The last two countries are home to the great mountain gorillas that do not exist on the eastern, more arid side of the Valley. Many scientists view the developing Rift as a zone of divergence in human origins, suggesting that the change from forest to savanna inspired the bipedal stance of hominids— descending out of the trees, as it were, because the trees became sparse. As we transcend from fertile highlands to semi-arid terrain, such an environmental shift (in color if not time) is demonstrated below.

Green hills swell. Then blond sediments appear, peppered with dark, dull gray shrub. North of Lake Baringo, ephemeral streams etch their potential return in the sand. Boulders of volcanoes lie dark and distinct on sandy terrain, where they were arrested by gravity and remain, testimony to their one act.

I study a roadmap on my knee. There are no roads to be seen below us. There are no charts for navigation. Leakey generally ignores the compass but navigates by the familiar shape of the lakes, the paths of rivers and streams, evergreen forest, and occasionally a curiously polka-dotted grassland, the result of termites.

To the northeast of Kito Pass rises the volcano Silali. Vents pocket Silali's slopes, where a hot spring attained a lofty position, producing a waterfall. To the west rise the Cherangani Hills, assigned vertical drama by erosion. Now we're over badlands. Camel paths link the horizons with loose, pale threads.

Two hours into the flight, Lake Turkana makes itself known, a mercurial shimmer suspended on the horizon, as if it floated above the actual shoreline. We cross Teleki's volcano and fly nearly three quarters the length of this 180-mile-long body of water, descending over crocodiles and hippos that appear along Allia Bay.

A sandy spit curls across the water like the toe of a Tibetan shoe—

Koobi Fora. The thatched rooftops of the research camp appear, a small cluster of flagstone huts. There is a hint of a dirt airstrip, which from my point of view appears equal in length to a suburban driveway.

Leakey tells me the strip at Koobi Fora was intentionally kept short to discourage visitors. (There is another strip for tourists visiting the Koobi Fora Museum, southeast of the scientific camp.) The total length of the runway is 428 yards; cross winds reach up to 25 knots at a 75-degree angle and pale grasses have taken advantage of absent traffic. The prop falls still. The pilot unfolds his six foot two frame and consults his watch. He announces that the wind should change its course. Within a few minutes, it neatly obliges. I suspect a pact.

Having landed smoothly, we make our way to the largest thatched-roof enclosure, surrounded by smaller *bandas*, or stone huts. A large open dining room is in the center, with storerooms and labs on the side; a verandah faces the lake, and the "kitchen," is a campfire out back. There are bones everywhere, stacked upon each other and on the concrete floor, stretching in piles across wooden tables: massive jaws of elephant and rhino, skulls of antelope, pig palates and pig teeth, hippo skulls and crocodile jaws. All these bones are contemporary and therefore white, bleached by the sun, with none of the hue of antiquity of fossils, though it's not always so easy to tell. When in doubt, a test is applied in the form of the discoverer's wet tongue: the tongue often sticks to a modern bone, still porous, but a fossilized bone might feel as smooth as glass. It's not foolproof; the final test lies in the geology and other fossils found nearby.

Contemporary bones are used for comparison in the second stage of identifying fossils. Ideally the first occurs in the field, though rarely does a hominid skull appear like the one I remembered seeing in the "Survival" film. The most famous skull to emerge from this terrain did so in three hundred pieces.

The original clues to the skull that became known as 1470 were discovered on August 27, 1972, by Bernard Ngeneo, a member of the Hominid Gang. They were light-colored pieces of the cranium, none more than an inch long. Some pieces were from the top of the skull, some from the back, and some from the sides. This collection, plus a few fragile facial bones, inspired a thorough sieving of the topsoil in the area, at the bottom of an eroded gully. More fragments were collected, wrapped in toilet tissue, then taken back to the Koobi Fora camp, washed, and laid out to dry. The very first afternoon they began to reconstruct the pieces, it became evident that the skull was larger-brained than that of the australopithecines found at East Turkana. Such a large brain suggested to Leakey (and others) that it was *Homo*. At nearly two million years old, 1470 remains the most complete ancient specimen of the *Homo* lineage.

Inside a stone-walled office, I am introduced to a fiberglass cast of skull 1813. (All original specimens are kept in the Hominid Vault in Nairobi.) Skull 1813 is not a prominently discussed hominid. It has none of the fame or recognition sparked by the mention of skull 1470. Its numerical code, like that of 1470, derives from its accession number at Kenya National Museums, a sizable inventory of all the fossils collected from Koobi Fora; 1813 is the one thousand eight hundred and thirteenth fossil retrieved from the East Turkana terrain. It was found in 1973 by Kamoya Kimeu.

The skull of 1813 is nearly complete, its braincase about the size of a softball. Underneath, the *foramen magnum* is low enough to indicate that 1813 walked upright. It has a reasonable collection of teeth, with small canines, unlike an ape's. The teeth indicate that 1813 was a young adult when it died. From time to time 1813 is addressed as a she, having been suggested by some as a female counterpart to skull 1470. Leakey disagrees with this, and thinks that 1813 may represent an australopithecine. Since debates center upon anatomical details, any addition to the skull would be useful.

A small triangular patch of bone on the front of the skull is missing. "This"—Leakey dips his finger in the void above the left eye—"is what we're looking for." During the flight Leakey had casually mentioned there were some fossils he had to "collect," the Queen's English for "pick up." I hadn't heeded the remark as perhaps I should have. There are five hundred square miles out there, and we're supposed to find a triangular patch of fossilized bone?

At the time I had no idea how carefully excavation sites were mapped, that the region of East Turkana was divided into over a hundred numbered sections, with detailed records of where every fossil and stone tool was found. Nor did I realize that the way fossils were found, and who found them, had changed dramatically. I assumed that Leakey led all of the surveys for fossils, by camel. There's not a camel in sight. "It was a romantic way to enter the field of paleoanthropology," he says wryly.

We climb into a Land Rover and head up the escarpment east of the camp, over soft passages of sand, round rocky ledges and scrub. Along the Koobi Fora Ridge the road leads to black sandstone, pocketed and bleak, a lunar landscape reflecting dry heat. Our destination is Area 123, but the road ends long before this site fifteen miles to the southeast of the camp.

Leakey flies on foot the way he does in his Cessna, with an occasional subtle yaw, as if his feet were too small for his agenda. As a teenager his Kamba friends called him Ostrich—coincidentally, the name applied to the black volcanic mountain tipped in snow, Mount Kenya (black and white like a cock ostrich, *k'enya*), and subsequently, the land where his missionary grandparents settled. Kenya, still a British colony when Leakey was born in 1944, influenced his demeanor, his outlook, his decisions, and to a great extent shaped his niche in our mind and his.

In a famous photograph taken during a 1969 expedition, Leakey was featured astride a camel, with lines as lean as the desert itself—sharp, refined, and determined. He wore khakis and smoked a pipe—the perfect advertisement for the adventure of the search during an era when art directors on Madison Avenue took to wearing safari jackets. As commercial images go, it made the Marlboro Man look like a greenhorn. Here was a man in his element, the photograph said, and that part was true.

Since my inclination is to extend the frame on this search, the photograph is as good a place to start as any. Leakey has since dismissed the pipe ("a nasty habit") along with the camels: "They carried precious little. The photographers rode up front while the supplies were carried in Land Rovers behind us," discreetly out of frame.

There's more. When published in *People* magazine, the photograph of this expedition featured Leakey alone. Yet in a display at the small Koobi Fora Museum, a second rider appears alongside him: Kamoya Kimeu, who has discovered more ancient hominids than any paleoanthropologist, including Leakey. Were you to include all the scientists who researched at East Turkana, the caravan would require an aerial photograph.

Now I study the rock-strewn surface, looking for something I've never seen—a fossil in the wild.

Bones, in modern feasts, require a quick filet. Bones are what the dog buries, what rattles in closets. There are wishbones, funny bones, and bone as a verb—to study up, to stiffen a corset, to importune, to level by sight, even to steal. A vessel plowing the sea has "a bone in its mouth"; we pick bones and make no bones about it. And to malaprop Marc Anthony, the good that we do is rarely inferred by our bones: they symbolize death and Halloween, poison and pirates.

In this search, bones impart elegance and malleability, the awe for their growth and form reflected by the names given them. Toes and fingertips are phalanges, and upper leg bones femurs; lower leg bones are tibias and fibulas; taluses connect to the foot, where metatarsals mock the metacarpals of the hand. The thumb of an ape is relatively shorter than ours, and less capable of a precise grip.

The bone of the kneecap is a patella, a diminutive shallow dish that in the enlarged anatomy of elephants affords a drinking cup, so employed by the people of Africa who find them.

The human skull rests on the summit of the vertebrae and is divided into two parts, the cranium and the face. There are fourteen bones to the face and eight to the cranium. The cranium, derived from the word "helmet," is described in the bible of bones, *Gray's Anatomy*, as "a case for the accommodation and protection of the brain." A lower jaw is a mandible, the upper jaw a maxilla. Given these names, bones take on eloquence and life; fossilization grants antiquity along with subtle grainy colors characteristic of the sedimentary matrix—literally, "womb." The surrounding sediments fill in the naturally porous tissue of bones.

Until recently the formation of fossils was as mysterious as the morphology the process preserved.* A similar chemical reaction occurs to create a ring in a bathtub. Animal fat reacts to the calcium in soap (like calcium in bones) to precipitate crystals of calcium carbonate, also known as limestone. The same chemical reaction that forms the ring around the tub acts upon bones—once buried in an alkaline-rich soil. The perfect environment exists in salinas or dried lakebeds, where evaporation concentrates the alkalinity in mires of mud. The volcanoes of the Great Rift Valley offer these conditions by pouring out alkaline. Fossils are rarely found in forests, where the soil is highly acidic; in fact, many suggest this is the reason no fossilized bones of chimpanzees have been found, since chimps favor forests. Occasionally volcanic ashes settle in forests; this is why Kenya is so wonderful and strange, for on the once forested islands of Lake Victoria, volcanic outpourings were so great as to preserve not only bone but flesh.

The odds are against burial, with most bones dispersed by predators or weathered to nothing by rain and the sun. But if buried in a highly alkaline environment, like those created by the volcanoes of the Great Rift Valley, bones maintain their form. With extreme alkalinity, other details can be preserved. One can find fossilized seeds and ants, caterpillars and grasshoppers, and theoretically, a hominid face.

Not ten minutes into the field, I notice a pink, textured "rock," with a small head on a neck at a tilt, contours that bespeak function. "What have you there?" Leakey takes the fossil from my hand, proclaims it an antelope femur, unworthy of collection, then resumes his pace, tossing over his shoulder: "Here, there are fossils everywhere."

We trek about eight miles across uneven blackstone that nonetheless reflects an even heat normally associated with an oven. Winds of 30 to 40 miles per hour do nothing to disturb the temperature, but sandblast sunscreen number 8 off the back of my legs. I carry two Nikons in a canvas bag, not the least bit heavy; so far, fossil finding is a piece of cake.

---

* I asked many scientists how fossils were formed: John Van Couvering, who once worked as a geologist with Louis Leakey, provided this eloquent explanation.

An area clean of boulders marks an excavation site, made official by a pyramid of stones, a cairn. With his hands behind his back, Leakey walks in a circle, then spies a set of jackal's teeth. He squints with concentration, turns the jaw over in his hand, then hides his find under the cairn. This is the procedure. It will be collected by a member of the Hominid Gang, washed with water from the lake, then given a free trip with Leakey to Nairobi.

The duties of the Hominid Gang are not confined to fossil finding. Kamoya Kimeu, when not searching for fossils, oversees operations at the various museum sites around Kenya; Bernard Ngeneo, the discoverer of 1470, was my guide during a subsequent trip to Olorgesailie. And Joseph Mutaba works not only in the field excavating fossils but in the laboratories at the Nairobi Museum, where the next stage of discovery on these jackal teeth will continue.

On the third floor of the museum, the fossil is cleaned with dental picks and brushes, and if the surrounding matrix is ensconced, with an airscribe—a sensitive air-powered hammer with a microscopic view; when Leakey was young it was hammer and chisel. A fossil the size of jackal teeth will be placed in a plastic bag with a paper label indicating: Site, Area, Date Found, Description, Family, Genus, Species.

This particular set of jackal's teeth would be denoted as *Canis* sp.—*Canis* indicating the family name for dogs, wolves and jackals, *Canis* sp. meaning Dog, unknown species. That there is kinship among *Canis* is not confined to such formalities. A dog called Nzuma, or "the Wanderer," that frequented the Koobi Fora camp bred and hunted with wild jackals.

"The fossils we're looking for," Leakey finally says, "are under a cairn like that." We come across several cairns, but not the right one. "I've lost my instincts," he confesses. He hasn't been to Area 123 in nearly six years.

I ask about maps. They're in the United States being microfilmed. He begins to wander, sinking and resurfacing in the folds of the land. I wouldn't recognize a fragment to 1813 if it fell on my head, but surely I can find a cairn. I establish landmarks. The earth swallowed the Land Rover long ago. On the eastern horizon, there is Lishode Peak and Puchoon Ridge. I decide to search in the opposite direction of Leakey; barely an hour into the field and I feel competitive!

The possibility of finding the right cairn leads to a general state of engrossment for a period of time that it does not occur to me to measure. When I finally look up, the ridge and the peak have apparently been leveled by sudden and fierce winds. I make smaller circles, in case I am in need of discovery. A few minutes later Leakey appears on a hill in front of me. "I'll have to come back next week." Next week I'll be in New York. My cameras double in weight.

We pass familiar cairns swiftly now, backtracking. A cairn we missed on the way out appears against a drift of sand. "Of course!" he exclaims, "I'd confused the carnivore site with this one!" He crouches, drops his canvas pouch, and begins to unstack the rocks one by one. There, exposed, are fragments that don't look anything like the one I found, but like dried mud. They're covered in calcite. Leakey sits, turns them slowly—an appraiser. He cuddles one fragment—not an inch long—in his palm, puckers, and blows dust from what normally returns to dust.

Leakey wraps these gifts from the wind in toilet tissue, slips them into his pouch, pulls the drawstring, and smiles. We walk back to the Land Rover and drink water from a canvas bag.

The fragments were discovered a week earlier, and in the field procedure that prevails, tucked under a cairn to protect them from erosion or trampling by camels or goats. They were discovered not by a member of the Hominid Gang but by a keen-eyed geologist from Utah named Frank Brown, who informed Leakey. The same procedure is maintained with the Hominid Gang and any other scientists who work in Kenya. Contact with the various sites is maintained by radio phone, and when Leakey goes into the field, he already has a preliminary report on what's been found.

The report on 1813 remains preliminary. Leakey gave an estimate for its age, but insisted it not be published until Frank Brown had finished his geological survey. He was even more reticent when I asked what the skull was. He wasn't sure; he had some ideas, but he wanted to be cautious.

Hominid skulls are rare. Some paleoanthropologists have based their entire career on less. The naming of a new discovery not only inspires funding and recognition but grants bones long dead a new life, complete with an interpretation that is traditionally related to the disposition of their discoverer.

Homo habilis is of course the "Handy Man." This hominid, first found at Olduvai Gorge, is famous for being the oldest tool user, and symbolizes the "dawn of civilization"; its braincase was relatively large. An australopithecine found earlier, in 1959, was given a different name, that of *Zinjanthropus. Zinj* had exactly the opposite features to the Piltdown hoax—a small brain and massive jaws. A small brain is also a characteristic of Lucy.

Most people have heard of the famous partial skeleton found in Ethiopia by American paleoanthropologist Don Johanson, and despite the absence of a whole skull, her bones confirmed that an upright gait evolved before the large brain, which had been suggested by the australopithecines from South Africa. The bones of Lucy (named after the Beatles song, "Lucy in the Sky with Diamonds") are prominently linked with the phrase "our oldest human ancestor." She is not; other hominids of her kind from Tanzania are half a million years older. But the bones and illustrations of Lucy convey the notion better than a lower jaw, and it's a much catchier name than *Australopithecus afarensis.*

These glib portraits of discovery are unfair and incomplete, but recounted in the popular vein for a reason. Humans tend to give things labels. Scientists assign their discoveries significance, and reporters give their story handles. But there were many debates about the naming of *Homo habilis*, and many about the naming of *A. afarensis*, which includes Lucy. There remain doubts about the very first use of tools and which hominids deserve credit, and doubts about the ancestral status of the australopithecines. In science, a few members of the jury are always out. New perspective surfaces with all the predictability of these new fragments.

That a skull so complete as 1813 had no designation initially struck me as odd. Its potential significance remained uncharacteristically couched in caution. And if the earth does not impart such clues easily, this time it had sent a little reminder, a notice of compounding interest, to the scientists. I learned that another complete skull found at East Turkana endured the same identity crisis. It was known simply as 1805. Both skulls were tabled in what's known in the trade as the Suspense Account. In over a decade of searching this 500-square-mile region, only eight hominid skulls were found. That leaves a quarter of the valuable evidence locked in mystery.

That evening, I sat in front of the camp, facing the lake, contemplating all this. The questions I'd so carefully prepared no longer seemed appropriate. What did our ancestors look like? Well, they really didn't know. Only in rare cases, when they found a lot of the skeleton, could they estimate height. Several artists fashioned reconstructions based on the bones of the face; well, some of the bones of the face. The brows and the mouth jutted forward. The nose was depressed, the forehead inclined toward a small braincase. Artists usually put hair on the face, and paleoanthropologists frequently surmised an ability to speak, but this was conjecture ("Words don't fossilize"). Did our ancestors employ fire? Patches of reddish-orange circles in sediments dated at 1.5 million years old were found at East Turkana, but this could also be the result of a tree trunk burned in a natural fire. Was 1813 a male or a female? They really couldn't tell without a pelvis; to be certain, they needed the pelvis of the opposite sex. Other clues for what's called "sexing the bones" are not foolproof.

By six o'clock I'd put all ancient hominids back into the Suspense Account. I threw in the tools. Had I known then what I do now, I would have thrown in Lake Turkana. I wasn't dismayed; I was hooked. The search appealed to me as one of the last frontiers of discovery on earth. I was dazzled by the context, both in a geological sense and an ironic one, that during an era of high-tech science and all-embracing theories like TOE (the Theory of Everything), the account of our own origins on earth remains largely unknown.

Had those fragments fallen from the sky, I could not have been more amazed. They didn't look like fossils, nor did I believe they belonged to the original skull. The circumstances, I thought, were too fantastic. Furthermore, even though the skull had been around for nine years and studied with the scrutiny due its appearance, it had not been officially proclaimed either *Homo* or australopithecine.

This, supposedly, was part of a science long on assertions and short of evidence, where fossil finders are quick to hold any discovery aloft. None of these givens prevailed during my initiation to the search.

Leakey defied labels as well. "You journalists stereotype me," he complained during dinner. "You've got me out here digging for fossils all the time." And in the same breath, "Fossils, after all, are simply a hobby of mine." Ninety percent of Leakey's day in the office has nothing to do with stones and bones, he explained.

Of skull 1813: "We don't know what to make of it. It's odd." "We" includes two scientific colleagues who co-author scientific papers with Leakey: his wife Meave Leakey, an erudite scientist whose specialty is monkey fossils, and anatomist Alan Walker. Leakey prefers to leave the reconstruction of fossils to them; the addition of the new fragments would have to wait until Walker, who teaches at Johns Hopkins Medical School in Baltimore, returned to Nairobi.

Because there is always so much controversy surrounding the naming of a new species, I was keen to see how scientists came up with the interpretations they did. When I learned that Leakey was about to embark on his semi-annual lecture tour in the United States, I asked permission to record his informal discussions with scientists at the University of California, Davis. There, the naming of 1813 would be put into context. What I learned was far more revealing, a behind-the-scenes glimpse of the way this science works. There was a new scope to this inquiry, one that shifted the focus from fossil finders to a vast fleet of researchers in seemingly disparate disciplines. It all began in 1967 with the Omo expedition.

2.
The Legacy
of
the Omo

The crack of breaking bones provides ruthless punctuation for Leakey's words. "I really didn't like the Omo project"—he pops a leg bone in two—"there were too many chaps ahead of me—all sorts of serious, senior scientists"—Crack!—"I was very much on the bottom of the pile."

For one who protects bones in a bombproof vault, Leakey dispatches the few before him as if he were preparing kindling for a fire. He is making chicken soup in a California kitchen, and remembering 1967, when he was the Kenya leader on an expedition into Ethiopia's Omo River Valley.

The Omo is inspired by the heavy rains in the Ethiopian highlands; the river extends seven hundred miles south of Addis Ababa, crossing the Ethiopian border to feed Lake Turkana. Much like the Mississippi, the lower Omo is marked by meanders and crescent lakes—oxbows that denote its former course. Richard Leakey described it as "a moody, slow-flowing river, brown in color," which is a nice way of saying muddy, for at this point the river is rich in sediments. (As might be imagined, I am familiar with such sediments on the lower Arkansas, which shaped the delta for which I was named.) Contained within the banks of the river, these sediments made the Mississippi "too thick to drink and too thin to plow," as Mark Twain noted. Along the Omo they preserved bones.

The French were the first to explore the ancient banks for fossils; during the 1930s, an expedition led by Professor Camille Arambourg collected over a hundred tons of fossils in a mere two years. During World War II, Louis Leakey took advantage of British troop movements along the lower Omo, arranging for one of his most trusted assistants to explore the region. Heslon Mukiri might be considered the first member of the Hominid Gang, although Mukiri found fossils two decades before the name was coined.

In 1959, F. Clark Howell (now head of paleoanthropology at Berkeley) conducted a brief survey along the Omo, but the small sample of fossils he collected was confiscated at the border. There had been some confusion about his permission to research in Ethiopia, a problem Louis Leakey was the ideal person to solve, though it would be years before the opportunity arose.

In 1966, when Ethiopian Emperor Haile Selassie paid a visit to Kenya, President Jomo Kenyatta invited Louis Leakey to a meeting at the State House in Nairobi. Louis brought along a collection of fossils, and described the unusual treasures found in Kenya and Tanzania. The emperor was not immune to Leakey's infectious enthusiasm. How is it, Selassie asked, that there were no fossils in Ethiopia? Leakey told him of the rich deposits of the Omo delta, and was promptly invited to research there.

Leakey was determined that the Omo expedition be an international one, including teams headed by Clark Howell from the United States and Camille Arambourg from France. But by 1967, he had arthritis in his hips, which made fieldwork difficult. He appointed his son as the field leader of the Kenya team; on scientific matters, Richard was to maintain radio contact with his father, who would fly up from time to time. Richard's experience in planning expeditions suited the task; he remains the "organizing genius of modern paleoanthropology," which is how he was described in a cover story in *Time* in 1977.

The Omo expedition attracted a number of young graduate students who, alongside Leakey, aged twenty-three, would shape the future of the search. Geology student Frank Brown was part of the team; so were Raymonde Bonnefille, collector of fossil pollen, and Gerry Eck, studying baboons; and Todd Olson, Noel Boaz, and Don Johanson, all graduate students in paleoanthropology. Many fossils surfaced, but the hominids were fragmentary and poorly preserved. While they were disappointed not to find more hominids, many viewed the Omo as a turning point in the search, one that made the "field a laboratory," as Howell says, and one that inspired what they would naturally call a "speciation event," propelling various participants on to isolated populations of continuing research, some to become more famous and competitive than others.

At Koobi Fora, Leakey had said that he was no longer interested in fame or competition ("These things mean little to me now"), a statement credible in the sense that he no longer need cultivate either. Certainly he enjoys some aspects of his fame, and is fond of pointing out that the issue of *Time* featuring him on the cover sold more issues than the one featuring model Cheryl Tiegs. But behind the scenes, he cultivates the team effort, one that diminishes the personal views of an individual paleoanthropologist. This inclination is not evident to the public, nor was it self-evident in 1967, when his priority was to move as far as possible from "the bottom of the pile."

He did so swiftly. In a February 1968 presentation to the National Geographic Trustees, Richard requested that the $25,000 earmarked for the Kenya team in Ethiopia be diverted to a project a bit south, just inside the Kenya border. Among the distinguished gentlemen gathered in the Washington, D.C., boardroom was Louis Leakey.

Surprised by his son's proposal, Louis spoke against it, arguing that at least the Omo held a known quantity of fossils; the young man's bravado represented mere impatience in a project without instant prizes. Louis had expected Richard only to report on the Omo expedition.

The trustees excused the two. Behind closed doors, they admired Richard's "cheek and initiative." When awarded the grant, Richard was warned that a great deal of trust had been placed in him, and if that trust was misplaced, he was "not to come knocking on our door for money again."

During the Omo expedition, he had gone south to Nairobi for supplies. Returning in a chartered six-seater, his pilot detoured around a storm, banking to the east, flying along the eastern shores of the lake. Leakey—bored with the Omo expedition, feeling some sense of failure because the French and American teams were collecting better fossils—gazed out the window, to see vast stretches of light brown sediments cut by erosion. Exposures.

In making order out of memories, one has to admire any attempt to rescue the past from hyperbole. The man who once said, "Somewhere down there, I thought, was the key to our existence, and I would be the one to find it," now allows, "I needed a project that was good, big and attractive."

Richard arranged to charter the Omo expedition's helicopter to do a little survey. Within minutes of landing at East Turkana he held a stone tool. Nearby, there was a fossilized jaw of an extinct pig. He decided to explore further, directing the pilot to touch down here, touch down there. "Everywhere we stopped there were fossils." In his excitement, he forgot to note the exact location where he'd found the jaw and the tool, or any of the other sites. He knew only that he was northeast of the lake. In the end it hardly mattered; plenty was pinpointed. Five thousand fossils were retrieved from East Turkana over the next decade.

People talk of Leakey's Luck. Richard spent the better part of his first twenty years being exposed to exposures. The Leakey family camped near them; new roads, if they held any promise, led to new exposures. His Search Image (as paleontologists call their focus or scanning template), is not confined to exposures, or for that matter, fossils.

When Kay Behrensmeyer, a Harvard graduate student in geology, found stone tools during the early days of research at East Turkana, Leakey went to the area that would eventually be known as KBS (Kay Behrensmeyer Site) to examine them. He thought these tools looked familiar, and returning to a site he had surveyed a year earlier, pointed out even more stone tools. When Meave Leakey found a hominid leg bone at Koobi Fora, Leakey took one look at it, only to say that he had seen a bone just like that. Because of the scarcity of hominid leg bones, considerable skepticism greeted this remark. Leakey left the group and set off in a Land Rover. A few hours later he placed another hominid leg bone on the table.

When he first began to fly on his own, he noticed the sediments surrounding Lake Natron, Tanzania, which produced a complete lower jaw of a two-million-year-old hominid. On every flight he takes across Kenya, he studies the terrain. Leakey averages over one flight a week, around seventy-five a year. His course is not limited to Turkana; he flies to numerous sites, and to annex museums, northwest to Kitale, further west to Rusinga near Lake Victoria, to Kanam and Mount Elgon, east to Lamu, and from Turkana to the Masai Mara in the southwest of Kenya, with occasional excursions into Ethiopia and across Tanzania, beyond Olduvai to Dar es Salaam. In 1987, he recorded two hundred hours in his flight book, equivalent to a bird's-eye view of about thirty thousand miles of the Cradle of Mankind.

Once, when I asked him to show me what he had seen from the air on that famous flight over East Turkana, he flew on for some time, then northwest of the lake, just below the Omo, dipped his starboard wing toward long sections of earth burned red, eroded, and stratified, saying simply: "It looked like that." There was a lot of "that" below, which Leakey continued to study in silence. Finally he commented on the potential, turning to shout over his shoulder to Kamoya Kimeu who sat behind him, "Kamoya! We are going to die in these mountains!"

Leakey swats at cobwebs with a dishcloth: "What a mess this place is!" He threatens to put on an apron and "mop and hoover and dust, but I simply don't have the time." The kitchen near the University of California, Davis, provides refuge from a schedule that taxes the clock itself. Early this morning he has been on the telephone, to Boston and Salt Lake City, to New York and Los Angeles and London. At nine he lectured before an evolutionary biology class, at eleven a seminar, at noon a luncheon. There is a press conference. ("Did you not say that deeply religious people were crazy?" "I did not say it, nor do I impute it," which sent copy editors scrambling in their dictionaries for "impute.") He attends a tea reception where he patiently responds to questions from sophomores. ("What did your parents do?" Leakey recommends back issues of *National Geographic*.) This evening he will attend another reception ("His ideas are outrageous," whispers one guest. "Soooh handsome," another.) Afterwards he will address a crowd of a thousand plus in an auditorium called Freeborn Hall—a reasonably sophisticated mix of students, professors, and polyester-suited patrons who will give him a standing ovation after being informed they are apes. "The question of whether we descended from apes, or split from apes, no longer arises, because it hasn't yet happened." He pauses. "We are apes."

Leakey prefers to group the chimpanzee, the gorilla, and the orangutan with hominids, "and not separate us from apes at the family level." Hominid, derived from Hominidae, denotes the family of man. Yet hominids are *included* in the superfamily of all apes, Hominoidea. Leakey's point was to diminish the distinction of bipedality alone, and to emphasize the similarities. It was not an original idea, but one that had been brewing among observers, based on the more obvious links with apes.

We share the following characteristics with apes. We are both mammals, and we are both primates. We both have fingernails and toenails rather than claws. We both have an opposable thumb—or an opposable big toe. We both have four incisors in our upper and lower jaws. We both have a Y-shaped pattern on our molar teeth. We both have fur or hair, and we both nurse our young. We both have three separate bones in our middle ear. Our shoulder blades are at the back, rather than at the sides. With all these similarities, the bipedal stance would seem to be a small difference. Behavior and biochemical evidence strengthen the ties even further.

The classification of the earth's flora and fauna was officially begun in 1735 by Carolus Linnaeus, who suggested, "*Homo nosce te ipsum*: Know thyself, Man." Now, a new subfamily has been created to acknowledge the similarities: Homininae.

In making these distinctions, scientists are supposed to be influenced only by bones, behavior, and biochemical evidence. Strictly speaking, they are not to be influenced by time or geography. Should a five-million-year-old hominid surface in Alabama, for example, its classification should not be influenced by such. Yet the age of skull 1470 consumed its identity. When it was first discovered, it was thought to be three million years old. In time, arguments about its age split the search right down the middle, but its purported antiquity brought Richard and Louis Leakey together.

There is a famous photograph of Louis Leakey with a twinkle in his eye. It was taken in 1972, the year 1470 was found. The elder Leakey studies the skull that would make National Geographic Trustees proud, a find that had eluded him for decades—the most ancient *Homo habilis* skull. "He was delighted," Richard recalls. "I think that's one of the days I remember most about him—his absolute joy." Richard had flown to Nairobi to show the skull to his father, who planned a lecture tour in California. The rest of the Leakey family discouraged Louis's travel, for he'd suffered a stroke, but as Richard recounts, "We were like a yoke around his neck. We meant well, but it was quite natural that he would prefer the hero worship that surrounded him on these tours to our saying, 'You can't do this; you shouldn't do that.' " After driving his father to the airport, Richard returned to Koobi Fora, and Mary Leakey to Olduvai. En route to California, Louis Leakey stayed in London, as he often did, as a guest of Mrs. Vanne Goodall, mother of primatologist Jane Goodall. The following Sunday, he suffered a massive coronary, and Richard and Mary, receiving the news of his death, returned to Nairobi for a sad family reunion, where a week earlier there had been one of celebration.

The antiquity of 1470 confirmed the elder Leakey's ideas on the long lineage of man, or *Homo*, a theory to which both Richard and Mary Leakey continued to subscribe, a theory that does not acknowledge the australopithecines as ancestral.

Before the discovery of the first *Homo habilis* at Olduvai Gorge in 1964, the australopithecines were the leading candidate for our ancestors—a direct line was drawn between the australopithecines of South Africa and *Homo erectus* in Europe and Asia. But the discovery of these hominid fossils at Olduvai Gorge known as the "Handy Man" at 1.8 million years old proved that the lineage of *Homo* was much older than previously thought. With the discovery of a Handy Man initially estimated at nearly three million years old at East Turkana, the long lineage of *Homo* seemed confirmed.

But two events that occurred at about the same time, in the mid-seventies, challenged this. One was the 1974 discovery by Donald Johanson and his team of substantially older hominids in Ethiopia's Afar Triangle. At first Johanson viewed the finds as further evidence of *Homo*. But he was to change his mind, and with colleague Tim White, propose a new species, *Australopithecus afarensis*, a new, primitive form of australopithecine. (The species was named after the Afar Triangle.) Johanson and White suggested that *A. afarensis* represented the ancestor of *Homo*, directly opposing the view that *Homo* went back far in time.

Their argument was strengthened when the date on 1470 was challenged during what became known as the KBS controversy. The age of the KBS tuff was eventually revised to 1.89 million years, making the age of the skull around two million years old. The age of the hominids from Ethiopia, initially put at four million years, was revised to three—still substantially older than 1470. These events are detailed in subsequent chapters, particularly the difficulties of dating. All of this occurred after Louis Leakey died in 1972, only a week after he'd seen the skull he'd longed to find for thirty-five years.

Richard kindly attributes his father's opposition to his work at Koobi Fora to a ploy that Louis knew would only encourage him.

"He was a very powerful man," Richard says, acknowledging his father's role as mentor. "I admired his ability to inspire people. I try to pattern what I do in public on the same thing, when talking to students. I saw so many people go so far on his words."

During high school Donald Johanson had a passion for chemistry, but an account by Louis Leakey in *National Geographic* made him favor anthropology as a college major. "The name Olduvai, with its hollow, exotic sound, rang in my head like a struck gong. . . . Leakey's experience was proof that a man could make a career out of digging up fossils," he wrote in *Lucy*.

Donald Johanson is now forty-five, the same age as Richard Leakey. He, too, now looks quite different from the widely published photographs of a few years ago. He's trimmed the over-long, Elvis sideburns, and trimmed his weight. A few years ago his eyes were overwhelmed by dark, dramatic brows, but his general countenance seems to have lightened up, becoming more refined. A touch of gray in the sideburns now makes them disappear in most photographs, and his skin is pale, with none of the chevrons around the eyes associated with long seasons in the sun. He spends much of the year running the Institute of Human Origins in Berkeley and teaching at nearby Stanford, and only a few weeks in the field in Africa. He, too, lectures to audiences around the United States, and once served as host-narrator for the PBS "Nature" series.

The son of Swedish immigrants, Johanson was born in Chicago. His father, a barber on the North Side, died when he was two. His mother, who now resides in California, worked as a cleaning lady. A central influence in his youth was Paul Leser, whom Johanson considers his "adopted" father. Dr. Leser was a professor of anthropology at the Hartford Theological Seminary, and Johanson first came under his influence at the age of eight.

Johanson studied anthropology at the University of Illinois, relying on scholarships and working part time in the Physics Department; he measured atomic particles between midnight and four, a shift that offered an extra 25 cents an hour.

At the University of Chicago, Johanson's doctoral thesis focused on chimpanzee teeth: he compared them to other apes, and to the ancient hominids, and "began to get a powerful intuitive sense of what made an ape an ape, what made an australopithecine, and what made a human." Johanson's choice paid off; the study of teeth became increasingly diagnostic in the search for missing links, and in particular, a pivotal feature on the fossils discovered in Ethiopia.

Some of his graduate studies were supervised by F. Clark Howell, then planning the Omo expedition. Howell's no-nonsense stance suited his role as Johanson's professor (Howell was also a source of inspiration for geologist Frank Brown). He helped Johanson obtain a grant to extend his studies of primates to collections in Europe and South Africa; their meeting point was to be in Nairobi. "Then I really stuck my neck out," Johanson recalls, suggesting it would be a shame to go to Nairobi and not join the Omo expedition. Howell eventually approved.

During his first day in the Omo, Johanson nearly collapsed from the intense heat. He also realized to his horror that he could recognize very few of the mammal fossils that were found. But Howell was a patient instructor, and Johanson eager to prove himself.

In 1972, Johanson became an assistant professor of anthropology at Case Western Reserve University in Cleveland, where he also served as an associate curator at the Museum of Natural History. At the same time, he planned a research expedition to Ethiopia, at a locale substantially to the northeast of the Omo River Valley. The Afar Triangle is bound by the Red Sea, the Gulf of Aden, and three adjacent plateaus: the Danakil Alps to the north, the Hararghe plateau to the east, and the Ethiopia plateau that edges toward the capital city of Addis Ababa. As it is a geological hotspot, the Afar is also a fossil hotspot. In 1971, Johanson had met French geologist Maurice Taieb, who had surveyed the Afar region with American geologist Jon Kalb. Taieb, Kalb, and Johanson formed a research project, International Afar Research Expeditions (IARE), and the fossils they found during their surveys were extraordinary: well preserved, abundant, and just as old as those from the Omo.

After a quick survey in 1972, Johanson spearheaded plans for continuing research in Ethiopia, assuming a pivotal position on the American team. Within a year of his introduction to the Afar, Johanson was listed as Co-Principal Investigator on a proposal for further research there, which was approved by the National Science Foundation in early 1973. While Johanson did not have the field experience of Richard Leakey, he did apprentice with leading academics in the U.S., and was partly inspired by Leakey's bold move to East Turkana; "Richard had taken a chance and struck gold. Shouldn't I?"

During the early seventies, Johanson was a frequent house guest of Richard and Meave Leakey, and was invited to visit Koobi Fora.

Some members of the American team on the Omo expedition gathered for a reunion during a 1986 Berkeley conference; Clockwise, from lower right, F. Clark Howell, one of the organizers of the expedition, Raymonde Bonnefille, Hank Wesselman, Donald Johanson, Joan Merrick, Harry Merrick, Basil Cooke, Noel Boaz, Dorothy Dechant Boaz, Todd Olson.

When he discovered a knee joint of a hominid at Hadar estimated to be three million years old, he made a quick press announcement at Addis Ababa, then flew with his finds to Nairobi, where he was met at the airport by Meave Leakey. Meave was curious to see "the oldest evidence of bipedalism" that had been announced on the radio the night before. There were four pieces of hominid leg bone; two of them fit together to form a knee joint; the angle at which the two bones met seemed more like a human's than an ape's. Johanson expresses relief that the Leakeys agreed that the knee joint was indeed hominid. His initial comparison in the field had relied on a modern human bone, stolen from an Afar burial ground—an illegal act that had serious repercussions when it became widely known several years later. It was one of the infringements cited by Ethiopian officials who eventually banned any further research in the country.

Leakey initially encouraged Johanson's research in Ethiopia, and invited him to become a board member of the Foundation for Research into the Origins of Man (FROM), based in New York, because "we needed someone to help raise funds there, and Don's a very articulate spokesman." Leakey also says that he knew Don would find something at Hadar.

During the field season of 1974, within a week of establishing the Hadar camp, a hominid jawbone was discovered by a keen-eyed Ethiopian researcher named Alemeyhu Asfaw. The following day Asfaw found two more specimens; a fourth jaw was discovered the very next day. From his studies of primate teeth, Johanson noted characteristics both humanlike and apelike. The press announcement in Addis Ababa proclaimed "an unparalleled breakthrough" in the search for human origins, suggesting that the finds extended "our knowledge of the genus *Homo* by nearly 1.5 million years," a statement which, had it been true, would have merely confirmed what the Leakeys had been predicting all along—that the lineage of *Homo* was old. Yet Richard Leakey was cautious, since the definition of *Homo* relied on a large brain, and the fossils from Hadar included no evidence of this. But Johanson found that proportions within the dental arcade were more like *Homo habilis* than the known australopithecines.

Johanson invited the Leakeys to visit the Hadar camp. Richard flew up in his Cessna, accompanied by Meave and Mary Leakey, and paleontologist John Harris; they were taken on a tour of the fossil sites and offered a review of the hominid jaws and teeth, which everyone, including Johanson, agreed were more like *Homo* than the australopithecines. The next morning the Leakeys left Hadar to return to Kenya. The date was November 29, 1974. The following day Johanson found Lucy.

It was with some reluctance that Johanson set out for Locality 162. It was toward the end of the field season, and despite the dramatic sequences of discovery featured in documentaries, fieldwork can be mundane. Johanson was tempted to work on papers and correspondence at the camp, but after a cup of coffee, he set out for 162 with American graduate student Tom Gray, who was collecting faunal fossils. The two spent a couple of hours collecting: a monkey jaw, teeth from antelope and extinct horses, *Hipparion*. Around noon they decided to head back to camp, but Johanson suggested a detour to a nearby gully, one that had already been surveyed twice before. They found very few fossils at the bottom of the gully, but turning to leave, Johanson saw an arm bone on the slope. It was so small that Gray's first impression was that it belonged to a monkey. Johanson was sure it was hominid. As they looked around, they found more fossils—a piece of skull, a thigh bone, even ribs. No one had ever found so much of an ancient hominid skeleton before—this was twelve years before the discovery of the Turkana Boy—and these sediments were nearly twice as old as those at Nariokotome. The two men embraced each other and jumped around, howling with excitement. The afternoon was spent mapping, and by nightfall they were sure of something spectacular. By the time the stars rose they'd entered a state of euphoria, dazzled by the bones on a table while a Beatles tape played over and over again. No one remembers who coined the nickname.

Lucy is estimated to have been the size of a modern six-year-old. The braincase for *afarensis*, based on a reconstruction of other finds in the area, was only slightly larger than that of a chimpanzee; indeed, Lucy has been compared to an upright chimp. Curved toes and finger bones suggest *afarensis* may have spent time in the trees.

Additional finds from Hadar are substantially different from Lucy in size. Some scientists think two species are represented by these fossils. Johanson and White argue that the variation is within the range of any population, and lump the finds into one species.

At the time, Lucy was the oldest record of bipedalism, told by details of the pelvis and the leg bones. The partial skeleton was complemented by equally extraordinary discoveries the following season. In 1975, the fossil remains of thirteen individual hominids were found. None was as complete as Lucy but their range was exceptional, including adults and juveniles, and even the partial skull of an infant.

While Johanson's account of the discoveries featured prominently in *Further Evidence*, the FROM newsletter of January 1978, behind the scenes a tension brewed between him and Leakey that is described by a former FROM board member as that of "two male gorillas competing for the same females."

"I think Don simply couldn't stand me," says Leakey. "I think he found me a tremendous burden to live with. The thing that really upset him was—at a meeting, there would inevitably be differences between him and me." Johanson would take an opposing position "often just to be different, I think," claims Leakey. "I may malign him, but I think that's why." And even if Johanson had some support in the beginning, "the board always came around to my way of thinking."

"I said to him: 'If you're chairman of the board, one of the things you try to do is have certain political linkages so that even if you can't control that person, you have influence on somebody who can—so that you can ultimately get what you want. I mean, that's the reason you have a chairman, isn't it—to have leadership?' I said, 'Really, Don, all it is is that I'm a better politician than you are. There's nothing sinister in it.' Well, he didn't like that at all."

The tension reached its peak with the publication of the book *Lucy*. The dust jacket heralded the "first real and successful challenge to the 'Leakey dynasty.' " Emphasizing their opposing ideas on whether the ancestor of modern hominids was a small-brained australopithecine or a large-brained *Homo*, this tyranny of dichotomies was translated as a coup d'état.

Johanson is often described as the foremost critic of the Leakeys, but he is not alone. The search is shaped by people who have either attached themselves to, or attacked, the Leakeys, many in that order. For several years the dialogue between disciplines was divided between two opposing camps. Johanson was drafted as the candidate to speak for the opposition. He described the Hadar fossils as "dazzling enough to match those of paleoanthropology's certified supernova, Richard Leakey." Recently, during a 1987 lecture, he told an anecdote about explaining his trade to a stranger on a plane, who responded, "Oh, you must be . . ." "No," Johanson teased the audience, "I'm the other guy."

His scientific stance represents a healthy challenge; yet among many of his colleagues, the opposing camp is more anti-Leakey than it is pro-Johanson, indicating a political battle rather than a scientific one. The reason for this is perhaps best put forward by Mary Leakey, when describing the conflicts between Louis and Richard: "Richard was always a competitive person, and when he entered a new field it was with the intention of getting to the top, and the sooner the better. And who at that time was in possession of the summit, needing therefore to be replaced? Louis." The script for a CBS Universe program described Richard Leakey as the "king of the mountain"—until Johanson discovered Lucy.

When Leakey arrived at a FROM fund raiser in November 1980, he noticed stacks of the book *Lucy* which Johanson planned to distribute. He found Johanson and steered him away from the crowd. "Listen, Donald," he recalls saying, "I've read the galleys for *Lucy*, and I'm very sad about what you've written. Much of it is incorrect; you should have checked your facts more carefully. And while there will be no litigation, this book will not be distributed at a FROM function—not as long as I'm chairman." The books were put away. "I thought I'd been direct and fair, but Johanson later said I'd bruised his arm with my grip." Johanson recalls that Leakey was extremely upset and threatened to sue, saying a letter had been sent to his publisher; he describes their exchange as "provocative."

Johanson resigned from FROM and founded the Institute for Human Origins, based in Berkeley, in 1981. Several FROM board members and scientists formerly associated with research at the Kenya Museums followed him. Most influential was Tim White, who had an equally provocative exchange with Leakey regarding the age of 1470, and subsequently, an argument with Mary Leakey about her finds from Laetoli, Tanzania. Each defection involved a former friend who became an avowed opponent, and the man once known as Ostrich preferred personal ostracism; he stopped talking to them, and to a remarkable degree, he stopped talking about them. The opposite tactic prevailed in the Berkeley camp; one professor's course in anthropology was likened to "Anti-Leakey 105," and there were numerous overtures for debates. The Leakeys were accused of stifling the scientific process by refusing to debate, the Berkeley camp of character assassination. It was bitter and ugly, but presented to the public as the Superbowl of Science. In December 1981, *Life* magazine ran an article featuring a double-spread photograph with Johanson on one page and Leakey on the other. Johanson held a reconstructed skull of *afarensis*; Leakey also held an australopithecine, skull 406 (the one he and Meave found courtesy of a thirsty camel). The two men and their skulls were photographed separately, then pitted against each other in the "Battle of the Bones."

For the first five years of its existence, the defense budget of the Institute of Human Origins (IHO) for this "battle" was cut by a controversial and complex stalemate. The dilemma arose during Leakey's lecture tour.

October 15, 1982, Davis, California: The Berkeley team led by J. Desmond Clark and Tim White are still waiting in the Addis Ababa Hilton. The Ethiopians had ordered a moratorium on paleoanthropological research by foreigners. Archeologist Glynn Isaac brings this news from Berkeley, where he serves as a buffer between the opposing camps. Buffers are few. A thoughtful, bearded man, Isaac began his career working with Louis Leakey in Africa, and was co-director with Richard Leakey of the Koobi Fora Research Project. Now Isaac serves as a governor to Leakey's temper, urging him to focus on the quest for evidence. Isaac brings flowers for the hostess, Linda McHenry, wife of Davis Professor Henry McHenry. The McHenrys are hosting a small dinner party in Leakey's honor; Isaac's report is served before the other guests arrive.

The predicament of the Berkeley team qualifies as a classic nightmare. Lucy's fame has begun to fade, and fund raising for research depends on visibility. Johanson needs a sequel to Lucy, or even an occasional reminder, like "Lucy Gets a Younger Sister."* Too, none of the *afarensis* finds included an adult skull. The exposures of Hadar promise many skulls.

But the Berkeley team in Addis can't even get close to Hadar. Instead, they sit in the Hilton. The Ethiopians, concerned about the protection of antiquities, had closed the country to foreign researchers. This was partly inspired by a passage in the book *Lucy*, co-authored with science writer Maitland Edey, where the authors describe stealing a bone from a modern Afar burial ground. The offense was listed in the Ethiopian Ministry of Culture's decision to ban paleoanthropological work, and the passage subsequently edited out of international editions of the book.

Others say the ban was indirectly inspired by geologist Jon Kalb, who had initially surveyed the region with Maurice Taieb. During the 1973 field season, Kalb had taken "major issue" with Johanson in the field. Then, in 1978, after having formed his own research group for further research in Ethiopia's Middle Awash, Kalb was subsequently banned from further work after being falsely portrayed to Ethiopian officials as a CIA spy. The rumor was rampant among American scientists, and found its way into the reviewing panel of the National Science Foundation (NSF), which was considering a proposal that would allow further research by Kalb in Ethiopia. Kalb heard of NSF's concern over the allegations only after his proposal was rejected. While NSF officials insist his proposal was rejected on its scientific merits, Kalb was eventually awarded $20,000 by NSF in an out-of-court settlement.

Kalb's research team in Ethiopia had included Glenn Conroy of Brown University, Clifford Jolly of New York University, and several Ethiopian students, four of whom were awarded Fulbright Scholarships in the United States. The students felt excluded from research in their own country by the Berkeley team, and in 1981 filed a petition to Ethiopian officials, urging them to reconsider their policy on antiquities.

---

* A headline that eventually appeared in the June 1, 1987, issue of *Time*, as detailed in chapter 10.

Among the fossil discoveries found by the Kalb team was a *Homo erectus* skull. It emerged piecemeal during the 1976 and 1978 field seasons. Named after the Bodo region where it was found, the skull is particularly interesting because cut marks suggest this hominid was "scalped." One of the Ethiopian students, Tsrha Adefris, studying with Clifford Jolly at NYU, applied for grants to learn how to clean and prepare the skull. But the Bodo skull was in Berkeley, where it was given on loan for study. The Berkeley group had obtained the proper permission to borrow the skull, but Adefris, along with another student petitioner, Sleshi Tebedge (who'd studied under Jon Kalb at the University of Texas), began to lobby with Ethiopian officials to block the Berkeley expedition. They "acted as a catalyst for what many people were feeling," according to a former dean of science at Addis Ababa University.

Many people were feeling ripped off; the Ethiopian students felt their rights to their own antiquities were usurped; Kalb felt his reputation was tarnished; the Berkeley team felt the door was closed on a great potential they had discovered. Leakey felt the whole thing was a sad mess, with Ethiopian students being pitted against each other according to the claims of their American advisors. With all the accusations flying, it was inevitable that Leakey's name be entered.

In making their decision, the Ethiopians called upon Richard Leakey for advice, which prompted accusations that Leakey inspired the ban. But their communication made perfect sense. Louis Leakey originally inspired Emperor Haile Selassie to open his country to the search, and as the matter had to do with antiquities, what better counsel than his son, the director of the largest museum in all of Africa and Third World neighbor who had recently drawn up new laws on antiquities in Kenya?

Leakey, who'd initially encouraged the research undertaken by Johanson in Ethiopia, now had two hats to wear. As to his response to the Ethiopian officials: "I responded not as Richard Leakey but as a government official." There is a chorus among the dinner guests at the McHenrys: "But you *are* Richard Leakey!" Dinner is served for the director of the Kenya National Museums.

"I said—in my letter—that in view of the alleged rivalry between the work they were about to do and mine, I would rather not express anything other than a purely official position: In Kenya we had very good antiquity laws, and they might consider adopting something like that. I didn't feel personally obliged to extend a special intervention. At the same time, I felt it would be wrong to allow my personal negative feelings in part to influence how I advised the Ethiopian government." Leakey enclosed a copy of the Kenya laws on antiquities. ("We saw that letter," a member of the Berkeley team said later. "It was innocuous enough.")

The ban in Ethiopia was strictly on paleontological research. Primatologists and geologists continued to research in Ethiopia. Johanson was understandably frustrated. "The raison d'être of this Institute is not simply to study the bones we've found, but to do expeditions," he told me in 1985. "The ban in Ethiopia is related to their rewriting antiquities laws. Once these are finalized, they will invite applications for research. I expect in the next few years Ethiopia will reopen and hopefully the Institute will again be invited back." He added wistfully, "I don't know why it's taking so long."

The tension between Berkeley and Nairobi surfaced again in the literature on skull 1813. ("Never has so much been said about so little by so many," I wrote in my first account on the subject, words I would eat. Not a great deal had been written on 1813.)

A cursory mention in a 1978 *Scientific American* article, "The Hominids of East Turkana," by Leakey and Alan Walker, includes a brief description. Skull 1813 is suggested to be similar to the gracile australopithecine, like other finds from South Africa. If this is true, three species of hominids lived at East Turkana around the same time (1.8 to 1.9 myo), *Homo habilis, Zinj,* and whatever 1813 might be named.

The subtle and hidden argument is that if 1813 is an australopithecine, one that "survived" to live alongside *Homo,* the more gracile australopithecine did not evolve into *Homo,* since they existed at the same time.

On the other hand, there's no reason an ancestral form has to vanish. After all, chimps and gorillas still exist, and they represent our ancestral stock. But the argument nested in the concept of linear progress.

The concept relied on the notion of "competitive exclusivity"—that two very similar forms could not exist because they competed for the same niche and drew upon the same resources—that one would eventually supercede the other. The concept didn't work for rivalries either.

Johanson and White considered the subject of 1813 in *Science* (1979). Referring to Leakey and Walker, they said: "Some investigators have alluded to the existence of a third lineage in eastern Africa between 1 and 2 million years ago. The evidence for this third species, usually regarded as a northern gracile australopithecine, consists of three or four fragmentary crania," in other words, bits and pieces of skulls.

Walker and Leakey followed up with a letter to *Science* that detailed the evidence for a third species: "The more complete specimens include 1805 and 1813 from East Turkana, and OH-13 and 24 from Olduvai . . . these are calvaria [the dome of the skull] associated with facial skeletons and upper teeth; two even have associated mandibles and lower teeth. They are thus less likely to mislead us than more fragmentary remains."

Don Johanson was disappointed, complaining: "To drag us into a peripheral argument by citing fossils of his own that we don't mention, and by failing to discuss our fossils at all, simply dodges the main point: Is *afarensis* a valid species or isn't it?"

Johanson's question could be applied to many species. For example, the australopithecines from South Africa include gracile and robust forms. Some scientists consider the gracile, or *A. africanus*, simply to be the female, and the *A. robustus*, with its broad cheekbones and bolder skull, to be the male. Others see three species among the specimens. The finds from Olduvai that Walker and Leakey mentioned, OH 13 and OH 24, are classified as *Homo habilis*. Perhaps they belong in the Suspense Account along with skull 1813, which was no closer to definition. In Davis, when I asked about the additional fragments found at East Turkana, Leakey said: "They belong to 1813, there's no doubt. But there's a problem in trying to make them fit." The original reconstruction would have to change to accommodate them. Would the changes be slight or great? The fragments belonged just above the eye, or orbit, of the skull, an area filled in by the expansion of the hominid brain.

Leakey's stint at the University of California, Davis, included a lecture to a class in evolutionary biology; the subject—the evolution of the hominid brain.

He stands before a table littered with skulls. Most are casts of original fossil finds; there is one authentic human skull. He has three basic points for the class: (1) There's not enough fossil evidence to know whether encephalization (the growth of the human brain) occurred suddenly or gradually; (2) the measurements of skulls, or cranial capacity, based on reconstructions, deserve great caution; and (3) there are several specimens that do not fit neatly into any known category.

"In amongst all this mess of strange things," he refers to the skulls before him, "we do have fossils from Koobi Fora that are contemporary with *Homo erectus*, and this is one of them." Leakey picks up the skull known as 1805, and turns it level to his face, mocking Hamlet. It was discovered in 1972 and is often referred to as the Mystery Skull. Skull 1805 is around 1.5 million years old. Leakey points out that 1805 has a cranial capacity of just over 600 cubic centimeters. The average cranial capacity for *Homo erectus* is substantially larger, over 1000 ccs, so there's no need for confusion.

There are two common methods for determining cranial capacity. One is to fill the braincase with lead shot or seeds, then measure the amount. The second is to immerse an endocranial cast in water, and measure the displacement. Those witnessing the reconstruction of 1470 were so stunned by the size of the brain that they quickly measured it in sand from the shores of Lake Turkana; their estimate based on bone fragments taped together turned out to be fairly accurate.

An endocranial cast, like the fossilized one found in the Taung child, can be created artificially by filling the braincase with layers of latex. Cranial capacities were thrown around for decades as measurements of sophistication. In 1948, British anthropologist Sir Arthur Keith suggested that a "cerebral Rubicon" separates apes and australopithecines from *Homo*. Keith put the dividing line for complex thinking at 700–800 ccs. If this was true, *Homo habilis* made it just across the line, with skull 1470 having 750 ccs.

But brain size is scarcely a measure of intelligence; now the focus is on changes in the organization of the parts of the brain, the details that can be told by furrows and indentations on the inside of skulls. Skull 1470 has, for example, a little indentation known as Broca's area, which indicates speech. Details of the organization arose by making a latex endocast. This is exactly what was done with 1805 by Dean Falk, an investigator of paleoneurology, the study of ancient brains. Leakey refers to her work on 1805, saying, "For those who look at insides of heads, it's a chimp." Then he complicates the picture.

"But its teeth are definitely hominid, and"—he touches the concave sections behind the eyes—"it's got relatively little post-orbital waisting." Post-orbital waisting (as in the waist of a Gibson Girl) refers to the areas of bone just behind the eyes (post-orbital) that were filled in by an enlarging brain. This is extreme on the robust australopithecines, where the small braincase curls up like a big wave toward the eyebrows and the large cheekbones.

"It [1805] never comes up in the literature," Leakey continues, "and it's never included in any arguments for or against anything, because nobody knows what to make of it." In other words, 1805, like 1813, has no species name.

"I don't know what it is, but it's got to be considered in the scheme of things." He puts the cast of 1805 back in its cardboard box.

A chart is among Leakey's visual aids—an incomplete rendering of a family tree, with gaps along the branches so large that white paint appears to have been spilled over the illustration. For nearly two decades, from 1963 to 1980, a line was drawn from the recent hominid skulls that Leakey reviews all the way back to fourteen million years ago, to *Ramapithecus*.

Ramapithecus gained its name from the mythical Hindu prince, Rama; the modest collection of fossils representing these species were discovered in India in 1932 by G. Edward Lewis. (The name of a Hindu goddess, Siva, serves for a cousin of *Ramapithecus*—

Sivapithecus.) All these Miocene apes are grouped into a clade, or cluster of branches, toward the bottom of the chart.

The line drawn to *Ramapithecus* is interesting because it was considered not a hominoid but a hominid. The conclusion was based on very little evidence. There were no leg bones. There was no pelvis. There was no *foramen magnum*. There were parts of an upper jaw, broken in two, as mentioned. From these pieces, you could reconstruct a hominid, if that was your preference, and it was the preference of investigators at the time to think that hominids were that old, and that the thick enamel on the teeth and the shape of the reconstructed jaw were diagnostic links.

So, in the sixties, the "oldest hominid ancestor" was found in a museum drawer, the typical storage place for fossils. Several legitimate discoveries have been made by reexamining archives, so it was not unusual for Professor Elwyn Simons to take a second look at Lewis's fossils from India; in the thirties, Lewis had suggested these fossils were hominid, and Simons agreed. Over the next decade, Simons and his student David Pilbeam published many articles suggesting that *Ramapithecus* was the oldest hominid ancestor; in 1965, Pilbeam, by then a professor himself, wrote of *Ramapithecus*: "Hands were probably used extensively and perhaps tools as well."

The degree of this probability was substantially revised in 1981, after new discoveries suggested that *Ramapithecus* was not hominid. In a symposium entitled "Fossils, Genes and Time," Pilbeam spoke on the fossil record of hominoids: "I'll be using the terms 'very likely,' 'probably' and 'possibly' as modifiers in describing paleontological events. Cast in odds forms, these correspond roughly to 10:1 (very likely), 5:1 (probably), and 2:1 (possibly). . . . Consider them equivalent to statements about politics, the weather or horse racing." The five-to-one odds on the bipedal stance of *Ramapithecus* were, like any theory, tested. This testing created varying levels of uprightness in illustrations.

In Richard Leakey and Roger Lewin's *Origins*, published in 1976, *Ramapithecus* is portrayed in a partially upright stance, as if its spine endured a slight, perpetual stoop, and its posture had a less than confident mien. In other illustrations, *Ramapithecus* is safely featured near a tree. Leakey has some fun with this: "This way, it's never quite clear whether it's a tree climber having just come down, or a bipedal pondering going up. The truth is we have no idea of whether it was bipedal," he says.

In 1976, during a field expedition in the barren Siwalik Hills of Pakistan, an upper jaw, more complete than the one used in the reconstruction, was discovered. The site in Pakistan was about 250 miles from the original site in India where Lewis had made his discovery; the sediments that have washed down from the Himalayas over the years are nearly a mile thick. The jaw was V-shaped. David Pilbeam, who headed the expedition, began to have doubts about the hominid status of *Ramapithecus*. Challenges had already been rendered by two anatomists who did their own reconstruction, Alan Walker (Leakey's associate) and Peter Andrews of the British Museum. An additional blow was rendered by biochemical evidence suggesting that hominids were simply not that old. *Ramapithecus* is now considered by most to be an ancestor of the so-called man of the forest—literally translated: an orangutan.

"What this has done"—Leakey renders the mistake some charm— "is give the orang a very respectable past." He is masterful at this, fed up with the personal derision that follows such mistakes, sympathetic because he has made his own. When a discussion becomes mired in the mistakes of the science, he moves it forward with, "Well, one slides around these moments as best one can."

The mistakes of the science are the wheels that make the inquiry turn, a positive view of negative results. If they hadn't suggested anything about *Ramapithecus*, they would have gained less of an idea of what it wasn't. It wasn't hominid, but the jury is still out on which Miocene apes led to hominids, or how these clusters of branches were related.

"More evidence will tell," Leakey says. "We have very similar finds like this in Kenya, from the Miocene. They're called *Kenyapithecus*."

Kenyapithecus is not included on the chart. When Simons and Pilbeam did their analyses of *Ramapithecus*, they compared it to fossils of *Kenyapithecus*, discovered and named by Louis Leakey after the country in which they were found. Simons and Pilbeam concluded there was no difference between the two, and in an effort to make matters simpler, lumped them together under one species name. Because the name *Ramapithecus* had been coined first, by the rules of nomenclature, *Kenyapithecus* was wiped off the chart. Even as Richard Leakey spoke, halfway around the world more "*Kenyapithecus*" were being discovered.

An international venture comprised of Japanese and Kenyan scientists was at work in Kenya's Samburu Hills; the leader of the Japanese team was Professor Hidemi Ishida of Kyoto University, who was assisted by Martin Pickford, a paleontologist with the National Museums of Kenya, and Kiptalam Cheboi, who collected fossils at Lake Baringo in 1966, before the "Hominid Gang" was invented. It was the end of the field season, 1982. When they first began to plan the expedition, Dr. Ishida warned Dr. Pickford that he was not in a position to gamble. The price tag for an expedition into the Samburu Hills, just south of Lake Turkana, was substantial, and Ishida figured he could afford just one month.

The first ten days of his month were spent building a road to the Samburu exposures, where sediments ranged between seven and twelve million years old. On their first reconnaissance, the two men drove west from Baragoi, then walked ten miles to get to the nearest outcrops, or exposures of sediments, plus an additional ten miles to the southern edge of the basin. All this was undertaken in temperatures of 105 degrees Fahrenheit.

"Dr. Ishida's anxiety was understandably increased," Pickford recalls. "I had to do some fast talking about the tremendous possibilities of the area, the wonderful fossils we would find, the novelty of the time period, and so on."

After the road to the new site was completed, there was more trekking. The more ground they covered, the further they walked each day back and forth from camp. They found "precious little." The day before they were to break camp, Pickford was "desperately anxious." Only 30 percent of the basin had been prospected in what's known as the "initial survey and randomized screening program," and Pickford had reasonable fears that it would be impossible to get anyone to return to Samburu.

Then Pickford, accompanied by Kiptalam Cheboi, returned to an area where Pickford knew, from a 1974 survey, there were fossils. They collected a few and took them back to camp, which brought Ishida to Locality 20. It was the final day of Ishida's gamble. Pickford remembers, "At about eleven o'clock I found another fossil concentration which yielded giraffe and antelope foot bones, and many catfish." He and Cheboi, looked across a small hill, the last outcrop of sediments. Beyond was only a tremendous expanse of lava, glaring black, dull, without promise. But Pickford—Dr. Cliffhanger—excels at locating potential at the last moment. Working their way up the slope, "with Kiptalam slightly ahead," notes Pickford, Kiptalam stopped, stooped, and seized a jaw fragment which he passed down to Pickford, a fossil that "looked awfully piglike, but the molars were undoubtedly hominoid." They found a second piece, including part of a cheekbone. Professor Ishida agreed to extend the expedition.

The area marked as Locality 22 became a maze of activity. They mapped, measured, and collected. No one complained of the heat.

By the end of the season, fourteen hundred specimens belonging to twenty-two species had been unearthed at Locality 22. Of the jaw that Cheboi found, Leakey would say, "It's like nothing we've ever found before. It's odd. I don't know what it is, but it does make a mockery of a lot of things we'd thought." The teeth appeared more hominid than hominoid. But because they were eight million years old, caution seemed a good idea, especially with the dethroning of *Ramapithecus* as the oldest hominid ancestor.

Two revisions had been made to major stems in the family tree, revisions more bold than the addition of *afarensis*. Paleontologists had drawn up a tree with the oldest hominid at fourteen million years old, and placed the gorilla as the closest primate relative to humans. But new genetic evidence indicated that the chimpanzee was closest to humans, and that hominids diverged from hominoids around six million years ago. It was a stunning idea, to think that hominids diverged from apes so recently. If the biochemists are correct, a hominid can't be eight million years old.

Take Two: three weeks later, on October 16, Ishida prepares to pack up camp, again. The majority of the team is more concerned with locating missing blankets than missing links. Pickford decides to go for a ride. He invites geologists Drs. Mitsusrio and Makinouchi along. "While we were puttering around . . ."

In one afternoon, the remains of twenty-two hominoids were found. Pickford measured out, at random, three square yards for screening. All three yielded hominoid specimens. The fossils were concentrated in a thick layer of silt so soft that they could be uncovered with bare hands. Back at the Nairobi Museum, Pickford cabled the news to Leakey in California.

When Leakey called his office, he complained about receiving a garbled message from Pickford about *Kenyapithecus*. The word "dozens" was confirmed. This was one of the calls he made before heading for the classroom.

Leakey comes to the last box unopened on the table. His lecture has focused on skulls. He's held aloft casts of *Homo habilis, Homo erectus, Australopithecus,* and even a modern human skull to make his point. In each case he's described them in detail, and in each case he's announced their known affinity—except, of course, for the Mystery Skull 1805—and now this one.

He opens the box and takes out a cast of a nearly complete skull. Small fragments are missing above the left "eye." Leakey describes it only in anatomical terms, adding simply: "1813—a *hominid* from Koobi Fora."

"Since this was reconstructed," he tells the class, "we've found a few more pieces. In fact, the post-orbital waisting is slightly more extreme, so I think the ultimate value of the published cranial capacity will be around 500 ccs."

Leakey didn't offer a new name for 1813. The name that cropped up with increasing prominence was that of geologist Frank Brown. The potential of geological clues surfaced a couple of days later.

Leakey's right hand stretches across his brow, shielding his eyes from the glare of fluorescence, putting the upper half of his face in shadow. He sits at a large round table in the Davis Geology Building, Room 417, holding court at an informal session with graduate students. He is discussing the final stage of research at Koobi Fora, which has been converted into the International School of Archeology and Paleontology, in association with Harvard University.

Leakey outlines a series of publications in progress on the research at Koobi Fora, where a team of scientists will describe in detail all the discoveries made during their decade of research. While many of the fossils have already been written about in various publications, this is a comprehensive record of reference, a series of monographs nine volumes thick. These monographs are vast black books, 16 by 16 by 3 inches, unsuitable for subway reading. In the works for Koobi Fora are one that will feature geology, two on archeology, three on hominids, and three others on paleontology. Mary Leakey, writing up the monographs on her discoveries at Olduvai Gorge, referred to this final stage as the "consuming part of my work."

A grad student, in the eagerness of a quip, ventures: "Looks like the research at Koobi Fora is coming to a rapid close."

"I'd hardly call it rapid." Leakey lifts his palm to glance at the speaker, then lowers it again like a massive eyelid. "One can't really close down Koobi Fora in good conscience until all the work is done."

"I never worry about conscience," the student inexplicably blurts.

"Oh, you lucky man!" Leakey laughs in rapid fire. His pinky rises, inviting the next question.

"Where do you go from there?"

Leakey describes new sites, to the northeast of Koobi Fora, very near the Ethiopian border, at the tip of a lake called Chew Bahir. "There are sites there that are probably between fourteen and eighteen million years old, with some of the most rich surface occurrences of bone that I've seen at any Miocene site in Kenya." Then he mentions younger sites along the west side of Lake Turkana, "from three to five million years old. In three areas, we've got lots of fossils that have not been publicly alluded to. We've only been there for a few weeks, but there are hominids there." Of this area, which will become known as West Turkana, Leakey says: "This is a very important extension of our knowledge of the Turkana basin that could become a very major location in another decade." (At the time Leakey spoke, in 1982, the bones of the Turkana Boy and the "black skull" were still buried in the sediments of West Turkana.)

For two hours, the conversation centers on sediments and time, from the badlands of East Africa to the volcanic islands of the Galapagos; students come and go. To Leakey's right, Stan Margolis, a geologist, sits waiting, as docile as a panda bear, his hands folded over his briefcase. He does not speak until Leakey addresses him.

"When fossils are found," Margolis begins, "I wonder if any effort is being made to correlate that information with what we're finding in the oceans." Margolis explains that he is working with a research project called CENOP, for Ceno-paleoceanography.

"Ceno" is short for the Cenozoic era, from sixty-five million years ago to the Present, from the time of the last dinosaurs to ourselves. "Paleo" denotes ancient, or prehistory. Paleoceanographers delve into the prehistoric records of oceans, as paleoanthropologists delve into ancient anthropology.

Barely three decades old, paleoceanography is a relatively new branch of earth sciences, studying fossils from deep-sea drilling cores. The history of oceans, as might be imagined, is a central force to the history of life on earth, where changes in temperature, salinity, and sea level effect climatic changes that extend across continents. For example, when ocean currents shifted about twenty thousand years ago, glaciers formed as a result of lower temperatures in Europe and North America. When ocean currents shifted again, fourteen thousand years ago, a warming event occurred; the glaciers began to recede.

Leakey shifts in his chair to face Margolis, who addresses the results of his team's research in a time frame of six million years before the Present.

"We started out in the Miocene, the Late Miocene. We identified a horizon in just about all the world's oceans between six and six point two million years ago that we can tie in everywhere in terms of a very significant event in the global carbon budget."

Today's "global carbon budget" is largely influenced by the activities of modern hominids. Carbon dioxide is produced when coal, oil, and natural gas are burned; carbon atoms from these fuels combine with oxygen in the atmosphere, where they retain the heat of the earth. The stunning increase of carbon in the atmosphere led scientists to predict a massive warming trend on earth—the so-called greenhouse effect. One of the results of the warming trend would be the melting of polar icecaps, with substantial increases in sea level around the world. The predictions gain credence in the history of the oceans, for the global carbon budget that Margolis speaks of involves an ancient record of similar changes, and of mass extinction, which might be considered "a very significant event." Margolis is thinking big by examining the small.

Plankton is microscopic plant and animal life that drifts in water, its name derived from the Greek *planktos,* or wandering. Today, plankton is best known for wandering into the mouths of whales, or forming red tides. Deep-sea cores offer a long record of plankton, a compressed archive of fossils, that when correlated with those on land from the same time frame allows a plane, or "horizon," to be drawn between the same fossil species.

One of the things Margolis looks for in fossil plankton shells is heavy oxygen. (Elements like oxygen vary in weight; in other words, it's an isotope.) When he finds it in large amounts, he knows the icecaps at the time were large. Light oxygen in water vapor is often lost from the oceans when atmospheric moisture is transported to icecaps. For this same reason, the larger the icecap, the more heavy oxygen remains in the seawater. Alternately, lesser amounts of heavy oxygen in plankton indicate times when the icecaps were small. Bubbles of air trapped in icecaps, also obtained by drilling cores, confirm this variation in the global carbon budget. The record maintained in fossil plankton relies on the carbohydrate diet of these minute, single-cell plants that lived (as they do today) by photosynthesis, drawn from carbon dioxide and water.

The very significant event that Margolis speaks of included a time when plankton contained higher amounts of heavy oxygen.

"It happens to be coincident with a major cooling, and a lowering sea level, and it seems reasonable to tie it in with the Messinian Crises, when the Mediterranean dried up."

That the Mediterranean Sea had at one point actually dried up was familiar to Leakey: "You think the date on that's about six point three?"

"Originally it was put at between five and six but now they've made a positive correlation by studying some sections in southern

Spain that were coincident with what we found in the horizons in the oceans. And this has been positively dated by a number of different means at six point two." The horizons Margolis refers to tie his study in with those of similar fossils on land, but these studies are not confined to marine creatures maintained during a time the land was covered by the sea. Shells from lakes also maintain a record of oxygen isotopes. From the work of paleontologists, Margolis can extend his isotopic curves across continents. It is like a weather report from the past.

Margolis's next move is into the Middle Miocene, looking at "a warming event"; then he's going to have a look at the Miocene/Oligocene boundary, "moving up into the Oligocene."

"Do you come into the Pleistocene at all?" Leakey asks of the more recent era. With isotopic curves from the Pleistocene, Leakey would know when and where land bridges existed for the migration of hominids out of Africa. With maps that indicated precipitation and temperature, he might be able to pinpoint times and places of droughts that pushed hominids toward better food sources.

"There's a project called CLIMAP, with glacial coring by Nick Shackleton and J. P. Kennett," Margolis explains. "Some of the critical sites are in the equatorial Atlantic, and the Indian Ocean. So the climatic belt crosses Africa. We can give you a fairly good idea of what was going on in terms of the shifting of the temperature belts, and patterns of precipitation. Perhaps the lowering of the sea level could be important in terms of migration. . . ."

"One hopes to find something as major as that," Leakey comments. "There seems to have been a major migration between nine and eleven million, and there was another major change between one point five and two million."

"Do you have your isotopic curves here?" prompts the Forum's host, Jere Lipps, head of the Geology Department at Davis. Margolis offers a translation. "Basically, there is a warming, around six million, with a slight rise in sea level," he says quickly, adding, "We're going to have a very detailed series of maps." Leakey takes Margolis's card, saying, "I'd be fascinated to follow up with you on this. I didn't realize that this much had been done and it's of tremendous interest. It's quite clear that there were major events in human evolution caused by ecological events, and it's time we brought this information together, so we can understand what happened.''

That did it. Margolis had just handed Leakey an extraordinary clue. Margolis handed me a clue as well. A search that seemed confined to conflicting views on the names of hominid fossils had just been extended, back to the dinosaurs.

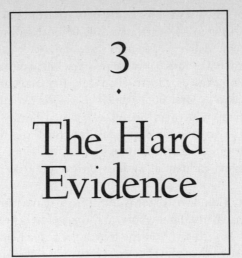

3

The Hard Evidence

The American Museum of Natural History in New York is famous for its dinosaurs. The 20-foot tall ceilings on the fourth floor of the Museum accommodate gargantuan relics of the Cretaceous. From head to toe, a *Tyrannosaurus rex* measures 18½ feet; from head to tail, 47 feet. The lower jaw is 4 feet long, with teeth 6 inches in height and 2 inches in diameter at their base.

The appearance of a lower jaw alone is mind-boggling, as was the case among normally blasé New Yorkers on an April afternoon not long ago, when just such a jaw glided across the avenues of Manhattan strapped to a mini-bike pedaled by Martin Cassidy. The curator in the Museum's Department of Reproduction was making an unusual personal delivery. I couldn't afford a whole dinosaur.

Cassidy's reproductions of dinosaurs stand tall in museums around the world, accompanied by instructions for assemblage and an invoice for $45,000. In a ground-floor workshop, fossils from Museum expeditions are reproduced in fiberglass, painted brown to resemble the color of the original finds, then air-freighted to isolated pockets of extinct creatures. That a *Tyrannosaurus rex* stunned one of the most prolific and influential authors on evolution is part of their fame.

Stephen Jay Gould writes for *Natural History* magazine, an organ of the American Museum—where, at the age of five, he was inspired by the *Tyrannosaurus rex* on the fourth floor. He held his father's hand and declared then and there that he would study ancient bones. At the time he didn't even know the word "paleontology," but he would come to study the growth and form of many creatures, and it is relevant to this inquiry that he chose snails for his attention. Gould's study of snails contributed to a theory of how changes may have occurred in hominid evolution.

Mollusks made their mark on East Turkana as well as other sites in the Cradle of Mankind, and alongside the plankton from deep-sea core drillings, provide the dips and rises to the isotopic curves of Stan Margolis, who had spoken of a "very significant event."

One such event captured the attention of the American public, entertained by fantastic theories on the extinction of dinosaurs. The significance of this event is often overlooked. Had it not occurred, we would not exist.

The global carbon budget was altered dramatically around sixty-five million years ago, during an extinction of so many species on earth that the episode is referred to as "crises." The plural is correct, for in addition to wiping out the dinosaurs that had prevailed for 100 million years, nearly all marine plankton disappeared. Geologists refer to their last crop as the "plankton line," for in the column of deep-sea cores they figure prominently, and then—at sixty-five million years ago—virtually disappear. Several theories are touted as to how this might have happened, brilliantly conveyed in an article (and subsequent lectures) by Gould. At the risk of repeating a highly publicized story of dinosaurs, a new angle is contained in this account, representing Gould's ability to look beyond his awe-inspiring dinosaurs in search of context, and the value of environmental influence in evolutionary change.

Gould described the notions as the "three primarily fascinating themes of our culture"—sex, drugs, and disaster. Two theories focused only on the extinction of dinosaurs; the last one offers an explanation of context, including plankton as well.

Sex: An increase in temperature rendered male dinosaurs sterile. This proposal relied on the knowledge that testes cannot function in very warm temperatures, which is why those of warm-blooded mammals hang externally.

Drugs: It was proposed that dinosaurs overdosed on angiosperms, the flowering plants that began to appear on earth around sixty-five million years ago. Then as now, some flowering plants contain mind-altering agents.

Disaster: A large comet struck the earth, sending up clouds of dust that blocked out the sun. Plants, including plankton, died from lack of sunlight, and lowering temperatures led to the extinction of dinosaurs.*

The disaster theory is also known as the "impact theory," and its impact on this search was threefold. It underscored the value of dialogue between disciplines; it emphasized the precarious position of hominids on earth; and finally, it provided unusual application to the future of hominids. Paleontologists like to say that they only deal with the past, that it is impossible to predict the future. In this instance, they made an exception. The results of such an impact were compared to those of a nuclear war.

The impact theory arose in dialogue between two disciplines. Luis and Walter Alvarez, father and son, were physicist and geologist, respectively, based at Berkeley. (Luis Alvarez died in 1988.) The central clue to their theory is found in a rare metal known as iridium. It is white, heavy, brittle, and so rare that it does not commonly

---

* For an explanation of why sex and drugs aren't the answer to everything, see Gould's essay in *The Flamingo's Smile* (New York: W. W. Norton, 1985).

appear in rocks on the earth's crust. It may arise from the interior during volcanic eruptions, but most of the iridium found on earth is brought to this planet by comets, asteroids, and meteorites. The enormous amounts of iridium found in sediments sixty-five million years old led the Alvarezes to contemplate the cause of the "crises."

Their scenario suggests that a shower of comets rained on earth, the impact sending up massive clouds of dust, enough to block out the sun for a decade. Dinosaurs starved and froze to death, it's suggested, but small, warm-blooded mammals found enough food to survive. In 1982, Luis Alvarez likened the results to that of a nuclear war.

Scientists heeded this analogy, and a group led by Carl Sagan prepared mathematical models of what was likely to happen if we drop the Big One. Massive clouds, blocked sunlight, lowering temperatures—a nuclear winter. Their report, published in *Foreign Affairs* for December 1983, inspired another dialogue between disciplines. This time it involved two disciplines that for centuries have been portrayed as dichotomous: religion and science.

Twenty scientists from eight nations joined forces with the Vatican. Pope John Paul II suggested a complementary effort: scientists would draw from the lessons of history; religious leaders would use the scientists' data in moral arguments against war.

What does all this have to do with the search for apeish skulls? To begin, it wasn't as if hominids filled the niche left by dinosaurs. Their extinction was the first in several significant events that led to us. What inspired our branching from chimpanzees? What was the significant event that triggered bipedalism? What triggered the enormously large brain of hominids? It would be wrong to imply that knowing these things might guarantee the future of *Homo sapiens sapiens*. Based on the fossil record, few species live beyond a span of three million years.

Of the eight known species of hominids, seven became extinct. Many, like *Homo erectus*, knew a tenure on earth much longer than ours. The success of *Homo erectus* spanned from 1.6 million years ago to around 200,000 years ago. Our own species has a brief record of a mere 40,000 years. We might insist that we're exceptional—so were the dinosaurs. Dinosaurs prevailed for 100 million years.

The myopic view of hominids was extended in a most unlikely setting, an homage to hominids. Some even called it "Ancestor Worship." The occasion was the largest international gathering ever of human ancestors, and it occurred in 1984, three floors below the *Tyrannosaurus rex* at the American Museum of Natural History. Record crowds, nearly half a million, filed through the turnstiles to glimpse the forty precious specimens, mostly skulls, displayed in an exhibit entitled "Ancestors: Four Million Years of Humanity." Behind the scenes, scientists involved in the search attended a separate exhibit beforehand, a private review of the fossils entitled "Paleoanthropology, The Hard Evidence."

The public exhibit opened on April 13, 1984. New York skies delivered a miserable gray drizzle, threatening a spring snow. Yet people stood on the sidewalks under bare sycamore trees. There were Hasidics from Brooklyn and students with backpacks, blue-haired matrons and Wall Street brokers. Impatience was remarkably absent for a New York crowd. When a child begged his mother to go elsewhere, she checked him sternly. "No, We're going to *see* this." The line was a quarter of a mile long.

The genesis of the "Ancestors" exhibit had occurred six years earlier and five blocks south in the Old Blarney Castle, a dark pub on West 72nd Street between two establishments of accounting, a bank and an undertaker. The notion was tendered by John Van Couvering, a tall, genial geologist who edits *Micropaleontology Press* at the Museum. Van Couvering had worked with Louis Leakey at Rusinga Island. Now, after nearly a decade of concentrating on tiny fossils like plankton, Van Couvering proposed "conceivably the most grandiose idea I have ever aspired to entertain."

The Museum itself is beautifully grandiose, with a granite facade that changes hues according to the season and the sun. The cornerstone was laid in 1874 by Ulysses S. Grant amid thirty acres of swampland. Photographs of this terrain, with herds of goats and dirt streets, bear a remarkable resemblance to Nairobi at the turn of the century.

Africa was a venerable source for the Museum. One of the early underwriters was Theodore Roosevelt, Sr., whose son's statue marks the Central Park West entrance astride a majestic horse. In 1909, Teddy Roosevelt sat astride the wooden cowcatcher of the train known as the Lunatic Express, which brought colonialism and white hunters into East Africa by the boxcar.

All of the game seen in the Museum's Hall of African Mammals, from bongos to giraffe, zebra, and an entire herd of elephant, were bagged in Africa, their bones shipped back to New York, where casts were made and the original skin of the creature stretched across its synthetic self. No detail was spared in reconstructing Africa within the dioramas; artists in pith helmets held their thumbs to the Serengeti; sample grasses, sand, and even entire trees were shipped back. But not one ancient hominid skull.

The search for human origins had yet to begin in Africa. At the time of Roosevelt's safari, Kenya-born Louis Leakey was six years old; Raymond Dart, in Australia, sixteen. Ironically, the Museum's Paleontology Department was established in 1891 by one keenly interested in hominids, Henry Fairfield Osborn ("For him the dry bones came to life and giant forms of ages past rejoined the pageant of the living," one can read below his bust in the Museum). But like most paleoanthropologists of his day, Osborn searched for missing links outside Africa—and found the Nebraska Man. A solitary molar from Snake Creek was proclaimed by Osborn as *Hesperopithecus*, "the first anthropoid ape of America." As mentioned, other finds at Snake Creek confirmed the affinity of the tooth—that of a pig. Osborn also endorsed the Museum's famous Missing Link Expeditions to the Gobi Desert, a seven-year survey led by Roy Chapman Andrews that stretched camels across the Gobi in pursuit of the "Dawn Man." Over 26,000 specimens were shipped back to the Museum, not one a hominid.

There are thirty-five million specimens in the Museum's vast inventory, but the specimens for the "Ancestors" exhibit were solicited from other museums around the world.

The Museum made security their guarantee to curators asked to loan their precious finds. An insurance policy of half a million dollars on each didn't mean much in terms of these hominids. The curators would have to be tempted by something else.

At a conference in Nice, the Museum organizers cornered potential curators, among them Phillip Tobias of the Witswatersrand Medical School in South Africa. Tobias inherited Raymond Dart's position of professor of anatomy at "Wits," and therefore is the official curator of the Taung child. "It was clear that the major motivation [for the "Ancestors" exhibit]," recalls Tobias, "was a counterblast at the creation-science movement." Tobias, along with other non-American curators, was unpersuaded: "We saw no reason to send our fossils over to fight the American movement." But Tobias came up with a more constructive purpose, characteristic of this gentleman and scholar, adept in both roles.

His sense of humor and decorum is boundless, as is his dedication to Raymond Dart and the australopithecine legacy in Africa. Legend has it that Tobias was conceived on the same day that paleontologist Robert Broom first visited Dart. "Broom's visit was on February 15, 1925," Tobias begins. "He entered Dart's office, and there was the Taung skull on the table. It is said he went down on his knees before the skull, in an act of genuflection, saying, 'Dart, I bend the knee before our common ancestor.' " In his own publication, Tobias itemizes the events from the discovery of the Taung child to the publication of Dart's paper describing the find in *Nature*—day by day— "The miraculous forty days," he sighs, his voice ascending, "like the forty days of the Flood, the forty days on the mount by Moses, the forty days of Jesus in the wilderness."

Tobias's bold stroke for "Ancestors" drew upon history. He cited three precedents. In 1938, Ralph von Koenigswald took all the Java Man fossils ("*Pithecanthropus erectus*, it was called in those days") to China at the invitation of Franz Weidenreich, a paleoanthropologist who worked in Peking, to compare them directly to the hominids known as Peking Man. The comparison led the scientists to lump both into *Homo erectus*. The second precedent occurred when Mary Leakey brought fossils from Olduvai for Tobias to review. She left them with her bank in London, where Tobias withdrew them and took them to Cambridge to study. Thirdly, von Koenigswald, based in Holland, wanted to compare his Asian finds with those from East Africa. He arrived at Cambridge with his fossils in his suitcase ("May 1964"). The fossils from Java and East Africa were spread across a table. "It was the most remarkable thing," Tobias recalls, "because for the first time we realized the parallels between human evolution in Africa and human evolution in Asia."

Tobias told Museum officials: "If we could have the opportunity to compare our fossils, I think you might sell us the idea." Tobias had just doubled Van Couvering's "grandiose idea."

Paul Beelitz, curator in the Museum's Anthropology Department, confronted a logistical nightmare. The creation-science movement was at its peak; would someone seek to destroy these agents of the devil? Even an accidental spill might invite bad press and leave rabid curators.

The comparison of fossils would take place in the Lounsbery Laboratory. Beelitz considered the current path from vault to laboratory too precarious; bumps in the floor were removed, along with doorway moldings. Carts to transport the hominids "became the monkey on my back." Beelitz searched the hardware haven along Canal Street for the right kind of wheels, eight inches in diameter, with ball bearings. "The slightest bump or smallest pebble in the wheel's path could stop them dead," he wrote in *Curator*. Shopkeepers teased: "What do you need wheels for, pal? Moving bones around?"

Meanwhile, exhibit designer Michael Blakeslee studied subway token booths and armored cars. The display cases had to be shock-resistant and secure; the final touch was bulletproof glass. New York's Finest supplied advice on lunatic violence and police escorts.

The hominids began to arrive: Neandertals came from Germany, Yugoslavia, and Israel. Cro-Magnon, at 32,000 years old one of the oldest representatives of modern *Homo sapiens sapiens*, came from France, as did a *Homo erectus*. The australopithecines, both gracile and robust, came from South Africa. The eldest hominoid, the thirty-three-million-year-old *Aegyptopithecus*, came from Egypt; the eight-million-year-old *Sivapithecus* from Pakistan. Some curators carried their fossils in aluminum camera-gear cases, thickly padded. Phillip Tobias and the Taung child flew in first class ("Friday, March 30"). At JFK, Tobias was met by a Museum curator and security officials and Port Authority police, "who sort of seized me, whisked me through formalities ahead of all the first-class passengers, and into a waiting limousine." Tobias and the Taung child were escorted by "a police car, making rude noises with its siren at seven-thirty in the morning." At the Museum, Tobias was received by an armed guard, taken up to the vaults, "and under my eyes," the Taung child was removed from its case, then put away under lock and key.

Yet Lucy, skull 1470, *Zinj*, and the original Handy Man did not make the party. In each case, the country of origin preferred not to send original fossils, so casts were used for the exhibit. Ethiopia, as mentioned, was undergoing a revision on antiquities, which precluded its loan of any of the *afarensis* fossils. Tanzania withdrew its participation at the last minute to protest the South African participation. (Ironically, Phil Tobias is anti-apartheid, but has subsequently been banned from an international meeting because he is from South Africa.) But the absence that caused raised brows were the fossils kept in a bombproof vault in Nairobi.

Richard Leakey was opposed to the transport of original fossils. Also, he had planned his own international exhibit—"not using originals, but casts and illustrations"—that eventually toured European cities, but not the United States.

When asked why he didn't attend the New York symposium, Leakey replied: "Well, I have nothing to contribute. The fossils in Kenya are unable to travel, and as I've seen all the originals that are to be there and we have far more of them here, a discussion around a few isolated originals didn't seem to warrant a trip to New York."

Leakey also preferred to diminish his role as public defender of an interpretation held by several scientists. The antiquity of the *Homo* lineage had become known as the "Leakey Line." Mary Leakey attended the symposium, though she preferred not to debate.

Since "Ancestors" was meant to be a highly publicized event, it would be ideal for more press coverage on the Leakey–Johanson rivalry, which Richard Leakey felt was misleading to the public. "There are many people involved in this search, and there are many schools of thought on various issues. It's got nothing to do with Johanson versus Leakey." Twice before, he felt that he was "set up" in opposition to Johanson by the media, once by a *New York Times* reporter, and more recently, in 1981, by a "debate" featured on a CBS Universe program that was taped at the American Museum of Natural History (detailed in chapter 12).

At the "Ancestors" symposium, Leakey's colleagues described him as conspicuous by his absence, and he became even more so on the opening day of the scientific sessions, when a small column appeared in *The New York Times* with the headline: HOMINID FOSSIL FOUND IN KENYA. The account described a jaw fragment estimated to be five million years old—a million years older than similar hominid fossils found in Ethiopia and Tanzania. "The discovery appears to be the earliest known specimen of the hominid line that was a humanlike precursor of modern man."

This hominid surfacing from the fossil gap was discovered by a team led by Yale paleoanthropologist Andrew Hill near a region of Baringo called Tabarin. At the end of the season, Hill and Kiptalam Cheboi were prospecting in an outcrop of the Chemeron volcanic formation when they discovered the jaw, which Hill described as resembling the *afarensis* finds from Ethiopia and Tanzania.

Leakey says he didn't expect the discovery to make the press, "but when it was proposed by NSF [the National Science Foundation, based in Washington, D.C.] that we put out a press release, that seemed a good day to put it out." The message was clear: You can talk about hominid fossils all you like; meanwhile, we're finding more evidence in Kenya.

The talk that brewed in the Museum's fifth-floor Lounsbery Lab was hushed as many scientists viewed original fossils they'd seen only in photographs or casts. Sunlight flowed from the tall windows stretching three quarters around the circular room, where padded tables four by eight feet held the fossils. Scientists were assigned tables, which is to say, each was encouraged to remain in his or her chair. They were given instructions in French, English, and German to hold the fossils over the table. But the opportunity to compare and talk inspired crossings between tables and into an adjacent room, where the rest of the fossils spilled over—so to speak. (There were nine such sessions during the week, with five tables of fossils. Not one nick was incurred.)

Because of the hushed voices and awe expressed by the scientists when viewing original specimens, the symposium was quickly dubbed "Ancestor Worship." It had glitter along with the antiquity. The opening program featured Raymond Dart, discoverer of the

Taung child, whose wife Margorie sat in a chair beside him on stage as he spoke, serving as a charming prompter. (Professor Dart died in 1988.) Don Johanson and Tim White were in the audience, as were Mary Leakey, Glynn Isaac, Phil Tobias, and even Jean Auel, the novelist (*Clan of the Cave Bears*, etc.), who devotes some of her literary profits to this search. For anyone who had read about missing links, the search came alive. Suddenly many names I'd noted had faces.

Geologist Frank Brown delivered a comprehensive revision to the dates assigned to hominid sites: "An Integrated Plio-Pleistocene Chronology for the Turkana Basin."

Two key points aroused my interest: Brown spoke of correlation to a comprehensive degree, comparing everything imaginable on the landscape, from the products of volcanoes to records of the earth's changing fields of polarity. Afterwards, his colleagues applauded "quality control" with expressions of both high regard and visible relief. The dating on many hominid sites had been controversial and subject to change. Brown had not only pursued a new, comprehensive method of approaching the problem, but worked closely with Australian Ian McDougall, who had helped to confirm the date on the KBS site, and was among the respected authors credited in the report Brown delivered.

Further context came from a carefully spoken scientist from South Africa, Elisabeth Vrba of the Transvaal Museum in Pretoria, who employed not only Brown's data in her report, but the very maps of isotopic curves that Stan Margolis had mentioned to Richard Leakey in California. At first her notion seemed as far-fetched as the link between dinosaurs and plankton.

Vrba focused on antelope. First, she compiled a census data of modern antelope in Africa—the hartebeest, the gazelle, the springbok, the wildebeest. She found that antelope "tribes" were excellent indicators of the vegetation that prevailed on the landscape.

After several hours of listening to scientific analyses that I was struggling to follow, here finally was a subject I knew well. I remember being fascinated by a sequence in a "Survival" film, *The Year of the Wildebeest*, produced by Alan and Joan Root. The script described the "browsing niche," where the long necks of browsers like the giraffe allowed them a niche of the vegetation out of reach of others; on the next level down were gerenuk, a long-legged antelope that frequently stands on its hind legs to feed from the tops of shrubs. On the lower level, sampling different kinds of grasses, were zebra, with large teeth adapted for tearing tough grasses, and topi, with their long noses good for finding the new, tender shoots. Adaptation aligned diet with availability.

So the link between certain kinds of vegetation and certain kinds of antelopes made a great deal of sense. Vrba studied current species of antelope and their dietary niche, then she did a census based on fossil antelope species, to try to discern the vegetation that prevailed in South African and East African excavation sites. She drew up a graph indicating antelope origins—when new species of antelope diverged. She put this alongside a chart of the family tree. There were two dramatic zigs as opposed to zags in the charts, one at 2.5 million years ago, around the time when *Homo habilis* is thought to have branched from the australopithecines, and again at around half a million years ago, when *Homo sapiens* branched from *Homo erectus*. Vrba suggested that the same environmental "pulses" that affected the antelope affected early hominids.

Alongside these charts, she put a third and a fourth. The third featured Brown's dates for the Turkana basin and her own in South Africa, fixing hominid discoveries in time. The fourth chart was drawn from the CLIMAP project of Nick Shackleton's deep-sea coring research, which features isotopic curves from the past 3.5 million years. The isotopic curves represent changes in temperature, and therefore changes in the vegetation. Again, there were two major "pulses"—one at 2.5 million years ago, and another when *Homo erectus* branched into *Homo sapiens*. Vrba also drew upon a study of microscopic scratches on australopithecine teeth by Fred Grine, which give clues to the type of diet these hominids may have consumed. Hers was a truly interdisciplinary salute, and while I had been sitting in California wondering why some paleoanthropologist hadn't seized upon Margolis's clue, Elisabeth Vrba had already done so.

Finally, she did a graceful and eloquent thing. She said: "It is important to recognize clearly the limits of what I am claiming here."

She served as her own critic on several points, sounding like a scientist's scientist; her ideas were meant to be tested. One was challenged instantaneously by questions from the floor. It had to do with a tiny item: fossil pollen.

Evidence of fossil pollen stretches back to 100 million years ago. Samples are collected from peat, wind-blown cave deposits, fossilized feces, and lake muds. The murky depths of lakes offer an exquisitely ordered archive of flora and fauna and even the dust from the trails of meteors. In an essay entitled "In Praise of Mud," fossil pollen collector Dan Livingstone describes the classic lake-bottom accumulation, occurring at a rate of about one meter per thousand years: "If wind stirs the lake completely, the sediment of several years may be resuspended and mixed together before final burial, but if the deep water of the lake is stagnant and devoid of oxygen, the playing-card-thin layers of each season are not disturbed. The careful observer might discern the strata of separate years, and count them back through time: 1988, 1987, 1986, . . . , for hundreds or even thousands of years."

The mud of some African lakes is two miles deep, offering an archive of the past twenty million years, back to the time of one of our better-known branches, that of the hominoid *Proconsul*. Records of recent hominid activities are found in the cores of European lakes, where the slash-and-burn clearings of Neolithic cultivators left a thin layer of charcoal, "overlain by pollen from the wheat they grew," Livingstone wrote, "from the weeds that bedeviled them, and from the regenerating bush that took over when they moved elsewhere."

Raymonde Bonnefille, who originally worked on the Omo, explores the pollen of the more ancient past, collecting her samples from sediments at hominid sites. Using magnifications up to 1,000, she identifies the pollen spores from 12 to 30 microns across, then counts the number of pollen grains to gain a proportional reading on former forests, swamps, and grasslands. All the species are plotted in a diagram Bonnefille considers "a dynamic image," with sediments and dates on a horizontal line, and on the vertical, the variation of each species through time. (Grasses, like antelope, are classified in "tribes.")

As a student, Bonnefille was inspired by a lecture Louis Leakey gave at the National Museum in Paris, on the discovery of *Zinj*. "The paleoanthropologists were looking for changes in the vegetations and habitats of early hominids, from forest to savanna," she remembers; "I thought I had a possibility by using pollen grains to give direct evidence for such." The classic notion is that when forests gave way to open savannas, our ancestors found it advantageous to walk upright. Vrba was suggesting that the same major influences inspired evolutionary changes in "pulses." Yet Bonnefille found evidence of savanna *and* woodland. From the eastern side of Lake Victoria, she found what she refers to as a "mosaic." Fossil pollen from eight-million-year-old sediments in the Ethiopian plateau indicates humid swamp forests. Three million years ago an evergreen bushland surrounded the Hadar site where Lucy was found.

Bonnefille's discoveries led her to dispute the concept of the most evocative visions of East Africa, that of vast, open grassland. She suggests that savannas are a misnomer. Dan Livingstone confirms this: "Vegetation is extremely complex in Africa. No true-blue pollen expert talks about savanna anymore."

The Serengeti plains in Tanzania are often referred to as savanna. "Serengeti" is the Masai word for open space. Yet Bonnefille's reference to a "mosaic" of savanna and woodland is apt, for there are pockets of trees in the Serengeti today. The hominid site of Laetoli edges the Serengeti. Laetoli is also home to the oldest record of bipedalism—evocative footprints found in 1976. The footprints were preserved by a layer of volcanic ash, which helped to date the site as 3.5 million years old. Based on fossil pollen from the site, Bonnefille was able to identify eighty species of plants that prevailed at Laetoli three and a half million years ago. The conclusion was that the vegetation around Laetoli was open grassland with scattered trees, much like it is today—a mosaic.

The paleoanthropologists agreed with Bonnefille's results. A couple of years later, Andrew Hill described the Baringo site where the five-million-year-old *afarensis* hominid was found: "Here we see evidence that the work of Raymonde Bonnefille might be reinforcing—that a simple change from rain forest to grasslands is not so simple as people might have thought." Hill sees environments much more diverse, "and maybe in the Late Miocene, Early Pliocene, more patchy in both space and time. This may support the idea of bipedalism being partly an adaptation for getting from one patch of woodland to another."

The concept of small portraits within the big picture is replacing many generalizations. Anatomists studying the evolution of the face and skull refer to a mosaic of changes; geologist Frank Brown pieces together his paleogeographic picture of the Turkana basin section by section. Among many disciplines, there is a general chorus: "It's more complicated than we thought."

Ron Clarke of South Africa has the final word. "With reference to the symposium title, 'The Hard Evidence,' I would request that we rid our minds and our writings of this misguided concept of evidence. After all, evidence is what is seen and not how it is interpreted. We can all see a bone and know it is a bone, but what it is evidence for depends on one's interpretations." Clarke suggested that the title be changed to "The Hard-to-Understand Evidence."

All of these issues highlighted during "Ancestors"—the fallibilities of human interpretation, the importance of Frank Brown's geological survey in the Turkana basin, the overlay of environmental influences and "pulses" in speciation—were seeds that would develop over the next few years. Because of the focus on hominid bones, there was no discussion of tools, no reports from biochemists, no papers from primatologists. Beyond fossilized bones, stone tools emerged as the first central clue to what our ancestors were doing and how they were doing it.

Some months later in Berkeley, Don Johanson talked about the new direction of the search: "In the first phase of paleoanthropology I think we've been taken by the discovery of hominid fossils themselves. Now we want to know how these hominids interrelated with their environment, and themselves. The excitement of finding a fossil is difficult to match, but the most pressing and perhaps most exciting question today is the investigation of what our ancestors were actually doing."

4.

Handy
Man

"Here's a stone tool," Don Johanson began, seizing upon what might appear to the uninitiated as a rock. "You look at it and say, 'It looks very simple; it looks very crude; how do you know it's a tool?' "

Johanson was speaking as a San Francisco video team recorded his remarks. The date was November 1985, and the occasion a press conference in Berkeley, on Ridge Road—an area referred to as "Holy Hill" because of the many religious organizations on these slopes. The Institute of Human Origins shares a building with a divinity school, their investigation of descent extending into the basement.

The former library of the divinity school is now a geochronology lab where Garniss Curtis and Robert Drake discern the age of both tools and hominid bones.

The camera team move in close on Johanson, who holds the stone tool aloft and turns it in his hand. "First of all we know it's a tool because it's foreign to the deposit," he explains. "It was brought in from quite some distance away." Stone tools are also identified by design, or pattern of flaking—the result of being between a rock and a hard place. The strike of stone upon stone leaves a concave space, and by repeated strikes, produces a pattern seldom confused with the accidental. Rocks bounced around naturally in a streambed are more likely to become rounded than flaked in the pattern that prevails among thousands of artifacts; rocks that split as a result of temperature changes reveal no symmetry in form, though a single natural edge may have inspired utility in the beginning. Students at Berkeley are often tested with a mix of authentic stone tools and rocks from the campus parking lot. How to discern an artifact from a fact of nature?

Stone tools appear in many forms, some named after what appears to have been their function—choppers and chisels, hammerstones and anvils, cleavers and scrapers. On some smaller, thinner tools you can see a deliberate series of little serrations, like the edge of a steak knife; the classical tear shape of an Acheulian hand ax (named after St. Acheul in France, where they were found in abundance) is equally definitive. Rocks foreign to a deposit are not always tools, and are described as manuports (implying manual transport), with no sign of alteration to the natural form; the assumption is that hominids brought in the raw material but didn't get around to flaking these particular rocks. Some rocks flake more easily than others, and among the lava rocks of East Africa, some types of lava were obviously preferred and transported from sources several miles away.

The tool Johanson holds is called Oldowan (Old'-one), for its style was first noted at Olduvai Gorge in Tanzania. In a search where names rarely impart a clue to the non-scientist, Oldowan is exceptional, for the industry is indeed the old one, first found in sediments 1.8 million years old. Oldowan tools surfaced all over Africa—in Tunisia and along the Ivory Coast, near the Nile delta, in Ethiopia's

Awash Valley, in Zimbabwe—as well as in Eurasia. In some sites the industry endured until a mere 200,000 years ago in its more developed form.

The Oldowan toolkit itself varies in form, depending on how each tool was flaked—a discoid, for example, has been given a sharp rim full circle by flaking on both sides of the rock; a chopper (thought to have been used for chopping meat or bones) has only a few fractures along one end of the rock.

Johanson reaches for his second prop, the lower jaw of an antelope, from sediments 1.8 million years old, when there were plenty of stone tools around. "We find many examples like this. Some ancestor was making stone tools, and either scavenged or killed this antelope—we don't know exactly—and was disarticulating the skeleton." Disarticulation is a kind way of saying butchering, as articulation refers to the connection between bones, largely muscle. Johanson points to cut marks on the antelope jaw, "where obviously they were cutting away the flesh, cutting away the meat, to disarticulate"—he stops short and simplifies—"take that mandible off the skull."

In the past, such scratches were rarely noticed by the naked eye. Nevertheless, there were suggestions of behavior when tools and bones were found in association, such as the hand axes and cleavers at Olorgesailie in Kenya, and the many broken bones of giant baboon found nearby, which led to the suggestion that hominids were smashing the baboon bones open to eat the marrow. There were similar broken bones at Olduvai Gorge in Tanzania, with the attendant hominid bones making the association all the more plausible (thus far no hominid fossils have been found at Olorgesailie, but plenty have been found at Olduvai). Because toolmaking was considered unique to *Homo*, the discovery of the first *Homo habilis* by the Leakeys at Olduvai Gorge inspired an examination of the fossils for unique features.

In *Gray's Anatomy* ("its appeal is not only to physicians and students," notes the dustjacket, "but to artists and the medically curious"), the modern human thumb is described as follows: "This is a joint of reciprocal reception, and enjoys great freedom of movement. . . . When the joint is flexed the metacarpal bone is brought in front of the palm and the thumb is gradually turned to the fingers.

It is by this peculiar movement that the tip of the thumb is opposed to the other digits."

Gorillas and chimps have thumbs that meet their fingertips, yet true finesse in opposability is assigned to hominids, as was, for a long time, the exclusive use of tools. The search for roots is also a search for identity, a survey of distinction by degrees. About the same time that Louis Leakey wrote that toolmaking in "a regular and set pattern" defined "Man," a young primatologist whom he'd inspired was making careful notes in her diary:

6 November, 1960: By the termite hill were two chimps, both male. . . . I could see a little better the use of the piece of straw. It was held in the left hand, poked into the mound, and then removed coated with termites. The straw was raised to the mouth and the insects picked off with the lips along the length of the straw, starting in the middle.

Jane Goodall documented other tool use by the chimpanzees of the Gombe Stream Reserve in Tanzania (now Gombe National Park), and found examples of "a regular and set pattern." (Goodall's comprehensive and fascinating observations are chronicled in *The Chimpanzees of Gombe* [1986], featuring wonderful photographs. The book covers a quarter of a century of observations; hers is the longest field study ever conducted, now in its thirtieth year.)

In addition to seeing chimps fish for termites (a high-protein delicacy enjoyed by the people of Africa as well), she saw chimps using leaves as a sponge to gather water (as in the hollow basin of a tree), and indeed as "napkins." Male chimps often wiped their penes after copulation, and one chimp tidied up his little brother when he sneezed.

The distinction of hominids then leaned toward tool manufacture; a recent (1980) publication prepared by the British Museum of Natural History notes: "No other living creature shares man's tool making behavior—it is a unique human characteristic." But as early hominids modified stones, the chimps of Gombe modified vines and branches to function as tools. They not only selected the most efficient length and width, but stripped off the leaves. Toolmaking and using were among many preconceptions of human uniqueness; it was once suggested that only "man" hunted cooperatively, but any keen observer of wild dogs, cheetah, or for that matter, chimpanzees hunting baboon, could see otherwise.

For primates, Goodall contends that the genius in tool using is not the object itself, but the contemplation: anticipation, modifying, and solving a novel problem.

A novel problem arose in West Africa, where chimps feed on nuts of palm trees. Some of the nuts are too hard to crack by biting; the chimps use a stone as a hammer, to smash the nuts against the roots of the tree. This doesn't always work, presenting yet another novel problem. The chimpanzees resorted to a hammer-and-anvil technique, transporting the two stones several hundred yards in anticipation. They knew which species of trees required this technique, taking two stones to those kinds of trees and not the others. Cynics suggest that chimps saw humans doing this and imitated their actions, making it fair game to suggest the reverse, if chimps were in a position to do so. They have as their eloquent spokeswoman a scientist who bridged what was once considered an unbridgeable gap—drawing up obvious links between human beings and our closest relatives in the wild.

Many hammerstones and anvils were found by Mary Leakey at Olduvai Gorge in Tanzania. Who made them? How were they used? And why were they left there?

The stone tools found in Tanzania inspired over half a century of searching for their makers, and careful documentation of one hundred and thirty sites rich in hominid bones, abundant fauna, and tens of thousands of stone tools. Like the Grand Canyon, these rich deposits in northern Tanzania were cut by a river, revealing hominid history in a stratigraphic sandwich—a slice of prehistoric life three hundred feet deep and twenty-five miles long into the Serengeti plains. Olduvai's place in the search for missing links was initially fixed in 1911 by Professor Kattwinkel, a German lepidopterist whose Search Image trained on an exotic butterfly that led him to the precipitous brink.

Kattwinkel proceeded down into the floor of the Gorge where he discovered fossils of a three-toed horse. The subsequent German expedition inspired by his fossils was led by Hans Reck, who found seventeen hundred fossils but no tools—or so he thought. Reck, like most Europeans, recognized flint tools only. When Louis Leakey visited Reck in 1927, he noticed that one of his "rock samples" resembled the hand axes that he had found in Kenya. Leakey invited Reck to join his 1931 expedition to Olduvai, betting him £10 that he could find a tool there within twenty-four hours. Leakey won the bet. Four years later he was joined in his investigations of Olduvai by a young woman who was to become the most influential archeologist in Africa, and the search for human origins itself. The seventy-six-year-old Dr. Mary Leakey's fame is such that a London shopkeeper, noting her name on a check, exclaimed: "Oh! Are you the Prehistoric Mrs. Leakey?" Mary laughed. "I suppose so."

Her interest in stone tools began in the rich sites of southeastern France, where she lived the greater part of each year with her parents. She was inspired to collect and draw tools by her father, an artist whose Turneresque watercolors hang in the living room of her Kenya home. As he searched for stone artifacts, she joined a treasure hunt that would continue for the next sixty years. By drawing tools, Mary gained insight into the way they were made. "I'd been handling tools since I was eleven," she told me. "They follow a given pattern."

That Mary Nicol, born in 1913, might contribute to the search for human origins is foreshadowed in her own origins. Her great-great-great-grandfather, John Frere, upon finding hand axes in Suffolk, England, suggested an outrageous and heretical idea in 1797, that they were "of a very remote period indeed, even before that of the present world."

It was Mary's illustrations of stone tools that brought her to Louis Leakey's attention. They met when he was at Cambridge; he asked her to illustrate his book *Adam's Ancestors*, and thus began a collaboration that made prehistory.

They were a handsome couple; young Leakey, tall, with dark hair, twinkling brown eyes, and a thin mustache, resembled Errol Flynn, in both his appetite for attention and his mischievous ways of getting what he wanted. When required to take a foreign language at Cambridge, Louis made certain that Kikuyu qualified, then, instructing his instructor in the language, passed with flying colors.

Mary may have resisted formal education, but she was a dedicated student of things she loved. She became a glider pilot at the age of twenty, and her impatience in classrooms transformed to discipline in the field. Africa was both a dream come true and part of an ongoing study. A photograph from that first expedition to Olduvai in 1935 shows Mary wearing a fashionable hat; the shadow of the brim didn't quite obscure the cigarette dangling from her lips, discreetly diminished by retouchers for its reproduction in *National Geographic*. Because she wore trousers and drove a car, she was occasionally addressed as "Mr. Leakey." Louis Leakey admired her spunk, and after their rendezvous in Africa, he divorced his first wife, and he and Mary were married. It was scandalous at the time, but for thirty years the Leakeys enjoyed a great partnership. In the end there would be professional disagreements and personal ones, reinforcing Mary's solitary retreat to her work in Tanzania. Louis's philandering, like his appeal to the public and his access to discoveries, continues to inspire critics surrounded by less to explore.

There is one story about Louis that only Mary Leakey can tell. It took place at an Olduvai site called FLK, named after Louis's first wife, Frieda Leakey; the K stood for *korongo*, which is Swahili for gully. The year was 1959.

Mary went for a stroll with her sleek Dalmatians at her side. Beyond the slope of the FLK site, awaiting her was the skull that would put ancient hominids on the map in East Africa, a skull that would inspire three decades of continuing support by the National Geographic Society. The discovery that became known as *Zinj*, however, was not the ancient hominid that Louis dreamed of finding.

The authors of *Lucy* described several versions of the discovery, one in which Louis was so disappointed it wasn't *Homo* that he dismissed the discovery as "nothing but a god-damned robust australopithecine!" Mary terms this version "Pure invention." She remembers Louis expressing "mild disappointment."

Leakey had hoped to find a large-brained *Homo*, but this skull had a very small brain like that of an australopithecine, which Louis was inclined to view as not ancestral, "an aberrant offshoot." The presence of numerous stone tools found around the skull presented a dilemma, which he solved by suggesting the discovery was so different from the robust australopithecines of South Africa that it should be called by another name—*Zinjanthropus boisei. Zinj* is the ancient name for the coast of East Africa; the species name honored Charles Boise, who had financed the Leakeys' research.

Following the discovery of *Zinj*, over the next twenty years Mary Leakey supervised all research in Tanzania. Her immediate priorities were detailed excavation and mapping of thirteen sites at Olduvai, plotting every inch with meticulous markers for the place where fossils and tools were found. "Mary's importance to African archeology is often underestimated," comments Andrew Hill, "because many of the techniques and methods she introduced are now regarded as commonplace."

The tools discovered at Olduvai Gorge were generally divided into two industries; the Oldowan were the oldest, and then, about 1.6 million years ago, a very different sort of industry emerged, the Acheulian (A-shoo'-leon). Based on careful study, Mary Leakey also discerned what she termed a "developed" Oldowan style; it was the first step in many to indicate that things were more complicated than they seemed. The three overlapped at points in time.

The Acheulians' most curious and beautifully fashioned tool is the hand ax, a large, tear-shaped stone beveled to long, twin-sided edges. Flexibility and longevity marked the Acheulian industry—stone tools that were the Black & Decker of hominids for one million three hundred thousand years. The Acheulian industry is thought to be the work of *Homo erectus.*

Tools are powerful links with early hominid behavior, and their manufacture and position on the landscape continue to inspire an investigation of details. Occasionally this led to assumptions about the behavior of the toolmakers. For example, the earlier use of tools was thought to employ a power grip, when the whole hand wrapped around a more primitive, round tool like a chopper, grasping it much the way you would a potato. The precision grip relied on dexterity between the thumb and the index finger, holding a thin flake the way you'd hold a razor blade.

The notion of a precision grip was applied to the discovery of the first *Homo habilis* at Olduvai Gorge. The name, meaning "Handy Man," was suggested by Raymond Dart. The distinguishing feature of the Handy Man is its relatively large brain; it is seen by many as a missing link between the australopithecines and *Homo erectus*.

The April 1964 scientific description of the Handy Man prepared by Louis Leakey, Phillip Tobias, and anatomist John Napier drew upon a wide collection of bones found at Olduvai amid tools. The fossils included the bones of the lower leg, several pieces of skull, a lower jaw, plus hand bones representing two individuals, one juvenile and the other adult. John Napier, studying the hand bones, found evidence of an opposable thumb.

While there were plenty of mistakes made in this search, a great deal was inferred correctly, often based on little or no evidence. Louis Leakey may have been personally inclined not to view the australopithecines as makers of stone tools, but so far, the evidence suggests that he was right. Long before biochemical evidence proved that chimpanzees were our closest relatives, Leakey suggested that close study of their behavior might shed light on early hominid behavior. (He was wise enough to hedge his bet, inspiring Dian Fossey to study gorillas, and Berute Galdikas orangutans.)

Yet pioneers, by definition, make mistakes, and often it seems that with such fragmentary fossil evidence, intuition is just as valuable as any sort of objective study that pretends to be rigid. When Darwin suggested that missing links might be found in Africa because this was the provenance of the great apes, he added, "But it's useless to speculate." Speculations that are testable are theories, and remain a vital sign of science as long as they're presented as such.

Subjective and highly personal decisions occur in many disciplines that tout objectivity. The true turns in discovery derive from ideas, and these derive from people. In providing an update, many early ideas will naturally be overturned. When the Leakeys first began to discover stone tools at Olduvai, their clues were as fragmentary and enigmatic as the fossils and their gaps. The Leakeys provided the matrix of discovery for other scientists to challenge. They were assisted in their efforts by a young man from South Africa who, like Louis and Mary, fell in love with tools at a very early age.

Born in Cape Town in 1937, Glynn Isaac's interest in stone tools began at the age of six, when a family outing produced authentic tools. By fifteen he was capable of identification at considerable speed.

"Stop the car!" he once shouted. "I see a hand ax!" When the family car was backed up to a heap of stones along the South African roadside, there was indeed a hand ax.

His parents were scientists; his father a botanist, his mother a research associate at the University of Cape Town. They did a remarkable thing: they managed to encourage inquiry and at the same time minimize rivalry between twin sons. With his brother Rhys, Glynn challenged "the Professor" in early morning debates with their father between shaves and baths. Rhys became a Rhodes Scholar, and was awarded a Pulitzer Prize for his work in American colonial history. Glynn won a scholarship to Cambridge, and in 1962 became the first assistant director of the Research Center for Prehistory and Paleontology in Nairobi. Isaac's early training in debates proved fruitful; he loved nothing better than a good argument. Of colleague Alan Walker, he once said, "The only way to change Alan's mind is to take the opposite view and get him arguing against himself." ("That's part of the game," notes Walker.) Following an expedition to Tanzania's Lake Natron, Isaac became friends with Richard Leakey; eventually the two co-directed research at Koobi Fora.

Isaac's dissertation for Cambridge was on the stone tools found at Olorgesailie, the archeological site south of Nairobi that served as my introduction to stone tools, in 1982. I've since visited the site several times, each time granted a slightly revised view based on the insights of a succession of scientists.

Isaac and others initially suggested that half a million years ago *Homo erectus* resided on a grassy plain surrounding Lake Olorgesailie. Today, this basin is arid and rugged. In the blinding white sediments, diatomites (algae skeletons rich in silica) crumble to the touch. From such graveyards of trillions of lifeless shells are mined products that polish, insulate, and provide the sparkle for lines on the highway. In this instance, the sparkle indicated a former lake. Mount Olorgesailie stands at the southeastern end; a shift in the earth's crust invited the Ol Keju Nyiro River to flow through the southern part of the basin. The western half of the basin lifted; red fault lines trace the actual shifts in sections of the earth's surface, fault lines not dissimilar to those that shaped Olduvai Gorge, less than two hundred miles to the southwest. The stone tools at Olor-gesailie were first noticed by geologist J. W. Gregory, after whom the eastern branch of the Great Rift Valley is named. On Easter weekend in 1942, Louis and Mary Leakey decided to explore the area further. I asked Mary Leakey what it looked like when these artifacts were found. "Just as you see it today," she replied. "All those tools were there together, just hundreds of them." More than a ton of stone tools were found.

A small museum with an elevated boardwalk has been built over the original site, with the tools below—vast spreads of stone cleavers and hand axes, lying on the surface of eroding lake sediments.

The tools found at Olorgesailie are Acheulian. In the first reports on these discoveries, the tools were thought to represent actual camps of hominids. The arrangement of the faunal and tool assemblages (which simply means the way they were found, or assembled, in groups) was reconstructed into "the activities of their hunting bands." It was suggested that the concentration of sites represented "a very popular neighborhood indeed, to which the nomadic bands returned repeatedly." Five separate campsites were distinguished in the main area, with "important, consistent differences in the size and shape of handaxes and in the proportion of handaxes to other tools. Though the various sites were certainly not in simultaneous use, there was probably no great time interval between them. Thus the differences are possibly due either to some kind of 'tribal' distinctions between occupants of the different sites or to the differences in the activities engaged at the sites."

The quotations come from a thin orange booklet entitled *Visitor's Guide to the Olorgesailie Prehistoric Site*, which I bought at the site for 2/50 Kenya shillings, less than 15 cents. They were written some time ago by Glynn Isaac, who encouraged a generation of students to challenge his conclusions. He inspired new disciplines, suggesting that students explore every conceivable angle from digging tubers to making tools. He urged them to look for "the scatters between the patches," meaning isolated stones and bones that might be found in between the more dramatic sites of assemblages. From this broader view, they were to seek patterns.

In September 1986, toward the end of the field season, I returned to Olorgesailie. My visit would coincide with that of a film crew sent by National Geographic for their television special, "Mysteries of Mankind." The Nairobi-based director carried in his pocket instructions telexed from Washington, D.C.: "Paint a picture of how early man lived here. As much as possible bring the past alive." Sent from such a distance, the telex bordered upon the telepathic. Rick Potts uses an approach called taphonomy, from the Greek *taphos* meaning burial.

To corner Potts before the film crew arrives, I set out before dawn, driving around the Ngong Hills on a now familiar road that drops me into desert sageland after only a brief introduction. From the vantage point of the escarpment, the volcanic Mount Olorgesailie appears to be the size of an eroded termite mound; in less than an hour I will be looking up to this mountain.

As the road levels out for the long straight stretch across the floor of the Valley, it rains on the right side of the road while the sun shines on the left. The eastern branch of the Great Rift is large enough to accommodate this. Within minutes the sun begins to win the battle, clouds sweep across the sky, and for a moment, it seems, the road itself, where there appears a flurry of white. A young Masai boy herds his goats across, offering an open palm held aloft before he disappears into the scrub brush. This boy will spend the better part of the day entertaining himself with the things he encounters on this landscape. It is not so unlikely that he might find a stone that intrigues him, a rock with an unusually sharp edge that he might keep beneath one of his favorite shade trees. It is this sense of accessibility that draws me back to Olorgesailie.

I'm not so sure that I would have been equally intrigued by this inquiry had I begun at a site like Terra Amata, in the foundation of an apartment building in France. Had a paleontologist there pointed out fossils of a giraffe, disbelief would have led me through a pile of textbooks until I found that giraffe once existed north of the Mediterranean. Here the former world is apt to parade.

A herd of giraffe assume the right of way at the dirt road to the

The road to Olorgesailie drops around the Ngong Hills and into the Eastern Branch of the Great Rift Valley. Mt. Olorgesailie can be seen on the horizon. The excavation site, where hundreds of stone tools are evident, is less than an hour's drive south of Nairobi.

Olorgesailie Museum. I find Potts waiting on the verandah, looking the part of a student: backpack, tan khakis, desert boots. He is short, thin, and carefully spoken; diplomacy and careful research catapulted him to a post normally reserved for scientists with three times his tenure in the field. A mere thirty-three years old, Potts has just been appointed to develop a human origins program at the Smithsonian Institution in Washington, D.C. His work at Olorgesailie continues an investigation he began on Olduvai Gorge in 1977. The question he pursues is: How did hominid behavior differ from that of other species on the landscape?

Two innovative researchers in taphonomy preceded Potts: Kay Behrensmeyer, and Andrew Hill. Behrensmeyer worked first at East Turkana, then at Amboseli National Park southwest of Nairobi, a vast sanctuary rich in elephant herds that parade before Kilimanjaro. In this beautiful arena, Behrensmeyer looked for dead bodies. She surveyed mudflats, open plains, and forested areas, measuring how long a carcass was exposed, when cracks in bones begin to occur—the kind of images capsuled in a time-lapse film segment on drought—so common here that Lake Amboseli is a euphemism: Land Cruisers zip across the "lake," sending up dust devils.

An exposed bone develops tiny cracks at first; these expand until the surface bone begins to peel; finally, the whole bone disintegrates. The entire process takes about fifteen years, unless the bone is buried. Knowing the stages of deterioration in a bone might tell something about the ones of mammals found at Olduvai, for the record at sites like FLK was preserved by a layer of ash. Because Mary Leakey was so careful in her excavation at the *Zinj* site, one can review the levels of bones in time frames marked by local stratigraphy. If the bones at Olduvai were the result of a temporary hominid base camp, certain levels should reveal the same degree of deterioration in bones. Such criteria figure in Potts's work, as does the inventory of bones.

Andrew Hill studied patterns of disarticulation, a statistical note keeping of what's left from a hyena or a lion's meal. By studying assemblages of bones, Hill was able to define a "death site," distinguishing the scene of the crime from a larder. Using this background, Potts could determine whether the bones at Olduvai were the result of a hyena or lion kill actually at the hominid site, or whether the bones had been collected by hominids.

The FLK excavation area where *Zinj* was found has been described as a living floor. Mary Leakey uncovered over two thousand stone artifacts and over forty thousand fossilized bones. In mapping out these discoveries on the site plan, she noticed something intriguing. One patch of stones and bones was densely concentrated, surrounded by a more barren zone. The concentrated patch held many smaller tools and mammal bones that had been smashed. The more barren area contained larger stone tools, and bones that, for the most part, were still intact—jawbones, hipbones, ribs. She then made an interesting observation. The smaller smashed bones were the kind that held marrow; the bones on the outer circle were not the kind to offer this soft, fatty tissue still considered a delicacy by some. Mary found similar patterns in other excavation sites at Olduvai. They were all circular in form, and in some cases, there were pairs of patches. Might these represent former campsites, like the domes of grass that the Turkana people still use today? It was a brilliant hunch, one that invited taphonomists like Rick Potts to ask, "What's wrong with this picture?"

Alan Walker motivated Potts "with the suggestion that maybe we don't have it quite right yet." Walker also suggested that a new tool be employed in the study of old ones—the Scanning Electron Microscope, or SEM.

At Olorgesailie, Potts shows me samples of bones with cut marks. I have to look twice. The normal width of a scratch is thinner than a single strand of hair. Seeing scratches with the naked eye often depends on the color of the bone. "They're subtle," he says, squinting. But the SEM magnifies in a high-fidelity image so powerful that it jiggles with the vibrations of a passing truck. Suddenly cut marks, like the one Don Johanson pointed out on the antelope jaw, began to appear everywhere—on baboon skulls, antelope bones, and on the *Homo erectus* Bodo skull found in Ethiopia.

The Bodo skull has cut marks near the eye that extend into the orbit, "which is a pretty unusual place to get any kind of marks accidentally," Potts says. But taphonomists are "shy about making broad assumptions about violence." Tim White, who has studied the

The excavation site at Olduvai Gorge where Zinj was discovered by Mary Leakey in 1959. The discovery was initially named Zinjanthropus boisei by Louis Leakey, and is informally referred to as a "hyper-robust" australopithecine, because of its prominent sagittal crest and broad cheekbones. The discovery was the first hominid accurately dated at 1.75 million years old, by the potassium/argon method developed by Garniss Curtis and Jack Evernden.

cut marks under an SEM, is convinced the marks represent a "scalping," but scalping could have been part of a postmortem ritual, or even ancestor worship. To know why the marks were made is considerably more elusive than knowing how they were made.

Potts's work on Olduvai bones was done in partnership with Pat Shipman. The two noticed cut marks at the same time, they insist, while working across the table from each other at the Nairobi Museum. Shipman is an associate professor in the Department of Cell Biology and Anatomy at the Johns Hopkins Medical School. Like Potts, she was encouraged to use the SEM by Alan Walker, who is her husband.

Shipman established a reference library of the various marks found on bones: weathering, scratches made by sand, root etching, carnivore tooth marks. All of these references exist on the African landscape today, but not marks by stone tools.

Back in the United States, Shipman and Potts made their own stone tools, and with raw material supplied by a local butcher, began to carve up bones. Then they compared their known experiments to the unknown.

Potts selected seventy-six bones out of eighty thousand gathered from twelve sites at Olduvai. Sixty percent had carnivore tooth marks; 20–30 percent were marks made by stone tools. ("Everything else was perforations undetermined.") "Either the bone surface was poorly preserved, the replica wasn't good enough, or we just couldn't decide on one cause versus another," he explained.

Some bones had both tooth and tool marks. With the SEM, Shipman was able to discern which came first, "much in the same way as old tire tracks are obscured by fresh ones." The overlaps were rare—she found only thirteen really good examples that she could trust, but of these, eight suggested the hominids made their mark *after* the carnivores did. Many mammals in Africa both hunt and scavenge for their food; there's no reason to think early hominids should have refrained from scavenging, unless it's a modern human preference. So hominids, like many creatures on the African landscape, may have been scavengers as well as hunters.

How were the bones at Olorgesailie different from those at Olduvai? For starters, there are no hominid bones. Potts digs in a lower geological sequence, less than a mile from the former shoreline of the lake. The National Geographic film crew arrives, headed by Mohammed Amin. Amin is best known for his dramatic exposé on the drought in Ethiopia in 1984–85. His images, broadcast by the BBC, helped to inspire awareness of the plight around the globe, and the rock collaboration "We Are the World." The first thing Amin wants to do is establish the setting with a long pan of the horizon, then focus in on Potts at work.

Potts leads us away from the better-known sites. "Many of those bones and artifacts were found in gravel and sand, which no archeologist believes was a primary place for hominids anymore. Hominids may have camped here seasonally, but some of the bones and tools were moved by water. Now we're looking for a primary site, one not created by streams but hominids."

We walk southeast, down a ravine; a herd of gazelle disappear into the scrub. A couple of miles from the museum, we climb along an escarpment cut by exposures, revealing neat layers of deposition, distinct in color and texture. Potts traces his finger along a bed of white diatomites, testimony to a "quiet" bed of water. Just above this is a brown bed of marsh sediments. Both are former boundaries of Lake Olorgesailie.

The lake was at least a mile across, contained on the east by Mount Olorgesailie. Just over a million years ago, the lake began to recede; it rose again, fluctuated, and then disappeared completely a half a million years ago. "That western ridge was probably visible to hominids when they were camping," Potts says, "or whatever they were doing." Potts found flakes along this western ridge. "It could be that the hominids were making tools there and bringing them to this area."

He finds most of the bones and tools in the brown bed, where marsh sediments covered the artifacts without the kind of disturbance that swept the original finds into their impressive piles. These assemblages are attritional, meaning they accumulated over a long period of time. "We've found more carnivores in the lake margin level, and very few in the channels. But we don't find any hand axes along the lake margin, they're all in the channel." Now what does this mean? That the two dined separately? If so, it was different from what prevailed at the Olduvai sites.

Amin directs Potts for the film: "Pick up the bone, study it; I'll do a slow pan first." Potts repeats great intrigue several times. Everyone's eyes are on the action within the frame of the camera. A member of the crew nearly steps on the bag of bones Potts had brought along. "Mind those bones," Amin cautions, "he makes a living from them."

Among the fossils Potts found were a hyena skeleton and a complete elephant. Around the elephant fossils he found forty-four stone tools, including flakes and cobbles. To determine whether this elephant was killed or simply died of natural causes, Potts makes latex casts of the elephant bones at the site. These include smaller casts of what look like scratches, to be subjected to the scrutiny of the SEM.

If the original view of some of the "living sites" at Olorgesailie has changed, so has the antiquity of the tools found there. Initially the sites where the hand axes were found were estimated to be 400,000–500,000 years old. Now this has shifted to slightly older: 600,000–800,000 years old. And the elephant site is estimated at just over one million, when the lake was at its fullest. A large cast, twenty yards square, was made of the elephant. A reconstruction of the site will become an exhibit at the Smithsonian.

In addition to all the elephant and hyena bones, Potts found three hundred and fifty stone artifacts at this site. Almost all of them were flakes. An archeologist who does not make a living from bones would sort out the mystery of the flakes.

A few months after my visit to Olorgesailie, I met Peter Jones at Gibbs Farm in Tanzania, a beautiful coffee plantation in the highlands south of Olduvai Gorge. In addition to coffee, there are mango, lettuce, carrots, and herbs—fresh vegetables and fruits that the Gibbs family often sent on a one-way journey to Mary Leakey's camp at Olduvai.

Peter Jones is the Sam Shepard of archeology. He bears a striking resemblance to the American playwright/actor. He is tall, his face angular, with short blond hair and a refreshing cockiness. He is careful to distinguish himself, his lifestyle, and his work from "Rick and all the rest." He's thirty-three years old; in 1976, when he first began to assist Mary Leakey in Tanzania, he was only nineteen.

Jones began making stone tools when he was twelve, working with flints in his native Denmark. Later he studied with François Bordes, a flint knapper of considerable renown, in some of the same Dordogne sites that inspired Mary Leakey's early interest in tools. Trained "à la méthode Bordes," he preferred to focus on the technology of tools—how they were made, how they were used—rather than only studying the final form. Tools were commonly divided into different "cultures" according to their position in the geological sandwich, and by comparing their design.

As mentioned, there was a curious overlap in tool "cultures" at Olduvai. While the excavation sites occurred at many places and on many levels, the geological survey of Olduvai, a monumental project undertaken by Richard Hay, granted order. Based at Berkeley, Hay had to determine the ages of strata, beginning with the older level, called Bed I, the order extended upward to younger sediments, or Bed IV, for the sites at Olduvai occurred on many different levels. Within these layers, the more primitive Oldowan culture was in Bed I, with a "developed" Oldowan industry extending all the way up in recent times to Bed IV. But in Bed II (when the Oldowan industry still thrived), Acheulian tools began to appear. Were two different species of hominids making two different sets of tools? Did they live at Olduvai at the same time? Too, the environmental "pulses" that Elisabeth Vrba found influencing species must have affected Olduvai Gorge; for example, the time of the sudden appearance of the Acheulian industry in Bed II coincides with the disappearance of Lake Olduvai. Did a new toolmaker pass this way on their migration to greener places?

In addition to this curious overlap, there was a curious reversal— the term used by geologists when they find an older section on top of a younger one. This "reversal" was not in the stratigraphy, but in the form of certain Acheulian hand axes. At an older site called HEB, the hand axes appear more sophisticated than those at a younger site called WK. The level of sophistication was based on the way they looked, not on a direct experiment of how they were flaked.

Jones went to the lava spreads around Olduvai and Laetoli, gathered rocks, and began to make stone tools. He concentrated on two aspects: technique and time ("I enjoy getting my teeth into the local stuff"). The first thing he discovered was that few of the local materials "behaved" like the flint he was used to working with in Europe. The next thing he discovered was that the pattern on a tool—its relative design—was related to the character of the raw material, not the sophistication of the toolmaker. For example, hand axes made with fine-grained phonolite (called a sounding stone because it rings when struck) naturally looked more sophisticated than hand axes made with the very coarse lavas. An elegant phonolite hand ax took him three minutes to make; a lava hand ax took fifteen minutes.

Mary was keen to see his results. "I was able to say, Look, it's damned easy to make a beautiful hand ax in this stuff, but it takes a hell of a lot of skill to make something that even looks crude in this other material. One material flakes beautifully, and with another it requires a whole different technique." This unraveled the curious reversal at Olduvai. The differences arose from the characteristics of the raw material.

If Jones could discover such things by making tools, what might he discover by using them? His dedication was tested during a culling operation by the Tanzanian Wildlife Department, when an elephant herd was trimmed. (At the time, culling was a common practice of wildlife management, when the number of elephants exceeded their resources.) "I almost turned away and didn't do any of the work at all." Yet he pressed on, timing himself, amid flies, blood, and a stench made thicker by the heat. "I did this for seven weeks, and by the time I got to the last elephant I'd reduced my cutting time to one tenth. I was tackling this in a way I assumed a single hominid would—taking as much meat as one can carry. Within an hour and a half I could easily remove twice my own weight in meat."

In 1970, two scientists (Vance Hanes and J. Desmond Clark) wrote a paper analyzing all the large mammal butchery sites, including Olduvai and sites in Europe. They surveyed stone tools lying around carcasses—elephants included. They found 75 percent flakes, 20 percent scrapers, the rest bits and pieces. They concluded that flakes and scrapers were used by early humans to butcher large mammals.

Jones began with "itty-bitty" flakes, efficient even on elephant skin, an inch thick. A flake may be only an inch long itself, but it works like a razor, yet is easier to hold, with concave grooves welcoming the precision grip. "If you get it just right, you can rip right down the whole leg." He slashes the air between us.

But the bigger and heavier the tool, even if the edge isn't as sharp as a flake, the easier the work. "You had a long cutting edge and you had a weight behind it." He found that he liked to work with a two-pound hand ax with a cutting edge twelve inches long.

He uses both hands, making incisions with the hand ax that he couldn't with a flake. As he's doing this, the edge becomes blunt. He knocks a few flakes off to refine the edge of the ax. By the time he finishes, there is very little of the hand ax left, but plenty of flakes on the ground. The first disposable razor was invented nearly two million years ago.

"I've been able to convince Mary [Leakey] that three if not four of the tools defined as tools are simply background to a single activity. They're by-products." For example, Jones thinks the chopper wasn't necessarily a tool, but often used for the production of flakes.

Jones qualifies: "Tool use is a very subjective thing. If you work very hard you could use almost any stone edge for almost any activity." He thinks many by-products were identified as a separate tool, purely on the basis of shape. Good examples are polyhedrons, subspheroids, and spheroids.

Polyhedron by name indicates many facets; a subspheroid is slightly battered, and a spheroid is of course round. Since tools were judged on shape and appearance, it seemed they graded into these forms, in stages of gradual sophistication. "Now, if you really look at it," Jones says, "most of the polyhedrons are lava, most of the subspheroids are quartz. So they can't really grade, one into the other, because the raw materials are different."

Now he's into disarticulation and efficiency, "finding this cuts easier than this; this edge is best for skin cutting, this one for meat cutting." His fieldwork relates to the discoveries of Pat Shipman. She found that different sorts of scratch marks prevailed, say, when she disarticulated a joint as opposed to when she made a long stroke to remove a tendon or skin, used by modern hunter-gatherers for clothes, bags, or shoes. In other words, the scratch marks on bones could be matched to the butchering purpose. It's a fascinating approach offered by new technology, "if," as Jones emphasizes, "you can find that one in ten thousand artifacts that's well enough preserved. That," he says, "requires a rather different personality than mine.

"I'm not a lab type," he adds unnecessarily. "I'm inclined to stay in Africa. I prefer being in the bush, not the academic scene." After several visits to the States and a brief stint at Harvard, he's come close enough. "I've got almost nothing in common with my colleagues. They live in the West, come out and do fieldwork for a few weeks, then go back. I like to follow my own research path, regardless of current scientific fads." Jones maintains a home in Arusha, Tanzania, where both he and his wife Annie supplement their research by working part time with tour operators Abercrombie & Kent. Annie Jones's research involved digging tubers with the local Hadza tribe, trying to figure out how early hominids might have gathered vegetables, what tools they used.

Jones runs his fingers through his hair, then leans back in his chair. It's just after six in the evening, when long shadows extend over the floor of Olduvai Gorge. At Gibbs Farm, a parade of visitors arrive; Jones is currently serving as a tour guide.

"There's very little money in the field, let's face it, there's also a lot of duplication. There are tons and tons of stone tools, all over the world, that haven't been studied. Yet people still go out and dig up more. It's like paleontology. If you find the right things, you can really make it. You'll be all over *National Geographic*! You can give lectures for a lot of money. It may allow you to obtain more funds, but it puts pressure on you to make a lot of what you find, and to find it quickly."

He remembers his initial frustration with Glynn Isaac in the field, "but at Harvard I realized how important he was for the whole field, because"—he pauses—"he had a conscience. He was trying to get people together, to get them to talk about ideas." Jones delivers a common complaint: "That's a problem in this field. It's dominated by personalities, and half the time they're just not going to talk to each other. It's destructive."

He sees the personalities propelled by glamorous projects, while he prefers to work "on a bunch of tiny problems, which I think might solve a hell of a lot. Most big projects are more publicity than results. But real discoveries often derive from a little thing like: I wonder why it's like this instead of like this. So I'm interested in small projects."

His next project is hand axes, "to find some clue to why you find some hand axes that are beautiful, hand axes that I know personally have a long, useful life in them because you can resharpen the edges. Were hominids so rich they could discard a brand-new hand ax?

"These ideas you only get if you're here," he insists. "I get a lot of ideas just being here. It's a hell of a kick to me to be working on zebra bones at Olduvai and look up on the horizon to actually see a whole herd of zebra."

As I watch, the pale flush of dawn strengthens in the east. The smell of new rain fills my nostrils. I have risen early, and write by lamplight. Last night I tried to write but my lamp blew out and the wind defeated my attempts to light it again.

Such winds can only indicate the setting of East Turkana. The extract is from a letter Glynn Isaac wrote to his wife Barbara in 1977. He was sitting beneath an acacia tree, at the camp dining table near Site 50.

The site is proving fascinating. We are extending the two trenches that Jack [Harris] dug, digging very carefully as to record the position, the preservation of even small pieces of bone . . . in one of our trenches, we are down to the level where we have started to find a little, thin scatter of flakes, mainly from one core, including conjoinable pieces (Yippie!). It really looks like the deposition of one fleeting occupation episode—the kind of atomic particle of the archeological record for which, as you know, I have of late begun to hanker. . . . This promises to be rich and complex.

In August 1985, Glynn Isaac made the familiar journey to Koobi Fora to introduce yet another student to yet another project. By this time Koobi Fora had become something of a second home, but he was pressed by other commitments, and quickly left Kenya for London, en route to Beijing, as part of a project for the National Academy of Sciences. Although he hadn't felt well in Kenya, he insisted on making the journey. In China he became extremely ill, and was transferred to the U.S. Naval Hospital in Tokyo, where he died suddenly, at the age of forty-seven, of fevers associated with hepatitis and filariasis, a parasitic disease transmitted by mosquitoes.

The following year two symposia honoring Isaac featured the work of the scientists he'd inspired. Stan Ambrose reconstructed the diet of early hominids by measuring carbon and nitrogen isotopes from bones found in Kenya, Tanzania, and South Africa. Jeanne Sept reported on early hominid food foraging "models," studying the way contemporary nomads around Turkana collect their food. Jack Harris talked about the earliest evidence for fire, patches of reddish-orange sediments in an archlike shape, with stones "thermally altered." Harris compared these from Site 50 to those left by the Turkana people today.

Jo Ann Gutin studied the isotopic variations in mollusks; John Barthelme reported on "site distribution patterns" around Lake Turkana, meaning the way bones and stones were found—like the taphonomy of Rick Potts, who reported on his work at Olduvai. Archeologist Nick Toth summed up Glynn Isaac's influence: "What I'm hearing, over and over, are students saying, when they confront a problem, a mystery, or new evidence, 'What would Glynn have done?' That," Toth concluded, "is as nice a legacy as anyone could have in this field."

On November 4, 1985, many of his colleagues gathered in the Geology Lecture Hall at Harvard to pay tribute. In their words they revealed not only Glynn Isaac's place in their search, but as people do when reminded of their own mortality, something of themselves.

Kamoya Kimeu, on his first visit to the United States, was among those paying tribute. At first Kimeu spoke slowly in English, then switched to the Swahili that Isaac understood. He told of the members of the Hominid Gang who had come to him. "We send you to say that we are all sad about Glynn."

"My words today are brief," Richard Leakey began. "Glynn was more than a friend, he was a companion, an invaluable point of reference for me over a period of twenty-five years. Most major decisions that I made in my career were influenced by Glynn's advice. . . . His complete sense of the way for our discipline to proceed was always visible and always reliable. Can we find among us another like him? As a tribute to Glynn we must build upon his ideals, make them the norm rather than the exception."

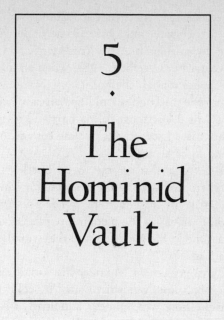

5.
The Hominid Vault

Among those hearing Leakey's words was Stephen Jay Gould. The scientist everyone expected to lose (everyone except Gould) was on the road to full recovery after a battle with cancer. His influence on the search was apparent during my first interview with Leakey in Nairobi. Leakey was careful to distinguish between evolution as fact and theory. That evolutionary changes have occurred, he explained, was a fact; *how* evolution actually works involves theories. "This is where the work of Steve Gould is so important, in proposing mechanisms." I later discovered that the invitation to Koobi Fora which I enjoyed was initially meant for Gould, who had planned a trip to Africa at the same time. Instead, he underwent four hours of surgery and began chemotherapy treatment.

His nadir occurred in December 1983, when an infection from an experimental application of chemotherapy caused peritonitis; he nearly died from the infection. Gould had already been subjected to heavy radiation; he'd lost most of his hair and sixty-two pounds. After the peritonitis, "I spent a lot of time convincing other people that I was going to be all right.

"There was nothing else for me to do but keep working," he insists. "I never stopped writing the columns for *Natural History*," which he credits in his introduction to *The Flamingo's Smile* for some of his will to live: "in the plodding regularity of these essays, who can surpass me in the good fortune they supply; every month is a new adventure. . . ."

At a Nobel Symposium in Minneapolis, Gould, wearing a little cap to cover his hair loss, was surrounded by colleagues, students, and press. The questions were endless, and finally a hand was raised. "Professor Gould has to rest now," Richard Leakey boomed, extracting Gould from the crowd. ("Richard behaved like a mother hen," Gould recalls.) Leakey escorted him to his hotel room, insisting that he rest. When Gould resisted, Leakey demonstrated on the second single bed.

The two men talked, Gould staring at the ceiling, Leakey keeping a watchful eye on his patient. At the time, the creation-science movement was gaining ground; they made a pact. "We agreed to use every public forum we could to promote the fact of evolution," Leakey remembers. "And I made it quite clear to Steve that he simply could not die before he'd come to Kenya."

January 1986, Nairobi: Richard Leakey leads the way to the Hominid Vault, taking long strides around a courtyard in the center of the Nairobi Museum complex known as the Louis Leakey Memorial Building. The grandson of missionary grandparents is accompanied by the grandson of a New York corset designer; Stephen Jay Gould does double time to keep pace, the top of his thick gray hair not quite level with Leakey's shoulder. Both men base their careers upon the investigation of the earth's clues to evolution, yet they are so physically and intellectually different, and their disciplines and backgrounds so disparate, that one might mistake them for the science's odd couple.

Gould's tool is the typewriter; his terrain, the literature; he works late. Leakey's airplane is his tool; his terrain, the Cradle of Mankind; he's up before sunrise. Leakey's forte is fossils; Gould's, ideas. Both rank among our most prominent spokesmen on evolution. Leakey was on the cover of *Time*; Gould, *Newsweek*. It took the evolutionary biologist forty years to achieve the name recognition that Leakey gained at birth.

Gould's career in taxonomy began on Rockaway Beach, Long Island, where as a child he collected seashells, classifying them as regular, unusual, and extraordinary. His decision to pursue paleontology at the age of five was unswerving; young Leakey was equally determined to do anything but.

While Leakey escaped the trenches of academia, Gould receives letters addressed to Mr. Illustrious Historical Professor Jay Gould; such find him at Harvard's Museum of Comparative Zoology, surrounded by fossils and erudite notions that buzz around his head like bees. He was among the first to be awarded a grant from the MacArthur Foundation, the so-called genius awards. As a graduate student at Columbia, he had no compunction about publishing on his early absorptions, dominated, as are his current ones, by the work of Charles Darwin.

The eloquence in Gould's scientific papers inspired the editor of *Natural History* magazine to invite him to write a column; "This View of Life" is now in its second decade. Gould is acclaimed as "the finest science essayist of our time"; his prolific expositions are republished in books with titles that seize upon "the particulars that fascinate": *The Panda's Thumb, The Flamingo's Smile, Hen's Teeth and Horse's Toes*. From these "particulars that fascinate," Gould finds "generalities that instruct."

With Niles Eldredge, of the American Museum of Natural History, Gould suggested a theory that requires paleoanthropologists like Leakey to view their fossils in a new way. While their idea drew upon the fossil record of trilobites (extinct creatures so named because their body was in three segments) and snails (the subject of Gould's study), it could apply to patterns in hominid evolution as well. This approach was essential. The rich data they studied supplied a comprehensiveness and longevity impossible in the brief history of hominids—a history, as Mark Twain put it, equivalent to "the last coat of paint on the top of the Eiffel Tower." Gould and Eldredge studied the basic parts of structure.

Their theory was granted the eloquent name of punctuated equilibria; to Gould's dismay, students promptly dubbed it "punk eek." It addresses the pattern of tempo and mode in evolution: perhaps changes in evolution do not occur gradually but suddenly, after long periods of little change; in other words, equilibrium is punctuated. In the time frames of the history of life on earth, "suddenly" is not to be confused with a lightning bolt; when people speak of "moments" of punctuation, they may be referring to a quarter of a million years.

It was a simple idea with profound implications. What if the hominid brain evolved suddenly? Then a large-brained hominid older than skull 1470 may not exist. What if our bipedal stance was an adaptation that evolved quickly? Then the search for this "moment" of change should focus on sediments around four million years old (just before the oldest evidence of an upright stance, the Laetoli footprints dated at 3.75 million years). In fact, "punk eek" suggests that some missing links may never be found, that certain changes may have occurred so rapidly that intermediary forms were simply not preserved in the fossil record.

All three of these possibilities offer potential challenge to Leakey's pursuit. He thinks that the large-brained *Homo* may be older and simply hasn't been found yet, and that bipedalism may have occurred as long as ten million years ago. And his general goal, assisted by the Hominid Gang, is of course to find missing links. Yet Leakey personally invited Gould to detail ideas that may prove him wrong. Gould expresses high regard for Leakey's pursuit of new evidence— "the doing of science." Leakey might be said to be dusting for fingerprints, Gould contemplating motivation.

Gould speaks as he writes, with mind-bending excursions from

the Cambrian fossils of Canada's Burgess Shale to the moons of
Saturn, and an occasional reference to Wagner and the wisdom of
Casey Stengel. This requires vision and imaginative reach, which
many scientists have, yet none match the translation for which Gould
is renowned. C. P. Snow once likened the relationship between
scientists and non-scientists to travelers covering the same ground
but not speaking because they hadn't been introduced. Gould per-
forms this introduction with invaluable asides. Leakey does the same
for the Cradle of Mankind.

Gould's comments in the field tend to be baroque expositions,
thick in parenthetical references and telling anecdotes drawn from
the history of the science. (They are also rich in sports metaphors.
At one point Gould says, "That one's too close to call," and while
Leakey accepts this, he is more familiar with the other American
pastime, referring to an enigmatic skull as "The Sixty-Four-Dollar
Question.") While Leakey's comments rarely require a semicolon,
Gould's call for a hailstorm of exclamation points; then with a pause
indicating the eye of the storm, he returns to the subject at hand,
with a series of questions for the keeper of the keys to the Hominid
Vault.

The vault itself is an unimposing space twenty by thirty feet,
with white walls, industrial brown carpeting, and the dispassion of
an empty locker room. (If human brains perspired, the room would
be unbearable, a concept that gains credibility.) The only entrance
is a six-inch-thick door, of bank-vault caliber. Inside, the ceiling is
high, dome-shaped, and concrete-reinforced; small, round skylights
tunnel up to blue skies. There is a guest book, a burglar alarm, and
a security camera.

This session between Gould and Leakey is nothing short of historical. Neither participated in the "Ancestors" symposium two
years earlier, nor were any fossils in this room a part of the comparative sessions. Here are two internationally renowned spokesmen
about to review the evidence. Were the news bureaus informed, they
might have attached a satellite hookup to that camera, their video
monitors revealing a newsworthy scene: The walls of the Hominid
Vault are lined with cabinets full of fossils.

"The evidence for hominid evolution would fit on a billiard table,"
noted *New York Times* writer Nicholas Wade, an assessment re-

Richard Leakey and Stephen Jay Gould in the Hominid Vault of the Nairobi Museum. Gould holds the 2.5 million year old "black skull" discovered by Alan Walker in 1985.

peated by Walter Cronkite on his CBS Universe program. Apparently neither Wade nor Cronkite has ever been in the Hominid Vault, or they failed to specify how high the bones were to be stacked.

The tall metal cabinets are common enough, where you'd expect to find airmail envelopes and Elmer's Glue. But here there are jaws and teeth and limbs and the occasional skull. There are skulls of australopithecines, robust and hyper-robust (or *boisei*) and the most impressive Handy Man, skull 1470. In the case of *Homo erectus*, there are several skulls, and there is the Turkana Boy, which means just about everything—ribs, toes, and teeth, femurs, tibia, fibia, and a pelvis that Gould has described as the most intriguing since Elvis's. There are mystery hominids in the Suspense Account, like 1813 and 1805. There are also four cabinets of hominoids, like *Proconsul*, and the "dozens" of *Kenyapithecus* found in 1982. Because of limited space in the Tanzanian Museums, several hominids from Olduvai and Laetoli are protected here on temporary loan.

The time span of the Hominid Vault runs from *Proconsul* at sixteen million years old to modern "saps" (as Gould calls *Homo sapiens*) a mere twenty thousand years old. This impressive inventory is capsuled by Leakey, who sweeps his hand quickly around the room: "Those are Plio-Pleistocene, there's Miocene, there's Holocene, and that's Tanzania." Air conditioning keeps the fossils at a steady 68 degrees Fahrenheit; the Hominid Vault is constructed to be bombproof.

Leakey introduces Emma Mbua, the curator of the Hominid Vault, standing sentry, smiling, cherubic and efficient, wearing a red silk dress. A ten-year veteran of the museum staff, Emma is of the Kamba tribe; her cousin works in the Museum Shop; her father is a cook at the Rusinga camp. The museum staff is an extended family.

Over the next two hours Emma Mbua will retrieve more than enough fossils to cover a billiard table. There are, for the record, 290 specimens of ancient hominids in the Nairobi Hominid Vault. (A specimen may be a whole skull or a single tooth.) Within this inventory (as of 1986) are 56 from Olduvai, 27 from Laetoli, 183 from East Turkana, 5 from Baringo, 4 from Chesowanga, 1 from Lothagam, 1 from Kanapoi, and 13 from West Turkana—the rest are archaic saps. Hominoids were not included in this count.

There are other inventories of hominids, in the Transvaal Museum in Pretoria, the British Museum of Natural History, the National Museum of Ethiopia, the Tanzania Museum in Dar es Salaam, and museums in China, France, Denmark, Greece, Germany, Italy, and the Iraqi Museum in Baghdad.

To steal one of Gould's metaphorical bases, a baseball diamond seems a more appropriate dimension than a billiard table, with *Aegyptopithecus*, the thirty-three-million-year-old, lemurlike skull (with the thirty-two teeth typical of hominoids) at home plate, and modern hominids (of course) in left field. This way there is sufficient space for imagining the unknown and the incessant rearrangement of the known.

In the center of the room is a long, padded table with a raised ridge running down its center, clamped with long-necked study lamps. The table assumes center stage, and like the annual Miss America pageant, becomes the foundation for an impressive display of anatomical details and empty-eyed smiles. Bright white spots fall onto the runway as Leakey switches on the lamps, one by one.

Leakey offers the "Professor" the only seat, a simple wooden Windsor chair, glossy with the rub of wool sweaters and (as Leakey jokes) "many famous rear ends." Gould assumes his position with certain relish ("It's quite a privilege to sit here in this great chair, and have some of the world's most important materials put before you"). A few days earlier, visiting Down House in England, Gould had slipped into the chair in Darwin's study where *On the Origin of Species* was written. One imagines Darwin would have relished Gould's chair; the man who suggested that missing links might surface in Africa died in 1882, forty-three years before the first australopithecine was discovered.

Gould qualifies that he is not an expert on human evolution, though he has written on the subject in an expert fashion. In this setting, Gould defers to Leakey and the literature. The review of the evidence begins with the older specimens, and therefore the lower branches of our family tree. "I'll run you through some Miocene things first," Leakey cues. Emma produces the most famous specimen of *Proconsul*, the skull found by Mary Leakey on Rusinga Island in 1948. It is sixteen million years old.

It falls into the group known as the dryopithecines, or "woodland apes." The wrist bones are like those of a monkey, suggesting that

Proconsul was a tree dweller, but its shoulder joints are like those of a chimp. It was about the size of a gibbon. That it is hominoid is told by several things: for example, the shape of the cusps—a monkey molar has four cusps; the dryopithecines have five. Too, the chest is broader, and there is no tail, but a vestigial one like our own. And relative to body size, their brains were larger than those of other apes of the era. The dryopithecines disappeared, or at least their fossil record did, around nine million years ago.

Proconsul was named in honor of a popular chimp in London vaudeville called Consul. At the time of this discovery, in 1948, it was Louis Leakey's policy that such finds be studied by colleagues in England. With the skull in a box on her knees, Mary Leakey set out for London in a converted RAF York bomber; when she disembarked in Cairo, the captain locked *Proconsul* in the cockpit. After a press conference at the London airport she carried the box to Paddington Station, where she took the train to Oxford, turning her carry-on luggage over to Le Gros Clark, who studied the skull and drew up a graphic reconstruction. In the fifties, Le Gros Clark had, by careful study, been the one to draw up the distinguishing characteristics between a hominid and a hominoid.

The following year, 1949, *Proconsul* was loaned to the British Museum for an exhibit. Twenty years later, when Richard Leakey became director of the Kenya Museum, he requested that the skull be returned. Officials at the British Museum claimed *Proconsul* had been a gift. Subsequent correspondence over the next decade did little except for stamp collectors at either end, until 1982, when Mary's secretary (everyone should have a secretary like Hazel Poitgeiter) found the original letter outlining the terms of the loan in the Kenya National Archives, an institution in downtown Nairobi quite separate from the museum. In 1983, thirty-five years after its discovery, *Proconsul* was returned to Kenya and the Hominid Vault.

Proconsul rests snug in its individually contoured bed of foam. Most skulls reside in a custom-built plywood case; legs, arms, pelves, and jaws find a similar niche; smaller fossils and isolated teeth are kept in plastic bags inside the same case. There is the occasional eclectic container; one portion of a skull from East Turkana emerges from a colorful tin labeled "Anti-Malaria" tablets.

"*Proconsul africanus*," Leakey announces, holding the tiny skull in his large hands. It looks like a mask carved of ivory. The back part of the skull is missing, and its bony face is a bit lopsided. "This is the original one that Mary found in 'forty-eight. Here's the basicranium [bottom of the skull], and the mandible." He fits the mandible, or lower jaw, into place, which results in a clicking sound like false teeth coming home.

"I didn't know it was that good a specimen," Gould enthuses. He turns the skull, examining a mouthful (thirty-two strong) of opalescent teeth. "It's got wonderful teeth"; the long canines protrude. "Look at that palate length," Gould refers to what we might consider a substantial overbite. Cracks in the skull denote the jigsaw puzzle that confronted its discoverers.

"It got horribly crushed," Leakey explains, "but it was possible to put the thing back together with a plaster reconstruction." He adds that *Proconsul*'s cranial capacity, based on the reconstruction, is under 200 ccs, about that of a present-day Colobus monkey. How this reconstruction came about tells much about the investigation that occurs not in the field but in the laboratory.

The 1948 reconstruction by Le Gros Clark was accurate, which is to say, it bore the same distortion as the original find. And the very back of the skull, the occipital bone, could not be attached accurately because two pieces that went in between, called nuchal crests, were missing.

Three decades later, Martin Pickford once again demonstrated his abilities as a keen-eyed paleontologist. Unlike the discoveries in the Samburu Hills with Ishida and Cheboi, this time his survey was in the archives of the Nairobi museum. Pickford noticed an entry in the field records for the 1947 expedition to Rusinga listing "possible" primate fragments from Site R106. He began to search through the numerous trays of fossil fauna from the Rusinga expedition. Among these were fragments of Crocodilia and Chelonia—the latter being turtles. Pickford became particularly intrigued by the turtle fossils. He picked out two fragments in the tray that were distinctly primate. Written on each bone was "Site R106." The *Proconsul* skull that Mary Leakey discovered came from Site R106.

Photographs taken during the 1948 excavation showed that the skull was found upside down in the sediments. In this burial position, the jaw was pressed down and back, the nuchal crests displaced by this pressure and therefore the first to surface. Discovered a year before the rest of the skull, they were marked as "possible" primate, but filed as definite turtles.

When the main skull was returned to Kenya in 1983, Alan Walker set about doing an accurate reconstruction, assisted by Richard Smith. The skull was cleaned. Plaster casts were made, lines of fracture scored; then the plaster was cracked along the scored lines. The result was a table strewn with fragments. The left and right lower jaws were joined, the lower incisors replaced. Before putting the upper jaw back together, they studied the wear on the teeth, positioning the jaw so that the teeth met (occluded) in a position that would have produced that exact wear on the teeth. Then pieces of the cheekbones were realigned, the frontal skull fragments added, the side parietals realigned. And into this, near the back of the skull, the two bits of "turtle" fit.

To round out the remaining distortion, a mirror was held to the fuller, more accurate side of the skull, and mirror modeling in latex offered the symmetry undone by natural burial.

The reconstruction by Le Gros Clark suggested significant prognathism, the forward jutting of the muzzle. With this more symmetrical and more complete reconstruction, the prognathism diminished. The nose moved. The nuchal plane lengthened. Overall, the cranium grew. For an ape of its time, *Proconsul* had a large brain. For several decades *Proconsul* was thought to be an ancestor of gorilla or chimp, but now it looks more like the last common ancestor of great apes and humans. That said, it was not a simple scenario, for two or three species (at least) were involved.

"The interesting thing about *Proconsul* now," Leakey sits on the edge of the table before Gould, "is the way we looked at it before. With more and more material coming in, it's becoming more and more difficult to classify. We now have *Proconsul africanus, Proconsul nyanzae,* and *Proconsul major.*" The differences are minor. A Splitter would be inclined to give a slightly different-looking specimen a new species name. In this instance, Leakey prefers to lump.

He places another small skull on the table, one discovered by Wambua Mangao, a member of the Hominid Gang. "This is yet another new specimen found last year on Rusinga. It forces a reappraisal of the taxonomy of *Proconsul*—because to me, these two specimens, found a few hundred meters apart, make a perfectly good male and female of the *africanus*."

Others think the two represent *africanus* and *nyanzae*. Thus begins one of the themes in any session with the evidence: Splitting and lumping comes up when sorting gracile and robust australopithecines; it comes up in debates over the *afarensis* finds from Hadar; it comes up with 1813.

Among living primates, sexual dimorphism—the female being smaller than the male—is less noticeable among smaller species, and greater among the larger primates. A male gorilla is nearly twice the size of the female. Yet among humans, the male is, on average, only 5 to 12 percent larger than the female. The differences were extreme in our ancestors, affecting the size of the skull as well as height.

"This dimorphism," Leakey suggests, "is well within the range of your gorillas and chimps today." To really argue his point, Leakey would need examples not of contemporary apes but of ancient ones, a range of evidence that normally eludes fossil finders. He positions four large wooden containers on the table.

"This is some of the new stuff from Rusinga." The "stuff" is extensive. "We've got literally thousands of pieces," says Leakey, "including at least thirteen different skeletons." This extraordinary collection was discovered during the 1984–85 field seasons.

Again, the initial clue arose from a sleuth in the archives, but this assemblage drew from so many distant sources that Gould would exclaim, "It's like putting together a Greek statue from all the spoils of pillages!"

To begin, Leakey displays some pieces of a *Proconsul* found by his father. "This was found in the fifties by Louis, and these fossils were all in blocks of matrix," which is to say, ensconced in hard rock, dense as concrete, yet the color of dark jade. There was no airscribe in those days, so the fossils were chiseled out, or at least, some of them were. "And blocks of matrix in the fifties were sent to museums all over the world for study."

Naturally some were sent to the British Museum. A student from

Bristol, writing about an extinct pig for his thesis, came across these blocks of matrix from Rusinga, and returned those unsuitable for his study to Nairobi in 1980.

This time it was Alan Walker digging around in trays. When he saw these blocks of matrix, he knew from the distinctive green rock that they were from the same *Proconsul* site where Louis Leakey had made his find. Using the airscribe, Walker extracted part of the leg and most of the foot of a *Proconsul*.

"We reckoned blocks of matrix around the world might have more pieces of *Proconsul* in them," recounts Leakey, who began dictating correspondence to seven museum curators in seven museums around the world. (So much for the romantic image of discovering fossils by camelback on wind-swept African horizons.) Blocks of matrix began to migrate to Nairobi.

"And out from this matrix comes a nearly complete skeleton!" Leakey exclaims. "A few parts were still missing, so we sent a team back into the field to relocate the original site."

No one had been to this particular site for thirty years, but they found the geologist's notes in the museum files. In 1983, Alan Walker and Martin Pickford set out for Rusinga Island, on Lake Victoria. Walker read from the notes as Pickford paced off the details of the map. Walker stood on a hill, directing. "Left a bit, right a bit." Pickford finished his paces. "I'm here!" he yelled. "But I don't see anything." From the top of the hill, Walker could see plenty. Pickford was standing in a patch of green grass—in the middle of brown grass.

The excavation site had, over the years, held water in the hollow that lent the grass its healthy color. Within this patch of green, thirteen by twenty-five feet, they found green rock with fossils in them. They began stacking. In less than an hour they had a mound three feet high. They were two miles from the Land Rover. "Forget it," Walker said. "We need a grant to do the job properly."

The grant was awarded in 1984. They scraped down the area, cleaning it of grass, and gathered up all the green rock with fossils— ten tons of it. They set up an assembly line around a table, gathering buckets of water to wash the bones. They brought along the airscribe, and a generator to power it. First, they washed the rocks. If anyone saw a bone in the matrix, they'd pass it on to the airscribe. If no bone was showing, the rocks were hit with a hammer, cracked in two, in fours, in eights, cracked down to something or nothing. The very first day they found what they needed—the missing bits. Now this *one Proconsul* skeleton is composed of fossils found during the original 1950 expedition, fossils retrieved from museums all over the world, and fossils discovered at the original site thirty-four years later.

During the "Ancestors" symposium, Alan Walker had expressed hopes of finding the missing bits to a single *Proconsul* skeleton. He didn't expect a baker's dozen. The team set out for another old site, downstream. "The surface was white with bones," Walker remembers, "every one a *Proconsul*: fingers, toes, bits of skull, bits of pelvis, vertebrae, wrist bones, ankle bones—everything littering the surface. There were two foot skeletons [with all the foot bones] and a yard away, an adult hand; a yard away, a baby foot. There were thousands of finger bones—babies have many more bones than adults," he explains, "long bones fuse as they mature. We found enough finger bones to fill up a museum tray. We'll have every bone of *Proconsul* before we're finished; we'll be able to track what happens all the way through from baby to adult." They can also study the sexual dimorphism in *P. africanus*.

Walker, who often says when "sensible people disagree, there's not enough evidence," delighted in this. "Too many trees have been wasted on academic arguments about what the wrist of *Proconsul* could do," he said. "Now we have four complete sets of wrist bones. We don't have to argue anymore."

Their return to Rusinga Site 114 presented another, more curious circle of bones. In the beginning, they saw only the surface. A dense collection of fossils were contained in space less than three feet wide. This circle held green rocks with bones; surrounding it were gray rocks, without bones. Walker thinks the circle represents a former tree.

Eighteen million years ago the area was thick with forests. Walker suggests that volcanic ashes surrounded the tree trunk; when the tree died, it left a hollow tube. "Animals used it; bats, snakes, lizards, small carnivores—one carnivore dragged in a *Proconsul*," he suggests. The surrounding rocks are dated at eighteen million years old. "Minus the time it takes for a tree to die," Walker said, "so are the bones."

They pursued the tree in a vertical fashion, carving outside the green rocks, tunneling down. When they got to six feet deep, the green column of bones was still there. They brought in ladders, and continued down to thirteen feet. More bones. They were still digging when Richard Leakey visited the site. "I'll believe it's a tree when you find the roots," he teased. This quest for roots remains unsolved.

The volcanic mud of Mfangano and Rusinga islands proved to be an extraordinary preservative. Their bounty included an earbone of *Proconsul*. Within this one can see the actual nerve pathway in the inner ear. The soft tissues rotted away, calcite grew in, producing a complete and perfect cast. There are fossilized centipedes and butterfly cocoons, locusts with legs and antennae. There is a tiny bird, with breast muscles and distinct impressions of feathers. The tongue of a lizard was preserved—muscle and skin as hard as stone. "Someday," Alan Walker predicts, "we're going to turn over a rock and find a *Proconsul* face."

Leakey hands the four wooden boxes back to Emma Mbua. "We've got rows and rows of boxes like this. We've got more material of *Proconsul africanus* than we do of any other Miocene, Pliocene, or Pleistocene primate," he says, adding a modest aside, "I don't want to bore you. But this should give you some idea."

Gould is anything but bored. "This," he proclaims, "gives you some hope of doing proper variation studies for the first time." Studying the range of size in a population would help solve the dilemma of different sexes or different species.

The sample from these islands on Lake Victoria is rare. Throughout the history of this very young science, most hominid discoveries have been singular. Comparisons were forced between a skull found in East Africa to one found in South Africa.

But thirteen seems to be the lucky number. Fossils representing thirteen hominid individuals, including infants, juveniles, and adults, were found in Ethiopia in 1975, the year after Lucy was discovered.

Called "the First Family," the finds from Hadar are also being studied for range and sexual dimorphism. Some scientists prefer to split, others to lump. Some say there is only one species at Hadar; others suggest two. The debates are covered in more detail in chapter 12, but so far, the hominids of Hadar and the hominoids from Kenya represent the only "populations" of species ever found.

More has been discovered in the last fifteen years than in the entire history of the search. In 1968, before research began at East Turkana, three hominid specimens were known from the entire country of Kenya. By 1984, one hundred and fifty specimens had emerged from East Turkana. During four field seasons in Ethiopia, twenty-three hominid specimens were retrieved. Leakey notes this by saying to Gould, "I think we ought to skip big teeth, little teeth, or we're not going to get through this today." In the past, big teeth vs. little teeth was sometimes all there was to evaluate. Enamel was measured for relative thickness, but it was difficult to tell what was relative. Large canines remain a crucial diagnostic feature in distinguishing hominoids from hominids; big and small "cheek" teeth, or premolars, figure among hominids. A gap in the tooth row, called the diastema, allows an ape to close its mouth without a collision of teeth. Hominids usually don't have any diastema; Lucy doesn't; other *afarensis* do. The further back in time, the more apeish. We're at fourteen million years.

"Let's move up to Fort Ternan." Leakey mentions the site northwest of Nairobi. Yet another cabinet door squeaks open. "This is *Kenyapithecus wickeri*." He hands Gould a jaw, with molars and canine teeth. "That's all there is from Fort Ternan."

But there are similar finds from the Samburu Hills, found during Leakey's California tour. Leakey lays out several upper and lower jaws with teeth, all fifteen million years old, about the same age as the one from Fort Ternan. They are slightly larger than *Proconsul*, but with a longer face. "We have a whole range of these things from Samburu," he explains, which means now there's a Third Family— yet another population group to be studied. "I think that whole clade or whatever you want to call it is going to sort itself out real soon. But you can see why there's been a lot of confusion."

The "clade" Leakey refers to is a cluster of branches that once included *Sivapithecus, Ramapithecus,* and *Kenyapithecus*—though the last, as mentioned, was viewed by David Pilbeam and Elywn Simons as so similar to *Ramapithecus* that it was "lumped" in with it.

The new genus and species *Kenyapithecus wickeri* was proposed in 1962 by Louis Leakey, based on the fossils from Fort Ternan. A heated debate followed, with more than fifty scientific papers published on the subject over the next two decades. Leakey also found more specimens at a site called Maboko, which he deemed different enough from the first to call them *Kenyapithecus africanus.* Here's the abbreviated history on *one specimen* of the seventy-two involved in the *Kenyapithecus* controversy, as chronicled by Martin Pickford. It involves a single upper jaw:

Maxilla M16649 was first assigned to *Proconsul africanus* by D. G. MacInnes in 1943. In 1950, it was described as the type for *Sivapithecus africanus* by Le Gros Clark and Louis Leakey. In 1965, Elwyn Simons and David Pilbeam lumped *Sivapithecus africanus* and *S. sivalensis* together, calling it *Dryopithecus sivalensis.* Two years later, Louis Leakey placed the specimen in *Kenyapithecus.* In 1983, Martin Pickford suggested the jaw differed in several aspects from *Kenyapithecus wickeri,* but was evidently from the same genus, *Kenyapithecus africanus.* Pickford based his view on new discoveries, returning to the original site called Maboko that Louis Leakey had excavated in 1947, to find more teeth of the same species. This, along with the abundant evidence from Samburu, proves that these fossils do not belong within *Ramapithecus.*

From fourteen million years ago, Leakey moves to eight million—though the source remains the Samburu Hills; the fossil in question is from younger sediments. "This is probably one of the most enigmatic specimens in this room," Leakey begins. "It's a very odd animal. Whatever it is," he adds, "it's the closest thing we have to something brand new at the other end of the fossil gap." First, Leakey lays out the teeth, five of them, black as pearls. They're huge, with deep facets, like those of a pig. "If you found those alone," Leakey says, "you'd think it was a suid [pig]." Gould agrees: "Historically, there's always been this problem distinguishing pig teeth from hominid teeth—like the famous *Hesperopithecus,*" the Nebraska Mancum-pig. Next, Leakey adds a jawbone, then a few fragments of cheekbones: "But if you view it together, it's a primate." Leakey then suggests that it may be a hominid.

"But doesn't its age of eight million make it an impossibility, as a hominid, I mean—with the biochemical dates suggesting the split around six?" Gould refers to the date of divergence suggested by the molecular clock.

"It's a fudge you can allow." Leakey doubts the biochemical dates. "It may well be one of the earliest hominids—probably is."

Gould is skeptical. He needs more evidence. "The key to all this is that fossil gap," he suggests, "finding those good sediments from four to eight million."

Leakey now produces evidence from the younger end of the fossil gap. They came from sites southwest of Lake Turkana. He presents a lower jaw discovered by Bryan Patterson in 1966 and dated at 5.5 million years old. Next, he produces an arm bone, much younger, about four million years old. The creature it belonged to was about the size of a chimpanzee.

Gould recalls that both were described as australopithecines. But Leakey views the designation as "sort of a bag in which everything was placed in the early days." He complains: "You know, anything that's hominid that isn't *Homo* has been called an *Australopithecus*, hasn't it? No one's produced an acceptable alternative genus other than *Homo*. And this specimen has been around for a long time—but it's just been ignored."

One of the reasons these fossils are disregarded is because of their poor preservation. Sometimes fossils are so weathered that details are lost—the antithesis of the finds from Lake Victoria, where you can see a record of feathers and nerves.

From four million years ago, we move forward in time to one of the most extraordinary preservations ever discovered. At Laetoli, Tanzania, a site dated at 3.5–3.75 million years ago, there are hominid footprints preserved by volcanic ash. These evocative paths are the oldest record of bipedalism. The footprints remain where they were found by Mary Leakey, but several fossils discovered nearby are presented in the Hominid Vault.

One is a lower jaw called LH 4, for Laetoli Hominid number 4.

It is worn and incomplete, yet it is the type specimen, or definitive model, to which all comparisons of the species are to be made. "This is the type specimen for *afarensis*," Leakey tells Gould, the species name assigned to Lucy, the First Family, and the hominids of Laetoli.

"Oh!" Gould exclaims. "Why did Johanson and White choose a Laetoli specimen when there is so much more material at Hadar?"

"I think that it was originally an attempt to honor my mother," Richard begins, "but she subsequently changed her mind when they decided on the thesis they put forward." Mary Leakey did not think the Laetoli hominids were australopithecine, but *Homo*. In his original description of the finds, Tim White also suggested they were *Homo*.*

Don Johanson answered Gould's question later: "When Tim and I realized that there was a new species involved, we chose the Laetoli Hominid 4 specimen because it had been fully described and published by Tim White. We also thought it was a way of drawing attention to the tie between the Hadar and Laetoli collections—and there's nothing in the code [the International Rules of Zoological Nomenclature] that prevents one from naming a species *afarensis* and using a type mandible from somewhere else. [Which is true.] Lucy was more complete but it was not described at that time, and we were in a hurry to get the thing published because we didn't want someone else to name the new species."

Gould points out a potential problem. "You don't usually choose a type other than the best available example. It invites terrible problems taxonomically. If they find something new, they're going to have to rename it." If, for example, a collection of skeletons were found at Laetoli that had a jaw like LH 4, but the rest of the body was quite different from Lucy and the First Family, then splitting would be required, and the finds from Ethiopia would require a new name. And the finds in Tanzania (aligned with the type specimen) would retain the name *afarensis*, after the Afar Triangle in Ethiopia.

But there are also *afarensis* finds in Kenya. The hominid discovered near Lake Baringo (announced during "Ancestors") has been described as *afarensis*, and several finds from East Turkana are also

* Charts of the family tree are featured on page 312.

afarensis. Leakey hasn't used them in any arguments because they are so fragmentary. His argument to Gould featured a complete skull now assuming every inch of the spotlight.

Its museum accession number is WT 17000, WT meaning it came from West Turkana, but it's commonly referred to as the "black skull" because the dark minerals incorporated during its fossilization gave it a manganese patina.

Leakey says nothing, waiting for Gould's reaction to this bold, almost blue-black fossil, with enormous teeth, a massive sagittal crest, and relatively tiny braincase.

"It looks like a hyper-, hyper-robust!"

Gould's impression extends the superative for a hyper-robust, like *Zinj* from Olduvai, and skull 406 from East Turkana, the discovery Richard Leakey made courtesy of his camel. "It's the oldest of its kind, at two point five," Leakey says.

He gingerly dips his fingertips underneath the skull snug in its bed of foam. "Let me get it out for you because it's very fragile." It doesn't look fragile; it looks like the ancestor to Darth Vader. He lifts the skull with both hands, then rests it before Gould on the padded table.

Gould runs the tip of his finger across the sagittal crest, on the dome of the skull, saying, "Massive, unbelievable," shaking his head. The sagittal crest of the black skull is the most prominent one ever found in a hominid. As the anchor for powerful jaw muscles, this particular ridge appears even larger because of the small cranial capacity, and it extends down the back of the skull, where it becomes compound—which is to say, it forms two small crests that diverge. The same lines, like a wishbone, figure on our own skulls in the forms of fused sutures. Just below the dividing line are two subtle projections called the mastoid process. You can feel your own by pressing behind your ears, halfway between the back of your ear and the very rear of your skull.

The mastoid process became a topic of focus during the "Ancestors" symposium, revived here to note that paleontologist Todd Olson presented a hypothetical drawing of an ancestral hominid that bore an uncanny resemblance to the black skull—discovered more than a year after Olson had devised his drawing. Leakey now focuses on this area in the back of the skull—the occipital, and the nuchal crests—the same area repaired in the *Proconsul* reconstruction by the "turtle" bits. Here exterior grooves and notches distinguish species, much as Raymond Dart noted interior furrows that distinguished the endocast of the Taung child. In addition to the black skull, the Mystery Skull 1805 has these same compound crests, called T/N for temporal nuchal, on the back of its skull, as does *afarensis*.

Gould furrows his brows. "I didn't know *afarensis* had a sagittal crest like that!"

One wouldn't, for several reasons. Of the thirteen hominid individuals found at Hadar, not one featured a complete adult skull. But a fragmentary specimen called A.L. 333–45 does have a T/N crest that suggests it had a sagittal crest; the dome of the skull was never found. The specimen was one of twelve different fossil specimens, or individuals, used to create a reconstructed skull of *afarensis*—"a synthesis" from the "available remains." The palate came from one individual, pieces of the face from another, a fragmentary lower jaw from another, a left canine from another, an incisor from another, and so on. The reconstruction, prepared by Tim White, Don Johanson, and Bill Kimbel, represents about two thirds of a skull; the forehead and brow ridges are missing along with the dome of the skull, and connecting pieces on the side.

"I think they've got the front of one species and the back of another," Leakey says. He suggested this three years before, in 1982, when addressing the evolutionary biology class in California, saying: "I fear a good part of the composite skull from Afar consists of a robust australopithecine, and other parts consist of something else." His hunches were based on the fragmentary specimens from Koobi Fora; he now suggests the black skull proves his point. "A weak argument," Johanson countered later, "which would involve the strangest set of taphonomic events ever. Why would only one species have its face destroyed, and the other species only the braincase?"

Gould responds to Leakey's argument: "There's always been this issue of the existence of several things at Hadar, and if you put a hyper-robust occipital with a gracile face, you might be led into thinking you had a primitive gracile. . . ." In other words, an

accidental combination of two forms might have led to their conclusions about *afarensis*—a primitive gracile australopithecine. "So
you think there were both gracile and robust at Hadar?"

"Yes," Leakey says, adding, "What I don't know about the Hadar
material is whether in fact there could be three things." He has
Gould's attention. "Now, let's have a look at 1813."

Two versions of 1813 make their appearance in the spotlight. One
is a cast, the other the original, with the new fragments retrieved
in 1982 on the side, yet to be added. The reconstruction awaits the
attention of Alan Walker, who's been busy over the past few seasons
with the *Proconsul* skeletons and the black skull.

"This is a much better specimen than I realized," Gould says of
1813. He thought it was only fragments, but it's a virtually complete
skull (as described earlier), with only a few fragments missing. So
the portrait is exceptionally complete. "Gracile australopithecine?"
Gould asks, which pleases his host.

Leakey too thinks it's an australopithecine; he explains that the
cranial capacity of 1813 is about 500 cc, then adds, "Other scientists
have called it a *Homo habilis*."

Gould is puzzled, as he should be. "But is that the cranial capacity
of a *habilis*?"

"No." Leakey offers skull 1470, the most famous Handy Man,
for Gould's review. The cranial capacity is 750 ccs, and because of
its large brain, the creature simply looks different. Its forehead is
fuller, and it has very little post-orbital waisting—the concave dips
behind the eye sockets which 1813 has.

The traditional view is that *habilis* slowly evolved into *erectus*.
Leakey now suggests that *habilis* represents a transitional species,
one that led quickly to *Homo erectus*. The *habilis* skulls from both
East Turkana and Olduvai are around 1.8 to 1.9 million years
old; the oldest known *erectus* is the Turkana Boy, at 1.6 million
years old.

"I wouldn't be at all surprised," Leakey expands, "if what we're
seeing in the transition from *habilis* to *erectus* is one of your moments of punctuation. You have speciation, you have selection for
the larger brain, and we actually have fossils to show it. I think the
whole thing is happening in less than 200,000 years. I mean, it's a
quite dramatic shift in a quite short space of geological time."

"But why *then*?" Gould asks.

"I really don't know," Leakey replies, "but I wouldn't be surprised if we found environmental evidence to support some dramatic shift in evolutionary change." The work of Elisabeth Vrba based on isotopic curves suggests a major environmental "pulse" around two million years ago. There are no large-brained hominids found before this time. Little change to sudden change qualifies as punk eek.

"My problem is I find your general take on this so congenial to my biases that I'm not going to be a very good critic," Gould says. His response is interesting. Where many scientists might have said, Great, here's proof for our theory, Gould tempers. Why? There's no evidence of that long stretch of *habilis* without change. Or is there, by another name? Louis Leakey called australopithecines "near man." Is his son about to position them there? Gould returns to the curiosity of 1813. "Why do they call it *habilis*? That's hardly the answer."

Leakey laughs and shakes his head. "You mustn't ask me these questions!" The skull is 1.8 million years old, which means it lived at the same time as *Homo habilis*. Both Leakey and Gould think 1813 is some sort of australopithecine. The consensus is that the australopithecines evolved into *Homo*. If so, they couldn't exist at the same time.

"Does everybody admit these two are contemporary?" Gould asks of 1813 and 1470, which gets a nod from Leakey. "Then why do they call it *habilis*?"

"I'll show you exactly why." Leakey turns to Emma and requests the type specimens of *Homo habilis*. The fossils he's requested, like the LH 4 jaw for *afarensis*, are the models on which all *habilis* finds are compared. *Homo habilis* is based on two specimens, one the type specimen called OH 7 (for Olduvai Hominid number 7) and a paratype, OH 13, meaning a second, complementary piece of information on the same species. Leakey doesn't think it's complementary.

"I'll show you why this is such a muddle," he begins, putting OH 13 next to skull 1813. "Now if you compare this with 1813 side by side, they could be brother and sister."

Gould agrees. "Yeah, I don't see any difference." And as Gould doesn't see any difference, neither did the scientists who called 1813 a *Homo habilis*, based on the model. But, as Leakey explains, he thinks the same mistake made with the *afarensis* reconstruction was made with the type specimens from Olduvai—that two species were combined.

"I think that a terrible mistake has been made." He points to the two type specimens for the Handy Man. "What they did was treat this as one species. Having done that, what has happened is that 1813 is then described as a *habilis*," based on the paratype specimen. Leakey suggests OH 13 is an australopithecine. If he's right, then the last two new hominid species named in the search have mistakenly combined two species where there should be one.

"But nobody thinks *habilis* and the gracile australopithecines are contemporary," Gould reiterates. "How are they going to get out of that dilemma?"

"I don't know how they're going to get out of it, but I'll tell you how I'm going to get out of it." Leakey places the other Mystery Skull, 1805, alongside 1813. He suggests that 1805 is the male, and 1813 the female, of an unnamed australopithecine. He slides OH 13 into this group, adding: "There are over thirty specimens from Koobi Fora related to this little issue."

"So!" Gould looks at 1805 and 1813. "This is direct evidence for a third species living at Koobi Fora?" *Homo habilis*, the hyper-robust australopithecine, plus one.

"Yes."

Gould wonders why Leakey hasn't published the idea. In 1978, Leakey and Walker did, but they buried it in a comprehensive report on all the hominids from East Turkana. "But you've got to write specific articles on the puzzle presented by 1813," says Gould.

"We haven't written it up because we wanted to wait until we got the stratigraphy at Koobi Fora absolutely straight." Leakey refers to the geological survey being done by Frank Brown, a monumental project that includes both East and West Turkana.

"Alan [Walker] and I felt that there would simply be no point in making further error by offering an alternative hypothesis that could be proven wrong. We felt it better to wait a couple of years and get the dates absolutely straight once and for all, then offer an interpretation." They also want to find more hominids around two million years old.

After their review of the evidence in the Hominid Vault (like visitors to the Ming Tombs), Gould and Leakey take tea. Emma Mbua emerges, the corpulent door closes firm on an impressive inventory, one that is being rearranged according to new discoveries like the black skull and the Turkana Boy, and by looking at old ones in a new way.

Many of the issues raised in the Hominid Vault will surface again in later chapters. Leakey's presentation and Gould's reactions were interesting to me because these two scientists look at things differently and still manage to admire each other. You could hear their bias, you could anticipate that Gould was warming up for arguments on the molecular clock, and you could discern a new flexibility in the Leakey Line when Richard said that australopithecines were "sort of a bag" that non-*Homo* specimens fell into. It was a hint that this third species might take the dichotomy out of the family tree, that the reason there had been so much confusion (and controversy) on the hominids from Laetoli and Hadar had to do with the labels being applied.

The session in the Hominid Vault covered more specimens than mentioned, and included some highly technical discussions. Their exchange was edited to offer a glimpse of some of the evidence, a sort of parade in chronological order, to emphasize that many discoveries occur in the laboratory, drawing upon archives begun four decades ago, or a mere four years earlier. Certainly the interpretations expressed are not shared by all scientists in the field; for example, the Berkeley team of Johanson, White, and Kimbel do not think their reconstruction of *afarensis* includes more than one species, nor do some biochemists believe that a hominid existed as long as eight million years ago, as Leakey suggested of the find from the Samburu Hills.

Before entering the Hominid Vault, I had been impatient for the reconstruction and naming of skull 1813. Naturally I had been impressed because of the way the additional fragments surfaced, which made me think that all sorts of clues remained unknown. The stunning additions to *Proconsul* suggested that I was right on one count and wrong on another: names themselves do not mean a great deal.

There is no clean progressive line of descent. Skull 1813 may be a missing link in the true sense that this skull (with 1805 and OH

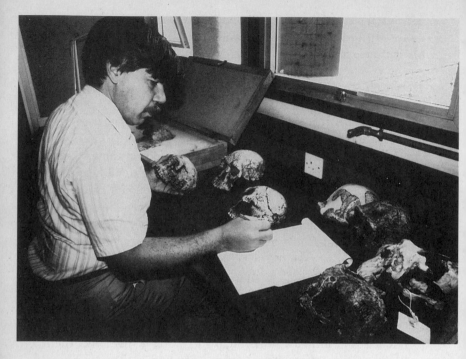

After his session in the Hominid Vault, Stephen Jay Gould compares hominid skulls in a Museum lab. He holds fossil skull 1813; on the table before him, from left to right, are casts of 1470, 1813, OH13, ER 3733, OH 5 and skull 406. The last two, with their massive sagittal crests, are examples of A. boisei, informally referred to as Zinj.

13) is representative of an experiment. It doesn't always happen that a primitive form glides into a more refined one. In fact, you can find examples of ancestral species that continue to thrive alongside their other forms.

Speciation implies that an isolated population of one species adapted in certain ways to its advantage—a larger brain, for example. And because of their advantage, they eventually succeeded while the original stock died out. But a missing link is by definition an intermediary form, and this is why Alan Walker might look at the large-brained 1470 and see many characteristics of an australopithecine. In hindsight, it's not surprising that two different species could be seen as one, or that Johanson and White might totally change their mind about what they saw in the same fossils. A species naturally combines the features of its ancestors. Over a century ago, the missing link was referred to in the singular. But every specimen in the Hominid Vault represents a missing link.

The family tree, Gould suggests, should be viewed as a branching bush, a concept that nature itself reinforced when we ventured into the field. The next morning, Gould and I met up with Richard and Meave Leakey for the flight to Lake Turkana.

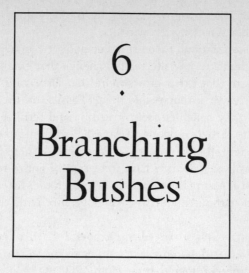

6

Branching
Bushes

Six canvas tents represent green in an area called Kalodirr, after the dry riverbed that snakes through our camp. On the map of the world we know, the camp is twelve miles west of Ferguson's Gulf on the west side of Lake Turkana and three hundred and fifty miles north of Nairobi, yet it marks an uncharted Africa, surrounded by sediments four million years old, sediments seventeen million years old, sediments a hundred million years old. Sediments embrace a broad term used by geologists to define earthly material that has been deposited, or laid down—by water, by the denuding of old rocks, and in a wider sense, by the wind.

The landscape around Kalodirr is a geology lesson, with no forests to obscure the patterns of terrestrial change that extend to the horizon. A scrub thorn that grows more than fifty yards beyond the ephemeral river is a remarkable thing. Fossils, on the other hand, appear as if they benefited from irrigation and fertilizer.

Four years earlier, trekking to Area 123 at East Turkana, Leakey had said, "Here, there are fossils everywhere." There I had to look to find a fossil; at Kalodirr I have to be careful not to step on them, for at certain exposures, especially in ravines, fossils litter the surface, a graveyard without hierarchy. Antelope mix with clams; turtles with elephant.

Kalodirr was first surveyed in October 1985. At the end of the field season at Nariokotome, sixty miles to the north, Leakey suggested to Kamoya Kimeu that the Hominid Gang spend an extra day in this region on their way home to Nairobi. "I think you're going to find something," Leakey told Kimeu, based on his own brief survey.

In this arena, Kimeu might be said to lead the Hominoid Gang, for the time frame of considerable display at Kalodirr—seventeen million years old—belongs to quadrupedal apes. On the first day of their quick survey, a jaw and a skull fragment of a small ape were discovered. Now why all the interest in these older apes, if they're not upright, not hominid?

If this is a search for roots, as it's often been called, then these Miocene apes represent our roots. Genetic evidence suggests that the chimpanzee is our closest living relative today. This information is based on current status. Chimpanzees didn't exist in the Miocene. Between our ancestor and the oldest hominids, there's the fossil gap. In this space from four to fourteen million years ago, no line can be drawn to our ancestors. After over a century of searching, the common ancestor that represents our split from the apes has yet to be found. In lieu of this, the more that is found on either end, the better patterns might be discerned. Is *Proconsul* the most likely candidate for our ancestor? It would help to know the form of all its neighbors, the entire cluster of species on a branching bush. The Miocene sediments of Kalodirr were ideal.

At Kalodirr, a site has been cleaned of surface boulders, and the soil sieved for smaller bits of fossilized bones and teeth. This is the first stage of excavation, following the discovery of fragments that have been washed to the surface by erosion. The discovery of a complete skull is rare; most emerge in bits and pieces, with careful and tedious searching. Two members of the Hominid Gang look for clues in a sieving screen.

Leakey shows Gould the 17-million-year-old skull excavated at Kalodirr by Kamoya Kimeu. The discovery, one of three new hominoids that surfaced at Kalodirr during the 1986 field season, was named Afropithecus.

We arrive on January 16, 1986, less than forty-eight hours after the Gang have renewed their search. Kalodirr is one of twenty-three new sites on the west side of Lake Turkana. Nomadic Turkana, who spend the night in domes constructed from scarce vegetation, refer to the camp as "green houses of cloth."

Because Kalodirr is distant from the lakeshore, a couple of shower stalls have been constructed and covered by the leaves of doum palms; imported water flows by tilting a two-gallon canvas bag high in the stall. Scorpions often appear on the "floor" of the shower, volunteering as conservation managers on the limited water supply. The sun is relatively unlimited, and a solar panel powers batteries for lights in the evening. Priorities feature in a large work tent devoted to fossils and food. ("All adaptations stem from the gut," as Leakey likes to say.) A refrigerator works off propane; empty wooden trays, brought from the museum in Nairobi, are placed on a tabletop, side by side, like empty picture frames. Twice a day, before lunch and before dinner, the Gang emerge from nearby Miocene exposures to fill the frames.

Smaller fossils, in the tooth-sized category, arrive in little plastic bags. Medium-sized fossils, in the jaw category, are wrapped in toilet tissue, tucked in a shirt pocket. Once, in a pinch for space, Kimeu stuffed fossils inside the pouch of his windbreaker, and on the long walk back to the Land Rover, aware of his fond embrace, explained, "It's my baby."

At 11:30 a.m. Kamoya Kimeu delivers. A team of three have been sieving since sunrise at a section fifteen by fifteen yards, a relatively small incision into the earth's past, where a small ape skull has already been found. They seek to find more. The morning's bounty includes forty plastic bags; other fossils tend to emerge out of pockets on a seemingly endless basis, like circus clowns spilling out of a Volkswagen. Richard and Meave Leakey break into the bags like kids opening party favors; Gould watches from the sidelines. Kimeu quietly announces that there is another ape among the finds.

To bring Gould up to date, Leakey produces the first ape skull found at Kalodirr this season, which had been sitting unnoticed among an array of bones. Gould turns the seventeen-million-year-old find in his hand, and wonders if this isn't proof of diversity among the dryopithecines, for this little ape skull is quite different from any *Proconsul* we saw in the Hominid Vault.

"We're not going to have a single-species hypothesis for apes!" he proclaims, referring to a theory on a long single line for hominids that was disproved by discoveries at East Turkana, now boasting two, possibly three species that lived at the same time. For a long time, hominid evolution was thought to resemble a ladder of progress, with one species leading to another. But the evidence for pruned twigs on the family tree—like the robust australopithecine—suggests long-term experiments with the upright form. The seventeen-million-year-old sediments of Kalodirr are quick to suggest diversity among the hominoids.

Leakey shows him a second lower jaw that was found nearby. As part of the morning bounty, Meave Leakey has a similar jaw in her hand; she lifts newly found fragments to match the grain of the bones, focusing and fitting quickly as if she were trying to beat the clock. Meave Leakey was key to the reconstruction of skull 1470.

Meave Epps was born in London and studied paleontology at the University of Wales. She ventured to Africa in 1965, in response to an ad that Louis Leakey placed in a British newspaper for a research assistant. She fell in love with Kenya and Louis Leakey's son. Their first date centered around the bones of an ancient monkey.

Meave's study is monkeys of all ages—from the Miocene when they first evolved, through the Pliocene and Pleistocene. Monkeys belong to the superfamily of cercopithecoids. But she, and they, are central to the search for hominids. Cercopithecoids are known as Old World Monkeys—"Old World" because they have only been found in Africa and Eurasia, as opposed to New World (North and South America). Modern cercopithecoids include Colubus monkeys, baboons, guenons. They branched from a common ancestor, as did Miocene hominoids, and from this arose the great apes—gorillas, orangutans, chimps, and us. Meave Leakey studies all sorts of fossils that emerge from East African sites to detail the long lineage of very distant cousins.

She works at the museum as head of paleontology, and her occasional entries into the Gould/Leakey dialogue are incisive; when checking her husband's "flights of fantasy" (his words), she does so with enviable grace. It is no coincidence that Meave Leakey's features are unpretentious—her dark blond hair cut short, her tan skin with no hint of makeup. She is by manner feminine and restful, even when tossing out the most piercing question. While she often compromises her own research in favor of her husband's, his territory provides exceptional access to the fossils for her research. She is so shy of the spotlight that she prefers not to be photographed, and stays in Kenya rather than accompany Richard on his lecture tours.

"It's not the credit I want," Meave explains, "I enjoy the work." Under the work tent at Kalodirr, when she inserts a fragment into its place, it makes a clicking sound. As she works, the two small apes begin to look more and more alike. Then the clicking sound stops.

"I *knew* this was going to happen," she protests, "Look at this; it can't go with that." What she has before her are two separate puzzles.

"There are two things here," Richard begins, "And if there are two species about the same size . . . ," he searches through the fossils on the table, "Where's that piece of skull you had?" As he looks up for his answer, Meave successfully clicks another piece into place. "Oh," he smiles, "I'll leave this to you." The two small apes that Meave Leakey pieces together may be alike, but they are unknown. They have never been seen before.

Richard prefers to leave the anatomical descriptions and matching of bones to others, having none of the passion for anatomy of Meave, Alan Walker, or paleoanthropologists like Sherwood Washburn, who as a student delighted in identifying bones with eyes closed. "She'll be at this for days," Leakey says to Gould. "You should see it when she and Alan race!" Gould can only shake his head in awe of her spatial sense: "That's why I work on *Cerion*," he sighs. "Snails invariably come out whole."

Richard looks at the array of fossils, to lament with satisfaction, "We should have brought more trays." He did bring six potato sacks. These will be filled with soil sieved at the excavation sites, then flown back to Nairobi where the soil is washed—every little clod of earth pressed between the fingers. Before the day is done it seems more potato sacks are in order.

Our first venture into the field moves from cairn to cairn, where fossils have been marked by the Hominid Gang. It takes a couple of hours, moving fast, to review what three people have found of interest in forty-eight hours. The more unusual finds included a clutch of tortoise eggs, perfectly preserved. Meave Leakey carefully digs away at some interesting-looking teeth, working with a dental pick and using preservative. "This is going nowhere," she says after well over an hour. Such is often the case.

Nearby is volcanic ash not contained by deposition; it's like walking over evidence of a community campfire left by the crowd at Woodstock. There are volcanoes to the northwest and the southeast; the land in between dips toward the lake. Gould meanders, trying to sort out the stratigraphy. I follow in his footsteps until my knee-socks are caught by familiar thorn scrub. Delighted to be able to identify something on the landscape amid all this paleontological finesse (Chenlonia, Cercopithecoidia), I shout out the local name for these thorns, requiring a step backward in order to move forward: "Wait-A-Bit!" Gould, ever polite, responds: "Oh, I will."

We join up with Richard and Meave again, to survey a totally new area. "We've got to try and find things before the rain," Leakey throws over his shoulder; "the changes from erosion can be quite dramatic." The changes on the landscape are slow to see, the effect on fossils is his concern.

The two men trek ahead of us across Miocene sediments. The juxtaposition of such modern hominids on a terrain that predates our existence by seventeen million years is not uncommon in Africa's Great Rift Valley, where the past wedges into the present in a landscape worthy of Picasso. Such an arrangement keeps Gould and Leakey alert.

From time to time their heads tip from side to side. They have yet to assume the classical pose of fossil finders, a posture aligned with that of wading birds, their heads brought lower to the ground, their backs parallel with the surface of the earth, their hands clasped behind. But they cannot resist casually looking for fossils as they walk and talk. Laughter drifts back, made hollow by the heat.

They rise up a hill naked of trees, the outlines of their arms and legs lost to the sky's incandescence. They will sink and rise several times, then disappear feet first down into a parched, eroded ravine. In this ravine their hands do not clasp for any length of time. So many fossils crop up that Leakey gathers stones to assemble a cairn. Discoveries occur quickly, as if reading from a list.

"Here's a piece of crocodile," he announces, gathering the bone made pink by iron oxide in the sediments, "and a little foot bone of a carnivore." Meave Leakey, not five feet away, holds aloft a fossil undeniably round. It's a perfectly preserved endocast—what was once a soft little brain is reported to the Present as hard as a rock. Gould is suitably amazed. "Look at that!" He turns it like an umpire checking out a spitball. "I don't know what it is, but you can see every sulcus and gyrus marked on it!" Gould refers to the furrows that outline the brain's organization, in this case, a little antelope whose brain favored smell, as did that of early primates, their muzzles long like antelopes'. If this little antelope was anything like the ones on the present landscape, this brain triggered locomotion nearing quadrupedal flight.

They return to their wading-bird position, entertaining individual pursuits and silence. Camels amble across the horizon, their languor extreme, the air suddenly still. Gould, the connoisseur of context, his feet firmly planted in the Cradle of Mankind, abruptly stands erect and with arms wide proclaims, "We're in a bed of clams!"

And so we are; everyone looks around and laughs, as if the land about our feet had suddenly been granted the status of an island by a rising tide. In this bed of mollusks Gould spies snails, his eyes trained from a dozen seasons of searching for the munificent forms of *Cerion*, a Bahamian land snail. "How do you find them?" Meave asks, her hands having seized upon everything but snails.

"It's my Search Image," he replies matter-of-factly.

Two hours later Gould would not see an extraordinary skull *in situ*. While we were discovering clams and crocodiles and antelope brains, Kamoya Kimeu was on his knees, brushing sand from the hint of a formidable skull. It was much larger than the earlier skulls presented on the work table. But it didn't look like a *Proconsul*. At seventeen million years old, it was new.

In mid-afternoon, we follow in Kimeu's footsteps, walking up and down rock-strewn hills, across eroded gullies, and into this Miocene site, which dips steeply. The skull remains buried in the slope of the hill; a few teeth protrude. Yet I stare at the patch of earth, as does Gould, our eyes finally directed by Leakey's hand. As the teeth come into focus for Gould, he renders two inevitables: "Wow!" and "What is it?"

"That's the big Sixty-Four-Dollar Question," Leakey says. "We don't know what it is. We're seeing these peculiarly big incisors sticking way out. They're Pongidlike," meaning the teeth are like those of an orangutan. As Leakey begins to brush away only a light layer of sand, hints of the bones of a long face appear, the same blond color as the surrounding matrix. No wonder we couldn't see the skull at first; the wonder is that anyone in the Hominid Gang could.

Kimeu led me to the side to show me something else he had found. I took far too long to find it, my eyes seeing only the general rubble and blond sediments. "Tell me, Kamoya," I finally said. "What do you see that I don't?" He leaned forward and with his right hand brushed away sand at points three feet from each other. Then he waved an open palm low and close over the earth's surface, like a magician recruiting. There, suddenly, was a substantial piece of elephant.

Now he resumes his excavation of the "Pongidlike" skull, working with his fingertips, a long, bold brush, and a dustpan. Kimeu has carefully ventured far enough down around the sides of these teeth to know that there is a skull underneath. Gould writes in his notebook: "ape skull with a long face, inflated nasal region, incisors worn flat, with a diastema [gap] a finger wide to the massive canine— almost like a beaver among apes." I am grateful for Gould's observations, for when the skull is finally lifted from the earth, the note I make into my tape recorder is limited to: "big sweet potato with overbite." The surrounding matrix will be removed by an airscribe in the lab in the Nairobi Museum, where the details of this new face will surface in a couple of weeks' time.

When viewing the bony face of a hominid like 1813, you can fathom human identity. But one look at hominoids like these, with canines and a very small brain, and a face half the size of ours, prompts wonder at change, and many modern humans, quite naturally, wonder how we're evolving now.

"I wish I had a buck for each time that question was asked!" Gould laughs. "I press this button on my chest and this comes out— it's a very elegant answer," he promises, "I've done it so many times. First, I give my 'Why paleontologists don't predict the future' speech, why it is that science is a history and not into prediction. That's part one. Part two is to review all the incredible things we've done, how all of civilization has been built in 25,000 years from Cro-Magnon to this, with no change in morphology [bone structure], so why should we expect anything else? Then there's point three, making the wry little comment that we seem to be able to do plenty with what we've got, so let's go with it."

"I say we can't tell," Leakey begins, "but it's most improbable there will be further evolution. For any evolution to occur would require isolation and time, which we're not going to allow ourselves."

"Yeah," Gould adds, "I usually make the point of isolation. There is the space colony hypothesis," which would allow an isolated population to evolve.

"If we wanted to evolve," Leakey continues, "we could in fact change humans by selective breeding—indeed, it had been thought about before the last world war, and it was banned, quite rightly." Leakey takes some pleasure in matching answers with Gould, clipping, "My answer's not dissimilar"—he smiles—"but perhaps less elegant."

Mary Leakey was briefer in her reply to a reporter who ventured to Olduvai, "in platform shoes," recalled Mary; "most ridiculous." When the reporter pressed for a futuristic vision of humans, Mary said firmly, "If you persist in this, I may get cross."

Richard Leakey playfully tosses a popular question back at Gould: "We've got you now: Why are there still apes if we evolved from apes?" (The quick and easy answer appeared in the comic strip "B.C."—"Some of the apes were given a choice.")

Gould laughs. "That the question is sometimes asked with good-will shows the extent of that old bias of progress and the chain of being. How anyone with any intelligence and education might think that apes evolved into humans bodily, that apes kind of turned into people . . ." He whistles. I don't say a word. I thought that apes bodily turned into people, over many generations. This was based on the charts of descent I'd seen.

Descent was the first hurdle. I must have seen Jacob Bronowksi's television series "The Ascent of Man" thrice before ever reading an excerpt from Darwin's *The Descent of Man*. Mind you, I had to think twice about Darwin's title.

The classic illustration of human evolution presented to us civilians is a ladder of progress, with nothing succeeding like success to the next rung, leaving the more primitive behind. The metaphor of neat rungs persists in climbing the corporate ladder (where lateral moves are ill-advised) and in generational change: A reviewer of *The Kennedys* noted that "In Jack one sees his father filtered and refined, one rung up the evolutionary ladder, at the point where gills turn into lungs."

Such bodily transformation is drawn up for television viewers. In the animation sequence for Leakey's BBC series "The Making of Mankind," and again in a 1988 National Geographic special, "Mysteries of Mankind," a quadrupedal ape literally walks toward uprightness, losing fur and other apeish features en route. In a 1951 illustration, from "Slinking Reptiles to Running Mammals," William King Gregory capsuled "the origin, rise and deployment of primates." Gregory, former editor of *Natural History*, portrayed the history of life in a rolling surf, with "Grandfather Fish" descending toward Man.

Yet descendants of "Grandfather Fish" continue to swim after amphibians crawled ashore, and the apes of Africa and Asia remain because they did not evolve into us but (among their ancestors) diversified, incorporating a subsidiary to the company of apes—a branch that would branch yet again. The ancestral stock for chimps is thought to have branched from gorillas around ten million years ago; the ancestral stock for hominids is thought to have branched from chimps around six million years ago.

How did this occur? Technically, the changes involve mutations. Mutations affect the constitution of the gene pool. Natural selection shapes the gene pool. Now we enter the land of scenario, for no one really knows the exact forces that produce evolutionary change. Scientists experiment with *Drosophila*, a fast-breeding fruitfly, to

mock nature's longer experiment. Hybrids are evident in farm animals, racehorses, lapdogs, and botanical produce—from tomatoes
to roses.

The classical contemporary examples of adaptation involve insects,
with short generation time. Moths in eighteenth-century England
had pale wings, which served as a camouflage against the pale, lichen-
covered trees. They survived because they fooled the birds intent
on devouring them. But as coal soot killed the lichen and blackened
the trees, moths with darker wings prevailed. Their adaptation concerned melanin pigment. The change involved only a few genes.
Even more rapid adaptation is seen in insects that evolve resistance
to pesticides.

While genetic changes relate to the changes in bone form, they
cannot be directly translated. For example, the blood proteins of
chimps and humans vary by only 1 percent, but almost every bone
of a chimp differs from that of a modern human.

The common ancestor would represent the first population of
species that branched from chimps, the first twig in the hominid
family tree. From this, there would be at least another branch to
afarensis, and at least other branches to the known hominid species:
the gracile and robust australopithecines, the hyper-robust, the various forms of *Homo*. The original stock, however, continued, to
evolve in its own way, to become the chimps of today. Gould brings
it all together visually.

The common chart of the hominid family tree looks like a saguaro
cactus. It presents a myopic view of only upright apes. With a
branching bush, Gould promotes a palpable template for our coexistence with apes. A profusion of branches aptly expresses that "splitting and twigginess are primary themes of human evolution." Our
story is marked by pruned twigs; extinctions impeccably reveal our
oddity. For a mammalian family to boast but one surviving species
is an odd thing in the general array of evolutionary history. "The
aardvark is in such a situation today," notes Andrew Hill. "So is
modern man, but he wasn't a couple of million years ago." A couple
of million years ago there were at least two hominid species living
on this landscape; seventeen million years ago there were so many
species of hominoids that the branches are referred to as clusters.

Proconsul was just three of many species of the dryopithecines, as *Sivapithecus* was just one of many species of ramapithecines.

Where does the large skull from Kalodirr belong on this branching bush? Everyone agrees, even before it's cleaned of its matrix, that it is not a *Proconsul;* they base this on the different teeth, and the longer palate. Nor does it match the *Kenyapithecus* skulls. It does resemble a find made two years earlier at a site to the northwest called Buluk, a jaw that Leakey and Alan Walker described as a *Sivapithecus.* But their definition of the Buluk find would be revised by this one from Kalodirr.

Later, Walker describes the revelation that took place in the lab. "If you cut the front of the face off here"—he levels his hand under his nose—"and you only saw the teeth, the lower jaw, and the palate of the skull from West Turkana, then you'd say just what we said about the Buluk specimen—that based on the parts you've got, it might be a *Sivapithecus.* But above the nose, it's nothing like a *Sivapithecus.*"

So the skull from Kalodirr underscored the value of a full skull, and the sort of mistakes that can be made when only jaws and teeth are named. "Even with a full palate and a jawful of teeth, you don't always know what you're doing," Walker expands. "When we wrote the Buluk paper, that's all we had to go on. And you can't make something new if you can't give it any differentiating characteristics. You can't say, 'I think it might be different, but I can't tell you what's different about it.' "

With substantial use of an eraser, the branches of the bush are drawn up slowly. The large skull from Kalodirr was so different from anything else among both the dryopithecines and the ramapithecines that the Leakeys felt it was a new species of a new genus. To distinguish it from the ramapithecines found in Asia, they named it after Africa.

The new skull from Kalodirr and the earlier discovery from Buluk were both named *Afropithecus* in a joint paper by Richard and Meave Leakey that was published eleven months later, in November of 1986. This long-faced ape, "almost like a beaver," also inspired Gould to write a three-part series in *Natural History* on branching bushes. He seized upon the Leakeys' view that *Afropithecus* combined several characteristics of a variety of Miocene apes: "The new genus represents a mosaic of characters which suggests an early radiation of Miocene hominoids." In other words, the characteristics nested in *Afropithecus* showed up in so many later forms as to imply a radiation event. That the later forms weren't that much older implied the radiation, or branching, happened quickly.

This radiation was underscored by the two smaller skulls found at Kalodirr, the ones that Meave Leakey pieced together, which represent a new genus they called *Turkanapithecus*. As Gould points out: "If one field season in uncharted lands could yield two new genera, how many remain undiscovered yet in the hundreds of square miles still open for exploration? Apes were bushier than we had ever imagined during their early days; human evolution seems even more twiggy, more contingent on the fortunes of history (not enjoined like the successive rungs of a ladder), less ordained, and more fragile."

The following season, Kalodirr delivered a third new twig for Gould's branching bush. Because the apes from Kalodirr were so different from those found on the islands of Lake Victoria, it implied a different ecology existed here.

The day after the Kalodirr skull was unearthed, we flew across Lake Turkana to Koobi Fora. That night at camp, Leakey addressed a much more recent branch on the family tree, the split of *Homo sapiens* from *Homo erectus*. He presents his case to the Professor as we sit around the dining table with Meave and Kamoya.

"The fossil record that I see thus far has increasingly suggested that wherever you're getting late *erectus* populations, you're getting the early *sapiens* populations at about the same time, throughout the world. You see it in Southeast Asia, you see it in Central Asia, you see it in East Africa, you see it in South Africa." The fossil record to which Leakey refers includes *erectus* finds such as the Solo Man from Java at 400,000 years old and the Peking Man at 700,000. Archaic *sapiens*, however, are still found in Africa as recently as 140,000 years ago. Leakey sees "a number of specimens that you simply cannot place comfortably" in one or the other species.

In the standard physical anthropology textbooks, characteristics that discern an *erectus* from a sap include:

- Saps have a larger brain size than *erectus*. Sap cranial capacities average between 1,000 and 2,000 ccs. *Erectus* cranial capacities average from 775 to 1,225 ccs.
- Saps have smaller molar teeth than *erectus*, and the canine teeth of saps look more like incisors. The canine teeth of *erectus* look more apeish.
- Saps have a chin, the "mental process." *Erectus* don't have an official chin; although the bone is there, it is less prominent.
- Saps have a more gracile face than *erectus*, and a more rounded skull.
- *Erectus* have thicker skull bones.
- *Erectus* skulls found in Asia have a sagittal crest, but this is absent from some *erectus* skulls found in Europe and Africa.
- Above the eyes (orbits), saps have two separate brow ridges, whereas *erectus* has a definite, strongly built brow ridge that connects as one across, the so-called beetle brow.
- *Erectus* have a bony bump at the base of the skull called an occipital bun (as in a lady's hair bun).

Leakey suggests that these differences are simply a matter of degrees, degrees too small for calling them two different species. He is not as concerned about lumping the species together as what this coexistence might imply. Did *sapiens* evolve in several different places? The standard view of speciation denotes a single point of origin, but Leakey thinks hominids may be an exception. "In terms of distribution and new environments, they are really different from any other organism. Did they move beyond the restrictions and limitations that under natural circumstances are being imposed on any other species?"

This would certainly be an exception, as Gould responds. "I always thought about a single point of origin for *sapiens*, because genetics predict a single origin for such a taxon." He then allows, "I'll admit the predisposition." Leakey argues that there was some earlier trigger for *Homo* that simply kept going, that *Homo sapiens* was simply a "further expression" of the same species. This would link *Homo habilis, erectus,* and *sapiens* as merely transitional forms. It would also put them together as one branch, rather than the three they now represent on the family tree.

Gould suggests one of the ways to make Leakey's idea tenable is by interbreeding. "But how would you get even a small enough genetic flow from Africa to Asia?" he asks. "You've got *erectus* in Java, and you've got *erectus* in Africa at the same time. How might the two have interbred? I mean," Gould adds with absolute sincerity, "they weren't sailing over there! They weren't flying over there!"

Leakey reiterates, "I simply think the fossil record is beginning to suggest that there isn't time for a single center for the rise of *Homo sapiens.*" In other words, the archaic *sapiens* appear in so many different places that if they did arise in one place, they really moved fast.

This is, as Gould puts it, the Problem.

"With culture," Leakey begins, "these distinctions would not rely on genetic similarity or differences, because there's been a constant genetic mixture until the advent of culture." The culture that Leakey refers to would include the more sophisticated society reflected in the world of *sapiens*: since language and behavior don't fossilize, the evidence of ancient hominid culture is reflected in Stone Age art, and earlier, in tools.

Prior to a mere 150,000 years ago, there's incredible similarity in the Acheulian toolkits found in Europe and Africa. Only in the last 150,000 years does the toolkit change to reflect cultural diversity that, to Leakey, reflects isolated populations.

"Just let me ask you," Leakey stretches his arms across the table, "how likely do you think it is that with an animal such as a bipedal primate, you're going to get almost identical selection resulting in new species form?"

This invites a quick "Why not?" from one who deems splitting and twigginess as primary themes of evolution. There are nine "almost identical selections resulting in a new species form" of hominids already discovered: five species of australopithecines, four of *Homo.* "I don't know what limited *erectus,*" Gould argues, meaning what limitations that might inspire the species to branch toward a better adapted form. He cites some of the textbook differences, adding, "I've never seen an *erectus* that didn't have an occipital bun!"

"But," counters Leakey, "you see saps with it!"

"I think that's just part of the transition."

"Ah ha!" Leakey seizes. "This is critical to accept. Because if you look at it one way, you don't see it. If you look at it the other way, you do."

"Maaaybe." Gould stretches, tipping his head to one side. "But it's kind of hard to think that modern *Homo sap* is anything other than the product of a single point of origin." It's also hard to think of *erectus* and *sapiens* as transitional forms, for they simply look like such different creatures.

"I don't suggest the notion is watertight," Leakey admits, "but I have a great deal of difficulty looking at large-brained hominids as series of true, separate species—I see them merely as stages." He rises to pour a glass of water from a canvas bag that hangs from a beam. "It's a fascinating problem. I think it goes back to the first departure from Africa. I think people were moving back and forth the whole time."

When Leakey returns, he sits forward, placing his hands on the table with fingertips together. "They were making the *identical* Acheulian hand axes at Java as they were at Koobi Fora. Then suddenly, about 150,000 years ago, the Acheulian tradition was abandoned all over the world!"

"That's the migration of the single population that somehow . . ." Gould begins.

Meave Leakey finally enters, to the point: "You could argue that one both ways. The sudden change in the toolkit doesn't really tell you whether *sapiens* evolved from one thing or were the result of many things interbreeding." The sudden change in the toolkit may have been simply the result of designing a new toolkit.

"Exactly." Richard honors Meave's point; tools are out as any indication of *sapiens* origins.

A gentle breeze slips across the open dining area. Having spun all these notions, the speakers are quiet. Finally Gould enters: "I admit this is all very puzzling."

Kimeu and I just listen and sit and wait—silent partners. Here are two men and one woman who might offer a key to this puzzle, yet nature has baffled even them on a fairly recent event, a time frame of human evolution with the most plentiful evidence. Here we sit, in the Cradle of Mankind, baffled.

Am I back to where I started? Four years earlier at Koobi Fora, when 1813 added a few more pieces to the puzzle, my intrigue began. I couldn't sleep, and went out to look at the stars, wondering if 1813 had done the same, if 1813 might think the stars were holes in the sky where the rain came in. I was drawn into the search because 1813 was in the Suspense Account. Now, *sapiens* are not in the Suspense Account, because they are named and described in detail. But names and descriptions do not tell us how they initially arose. The quandary is acknowledged with silence. Within this silence, wheels turn in five cerebrums granted by an event we seek to unravel. One of the five you can virtually hear.

"Take any species," Gould begins forcefully, "like mice, for example: mice in New York now, and mice in New York a hundred years from now. There's such a small number of mice alive now that will make any contribution to mice a hundred years from now. That's what the mitochondrial DNA studies show. Ultimately only a few breeds are successful. So the actual three or four mice that may be the ancestors of all mice a hundred years from now are carrying within themselves genetic material for reticulation. At a higher level, you can make the analogy for a limited point of our ancestors."

Leakey, unconvinced of the accuracy of the DNA evidence, prefers to judge from fossils. "It's increasingly difficult to look at these fossils and say whether an individual skull belongs in *sapiens* or late *erectus*," he concludes. "It may be the fault of the trade—maybe we shouldn't expect a split, but it's become very tricky. The more material that comes in, the more ambiguous it becomes."

Gould would not forget this argument. Later, he picked up the threads in his branching bushes trilogy for *Natural History*. After acknowledging the fossil evidence of *Afropithecus*, and the Leakeys' contribution, he asks: "Where is the teeny ladder of this ultimate twig? . . . Some paleontologists have identified *Homo erectus* as the start of an ultimate ladder, arguing that this ancestral species transformed itself, in toto and various places, into modern humans (*Homo erectus* and *Homo sapiens* become, in this interpretation, grades of structural improvement within a single evolving lineage, not proper species by the usual criterion of branching)."

Gould turns to the genetic data that inspired his "Take any species, like mice for example" argument. A molecular family tree drawn up by Rebecca Cann, Mark Stoneking, and Allan Wilson inspired Gould to conclude that "all modern humans are products of a very recent twig that lived exclusively in Africa until 90–180,000 years ago. We therefore branched from *Homo erectus* in Africa, the center of origins for all hominid species known so far." Single point of origin.

This argument was subsequently featured as a cover story in *Newsweek* (January 11, 1988) entitled "The Search for Adam and Eve—Scientists Explore a Controversial Theory About Man's Origins." "Eve" was described as muscular as Martina Navratilova. (With all due respect for Martina's muscles, this is one of the reasons you don't find effusive descriptions of early hominids in this book. For all we know, "Eve" could have had the muscles of Woody Allen.)

This source of modern hominids was traced by studying the DNA in babies' placentas donated by one hundred and forty-seven pregnant women from diverse geographical regions of the globe. The tissues provided large samples of mitochrondrial DNA, and a genetic blueprint was transposed to a family tree among modern hominids.

While it seems preposterous to suggest that a single female was the original source for all of us, every year a large number of human surnames die out, which is to say, among individual family trees, there is extinction. Also, many species arise from very limited populations, known as "bottlenecks." The Theory of Eve doesn't suggest that only one woman lived 200,000 years ago, but that the molecular evidence points to a single female, assisted in her efforts, of course, by one or more males. If the biochemists are correct in their time calibrations, this would be one female *Homo erectus* in Africa.

Leakey has said that he found the theory interesting but simplistic. In the *Newsweek* article, he and Gould were quoted at odds: "As the veteran excavator Richard Leakey declared in 1977, 'There is no single center where man was born.' But now geneticists are inclined to believe otherwise. 'If it's correct, and I'd put money on it, this idea is tremendously important,' says Stephen Jay Gould. 'It makes us realize that all human beings, despite differences in external appearance, are really members of a single entity that's had a very recent origin in one place.' "

If the Theory of Eve is tested and proven with other DNA samples, then the most recent branch on the hominid family tree seems to be an incredibly small twig. No wonder that with all those clades and clusters of radiation, the rest of the chart looks like a branching bush.

There rests, on a round table in Darwin's study in England, a little ape skull, not so very different from the *Afropithecus* one uncovered at Kalodirr, though seventeen million years younger. The differences are a matter of degrees, a rearrangement both subtle and profound of those characteristics of Miocene apes, an experiment that led to the current array of gorillas, orangutans, and chimps, the last Emperor of China and the first Wall Street broker.

It also led to two investigators who, while they may disagree on small points, are able to debate them despite "two huge egos," as Leakey once said. Just as they disagreed on the origins of *sapiens* one evening over dinner, the next evening they disagreed over the origins of bipedalism. The first debate had to do with place; this one involves time.

Leakey tries to put the time of our upright gait back to ten or fifteen million years ago. "I think bipedalism goes back beyond six point two." He picks on the date suggested by biochemists for our divergence from chimps.

"I don't," Gould says flatly.

"I think," Meave Leakey says firmly, "it's more around six point two, and not all the way to ten."

"Well," Richard, outnumbered, says, "we'll see."

"That would be something, though," Gould imagines, "to find a hominid that's absolutely ape in all other respects."

"We have from Buluk," Leakey refers to the site to the northeast, "a neck and a head of a primate femur, broken off on the shaft. But there's enough of that shaft there—not to *know* the angle but to *suspect* the angle." Leakey treads on precarious ground. "*If* you lay that bone on the table and ask any anatomist, it's an instant hominid. It fits perfectly. And it's seventeen million years old."

"To really know," Meave inserts, "you need the rest of the shaft."

"Well," Leakey says, "it's a hint. You add this to the fact that bipedalism is such a fundamental difference in locomotion that it *must* go back some time."

"Bipedalism just might have developed reasonably quickly," Gould says forcefully. He would prefer to see this adaptation occurring in a "moment" of punctuation, which Leakey agrees may be true. They disagree on when it occurred. "If you find a fifteen-million-year-old creature that is absolutely upright but otherwise completely ape, I'd be so excited I'd come back to Kenya to see it," Gould promises. "Just call it *Afropithecus gouldei!*"*

"Some ego!" Leakey exclaims.

"In memory of my refuting the idea." Gould shrugs.

Leakey stands to help Kimeu clear the table. As he turns away, one can catch the hint of a smile. Leakey, frequently criticized for his ideas, has gained from his sessions with Gould, severely edited for the consumption of non-scientists. It should be said that at one point Leakey qualified, "We haven't got enough material yet, but is it not possible—this is what I really don't know but the idea I'm pushing . . ." and continued with his arguments. The pleasure he takes in this vulnerability is in direct proportion to his admiration for his guest, who he privately confides is a "hero" to him.

At Koobi Fora, when Gould was late while we all sat in the Land Rover waiting, a suggestion to hoot the horn was refused outright. "He's too eminent to hoot," Leakey said, guarding the wheel.

Leakey gives the ignition key of the Land Rover its fifth turn. On the sixth, the passenger door opens and Kamoya Kimeu prepares to tend the engine. As Kimeu plants his first step, the engine finally turns over, sputtering toward a healthy rattle. "Thank you, Kamoya," Leakey says matter of factly, "I may ask you to do that again."

---

* Eleven months after Gould's visit, Leakey did indeed employ the name *Afropithecus* (but not *gouldei*) for the larger skull found at Kalodirr.

We drive over dunes that build from the Koobi Fora camp to higher ridges, the same road that Leakey and I took to Area 123 to retrieve the fragments to skull 1813. The wheels of the Land Rover climb a sandy escarpment dotted with commiphora bushes and euphorbia scrub. Leakey, over his shoulder, describes the horizons to Gould: "This is the last high stand of the lake. Holocene sediments sit on top of these deposits."

"What's the age of the indurated snail barrier?" comes the instantaneous inquiry, "indurated" meaning hard, "barrier" meaning boundary left by the lake, and snails being Gould's forte. "Here, about one point six million years old," Leakey informs. The mollusks serve as a "particular that fascinates, a generality that instructs," Gould's passion.

The mollusks from Koobi Fora represent the best preserved and longest series of lacustrine (or lake) assemblages in the Tertiary of Africa, Tertiary being the rather encompassing period of Pliocene, Miocene, Oligocene, Eocene, and Paleocene epochs that stretches from two million years ago to sixty-five million years ago. Peter Williamson, a colleague of Gould's at Harvard, collected over a million samples of clams and snails. From these he identified seven major zones that marked reinvasion by one species over another, and major extinction events. The regressions and transgressions of the lake drew up his storyline. Regressions, bordered by "stunted" forms, were followed by the lake's transgression, wiping out the old species with a new branch. Williamson saw in the lake's movement evidence of stress and isolation—the trigger for new species. He wrote in *Nature* that "Evolutionary patterns in all lineages conformed to the 'punctuated equilibrium' model."

Other clues on the landscape before us relate to the landscape that ancient hominids knew. Raymonde Bonnefille, collecting fossil pollen, found that the acacia, commiphora, and Salvadora that now dot the landscape once occurred in considerable density, and that a forest once existed here.

The only shadows to be cast upon the roof of this Land Rover today will occur far down the road, when we drive in a dry riverbed lined by trees. Before us now is a vast expanse of parched badlands.

"The fossil sites stretch down to those far hills"—Leakey points out the passenger window to volcanic hills near Allia Bay—"and about the same distance to the north"—he points out the driver's window. This sweep of the hand just covered 500 square miles. We head to the northeast, along the Karari Ridge Road, bypassing the turnoff for Area 123 where 1813 was found, on toward Area 131, home of skull 1470. Discovered in 1972, it remains the most complete and oldest skull of the Handy Man.

The *Homo habilis* 1470 was initially misdated at 2.6, then revised to 1.89 million years old. Criticism of the older date mounted alongside doubts of the antiquity of the *Homo* lineage in general. The controversy was sparked when younger fossil fauna from the Omo appeared to be very similar to that from Area 131, better known as the KBS site. Fossils that are well defined and plentiful often confirm or challenge a date derived from geological clues.

At the KBS site, the professor of geology from Harvard meanders, trying to sort out the confusing stratigraphy. The results of his survey: a nice set of baboon teeth, the inevitable snail, and his frustration with the stratigraphy. "You're right," he says to Leakey. "It's a mess," geological jargon for just that. "I mean there are no marked events you can trace. I've been playing this little game with myself, and I lost. I can't follow it."

"This tuff here," Leakey refers to a layer of volcanic ashes, "is 1.89 million years old; the other tuff over there is a bit less." When the area was first surveyed in 1970, it was initially thought that there were six volcanic tuffs that laced through this area. In the end there were seventy. At the time the samples were taken for dating, the stratigraphy had yet to be sorted out to this degree.

"But you always knew 1470 was below the KBS tuff?" Gould asks, knowing this would mean the fossil would be older if it was below.

"Yes," Leakey replies. "It was 45 meters below the 1.89-million-year-old tuff. But that time is criticized when leaning toward the maximum," he finishes wryly, exhausted by critics who suggest he personally tried to make the find older.

Handing me his camera, Gould asks to have his picture taken on the KBS. Leakey raises his own camera. "Maybe with a photograph of Stephen Jay Gould on the site"—he presses the shutter—"there would have been fewer problems."

There would have been fewer problems if 1470 weren't one of the most extraordinary hominid skulls ever found, and if Richard Leakey weren't Richard Leakey. But as the discovery granted him certain fame, and the older date supported his father's theory on the long lineage of *Homo*, its antiquity became central.

"It's unfortunate that the dating got involved in the theoretical issue of 1470 and the age of *Homo*," Gould reflects; "otherwise it probably would never have been so heated." He dismisses the dating mistake as one of the inevitable lessons of science being practiced in new frontiers, offering, "You can't expect to get everything right the first time."

"With all the things we know now," Leakey allows, "it's easy to say afterwards what went wrong. But people got emotional, attached and defensive." He includes himself among them.

"But everybody," Gould reiterates, "needs at least one big error to show for their autobiography, just to show the primary principle of the scientific process."

The primary principle of the scientific process had been demonstrated by the skull from Kalodirr. At first, Leakey thought it might be a *Sivapithecus* (or what was described as a *Sivapithecus*, from Buluk). But once the skull was cleaned and studied, it required not only a new name but a reassessment of the jaw from Buluk. When writing about the new *Afropithecus* skull, the Leakeys carefully noted that the age of the skull was estimated: "It has not yet been possible to date the locality but we estimate the age may be between 16 and 18 million years based on faunal comparison," from Rusinga, Buluk, and a third Miocene site to the south, Moruarot.

An accurate age for the Kalodirr site awaited an analysis by geologist Frank Brown. A few months after Gould's visit, the lanky geologist from Utah covered this same terrain. He noted the clam beds that Gould discovered, the iron oxide in the surrounding sediments, and standing before the vast volcanic ashes that we saw, inserted a broad-bladed *panga* (Swahili for machete) to select a sample. At Kalodirr, Leakey had acknowledged a range of sediments that spanned from the Cretaceous (100 million years ago) to the Present, saying of the various exposures, "but we don't know how they hang together yet."

Brown's business is time, but in fixing time, he reconstructs the environment where our ancestors lived by "hanging" beds, or layers of sediments, in order. Frank Brown's view of the KBS controversy, like most of what he does, put things into perspective.

7
·
Thin
Slices
of Time

There is an old geologist's saying: I wouldn't have seen it if I hadn't believed it. Frank Brown saw Lake Turkana, and he believed it. "That," he allows, "was a big mistake." Most lakes are "transitory things," he explains; "they don't last over a few hundred thousand years."

It is Brown's task not only to estimate an age for hominid fossils but to reconstruct their world—what he calls a paleogeographic picture. This portrait by numbers began with the Omo expedition in the sixties, extended through the decade of research at East Turkana, and now finds new momentum along the west side of Lake Turkana. As it happens, the route of Brown's career in the field circled Lake Turkana.

The central subject of his picture, a bold body of water that appears on every map of northern Kenya (its outline that of a wet sock hung from the Ethiopian border), became blurry around the edges; ghosts lingered in the background, as if the Turkana basin suffered from poor reception.

The oldest ghosts are rock-solid pentimentos of the past, as Lake Turkana formed over a Precambrian basement layer. As mentioned, the origins of the Great Rift Valley are found in the division of the earth's continents, the Rift being a further tectonic feature. It was named (as it was defined) by the British geologist John Walter Gregory, who set out in 1893 to discern the pattern responsible for the lakes. The Valley resembled the Grand Canyon in the sense that it appeared to be eroded by a river, but Gregory discovered faults, testimony to a splitting of the earth's crusts, along with matching rocks on opposing but uneven escarpments that had slipped down. The latter is especially visible near Lake Baringo at the Kamasia slab. Faults are apparent from the Red Sea to Mozambique; the width of the Rift is remarkably proportionate to the thickness of the earth's crust.

Certain lakes on the Valley floor are cut on one side by antithetic faults—breaks in the rocks that indicate movement in the opposite direction of the Rift. Brown noticed such contrary faults west of Turkana, to suggest that this basin is not really a part of the Great Rift. There is no well-defined valley at Turkana, but a rift is defined by parallel faults.

Geological faults are among the larger features that Brown uses, alongside beds of clams that mark the former boundaries of the lake—and here the ghosts really move. Shorelines are marked by the transgressions and regressions indicated by Peter Williamson's mollusks, by the grassy swamps reconstructed from fossil pollen by Raymonde Bonnefille, and by fossil fauna—the clams and crocodiles and turtles found at Kalodirr—details that Brown assembles to offer considerable complement to the search for missing links. Such an exchange is historically fruitful.

Charles Darwin, in devising his theory of natural selection, relied on the work of a great geologist. "By following the example of Lyell in Geology, & by collecting all facts . . . some light might perhaps be thrown on the subject," he wrote. Sir Charles Lyell's *Principles of Geology*, published in three volumes between 1830 and 1833, was among the treasured books carried on the voyage of the *Beagle*. Lyell honored time as no geologist had before, explaining the present landscape by changes that occurred over epochs and eras and periods vast. He reconstructed a paleogeographic picture that was considerably longer than anyone expected, a past where geological divisions explained many mysteries about the current organization of creatures on earth. With Lyell's framework, Darwin pondered the origin of species.

Branches on a family tree often occur as a result of a geological barrier that divides a single species into two populations. A most outstanding and gross division is that of Old and New World species, the Old World being that of Africa and Asia, the new one the American continental mass that split off. The widening Atlantic Ocean presented a barrier for flightless creatures around eighty million years ago. Birds of Australia and South America were split. Old World monkeys of Africa and Asia were split from New World monkeys (like the howler and spider). French paleoanthropologist Yves Coppens suggests the Great Rift Valley inspired the split between hominids and hominoids (if so, the Rift might be regarded as the Greatest Splitter of all). The more Brown learned about the Turkana basin, the more it repositioned boundaries that presumably affected the lifestyle of early hominids. For example, a couple of million years ago, Lake Turkana was not where it is today, nor was it a lake. As he details in a series of maps, Brown thinks the Omo River once flowed through the Turkana basin. To understand how such changes occur, consider the general arrangement of East Africa.

As opposed to the basin and range topography of the North American West, the African Rift combines valleys and swells, valleys and swells. A major sag in a swell is Lake Victoria. A superimposition on a swell is Mount Kilimanjaro. The 11,000-feet plateaus shouldering the Ethiopian Rift contain marine fossils, testimony to a time when these "plateaus" were below sea level. During the upwarping of rift shoulders that occurred over the last 2.5 million years, the Victoria Nile was forced to find a new route into Lake Albert. Where the Nile once found it convenient to flow west, a substantial uplift sent it along a circuitous path into the northern end of Lake Albert; consequently Lake Kyoga in northern Uganda became a pond.

At the Rift Valley's eastern wall near Lake Naivasha, the earth takes a nose dive for fifteen hundred feet from the Kikuyu escarpment down into the Valley floor. At the turn of the century, when tracks were laid for the Lunatic Express, the escarpment posed engineering problems on a grand scale. The incline that today inspires a shift to low gear in 1900 invited disaster for trains negotiating gradients so steep. Flatcars used for construction opposed gravity by being pulleyed up and down in tandem. Despite their near-vertical descent, the flatcars remained just that; front wheels were positioned ten feet below the rear wheels. Seen on the floor of the Rift, they were the picture of ridiculousness, except to the railroad engineers, inclined toward utility.

The most dramatic era of plateau uplift occurred during the Plio-Pleistocene era, the time frame for Brown's study.

Plio-Pleistocene sediments, from one to five million years old, are found in extensive exposures all around the Turkana basin. Hominid fossils surface amid vast formations of volcanic rocks, in the Usno and Shungura formations of the Lower Omo Valley, the Koobi Fora Formation on the east side of the lake, and to the southwest of Turkana, in the Lothagam and Kanapoi formations. The Plio-Pleistocene formation directly west of Lake Turkana was unnamed. (The formation has since been named Nachukui.)

Brown's revised view of the Turkana basin sailed forth as a piercing, hold-everything whistle to every scientist involved in the search. The background to portraits of hominids like 1470 and the Turkana Boy changed. Trees moved, sands shifted, and rivers ran in the opposite direction. Even the winds would have been different, along with the character of the clouds, the extent of the rains.

Lake Turkana, in current fact, is synonymous with the search for missing links. This body of water, 180 miles long with an average width of 40 miles, has provided the bath at the end of the day for members of the Hominid Gang for two decades; fresh tilapia (like

North American crappie) commonly figure on the dinner plates at Koobi Fora. The deltas that wedged these shorelines imbued bones with antiquity.

Like most hominid finds, the lake goes by more than one name. Old-timers still call it Rudolf, honoring the Crown Prince of Austria for whom it was named in 1888. In 1975, the lake became Turkana by government decree; it was independent Kenya's stance to rein-state the African identity usurped by European explorers—a sort of cultural reclassification of habitat. (As paleontologists "sink" sci-entific names no longer appropriate to species, President Jomo Ken-yatta's regime deep-sixed colonial nomenclature.) The Turkana basin still belongs to the people of the lake—the El Molo, the Dassanetch, the Turkana—despite the occasional invasion of *shifta* (bandits) from the north, tourists from the south, and these people who scour the landscape as if in search of a lost contact lens of God. The nomadic Turkana deliver their goats to the Hominid Gang in exchange for flour and water; their songs and grace they render free. (On the other hand, bracelets of sharpened steel demand a hefty price. One Turkana bargained offhandedly that only by this utensil was he able to eat.)

We begin our discussions out of context, sipping espresso in the Utah Student Union. Brown borrows clean gold paper place mats so as not to confuse the issue with coffee stains. Then he renders several versions of Lake Turkana in black felt tip.

The boldest superimposition is a meander that resembles the Mis-sissippi. With a squeak from the felt tip, Brown extends the Omo River through the "lake" and on its way to the Indian Ocean, a condition that he says "obtained" between four and two and a half million years ago. Prior to four million years ago, Brown's "not really sure what was going on." He indicates uncertainty in dots and dashes. "It's clear there was a big lake, but more to the west than the one we now know." Uncertainty resumes after 2.5 million years ago, the time frame for most of the known hominids in the Turkana basin.

"Now," he says, meaning after 2.5 million years ago, "you have

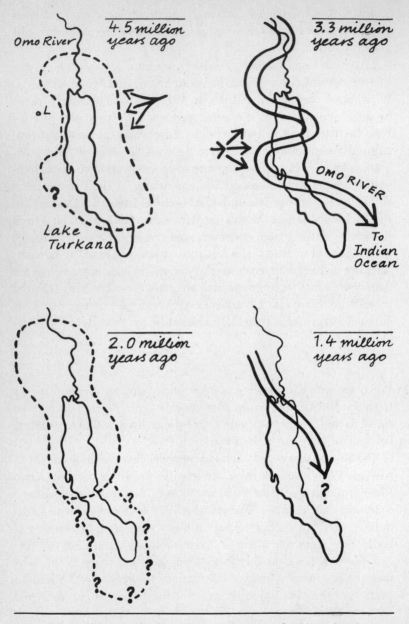

Brown's drawings of Lake Turkana in the past, refined by Bob Gale.

a number of things happening." He knows of deposition at certain points on the eastern side, erosion at certain points on the west. Around the KBS site at East Turkana, he found lacustrine deposits, or lake beds; the *habilis* represented by skull 1470 may have lived near the lakeshore. The Turkana Boy, however, may have lived along an oxbow left by the Omo. The first hominid collected from West Turkana was found in an ancient alluvial fan. Alluvial (river) fans are cone-shaped deposits at the bottom of a slope, rocks and pebbles indicating that a river or stream fanned out as the terrain became less inclined. This hominid may have lived here; it may have lived upstream.

The cautionary "may have" is itself a discovery, for just as some of the tools of Olorgesailie were transported to their current position by water, there's reason to think that some these hominids enjoyed the same transportation. Richard Leakey often warns that creatures may not have lived where their bones were found. In Africa you see predators like leopards moving their prey; you also see, as Leakey had noted on the Omo, giant forest hogs floating for great distances downstream. A pile of monkey bones found near a hippo skull doesn't imply the monkey was aquatic. A hominid skull found in lacustrine deposits doesn't imply that hominid lived on the lakeshore. An accurate paleogeographic picture that features habitats requires hundreds if not thousands of examples that reveal a pattern, and cannot be drawn from single examples. As Andrew Hill once remarked, "The only thing we know for certain about those bones is that they're dead!" He was being modest, but his point was made: posing more questions than answers was indicative of a new sense of caution in the search.

Brown tentatively extends the southern boundary of the lake, putting question marks around the Sugutu Depression, just below Teleki's volcano. At the top of the lake, he says simply, "This closes off, pushes up." When? How? Until he finds out, Brown prefers to draw in a lake that would have covered the Omo "River" Valley.

This quandary is delivered in an easygoing California accent. Frank Brown was born forty-five years ago in Willits, population 3,091, in a region worthy of his early investigations, the Mendocino Valley. A love for being outdoors led him to ponder rocks.

By his dress and demeanor, his beard and his perennial tan, he could pass for a wildlife photographer or a biologist. By his own admission he could not be a chemist. ("How'd I get into geology?" he laughs. "I hated chemistry!") Nine months of the year he teaches at the University of Utah, and nearly every summer for the past two decades has gone to East Africa to collect samples of the earth, which return to Salt Lake City in plastic bags. In a fifth-floor lab of the University Mineral Science Building (set amid meticulous landscaping) he reconstructs a vanished landscape.

The first treatment Brown gave the canvas for the Turkana basin was to erase the Present. The lake so familiar to the Hominid Gang was taken off the map. When he announced this one evening at the Leakeys' home in Kenya, Meave Leakey entered a gentle protest, "You just can't take our beautiful lake away!" But Brown did, and took away the Koobi Fora spit while he was at it. (The spit did not exist on maps drawn as recently as 1888.) The ephemeral nature of a sandy spit was something everyone could handle, but the lake had been written into many accounts dealing with early hominids, both scientific and popular. It was also visually rendered. Artist Jay Matternes, who does portraits of early hominids based on anatomical reconstructions, found some of his backgrounds altered dramatically by Brown's view.

"Basically what the hominid people want first is age," Brown explains. "But they don't get excited until all the fauna is stuck into their depositional environment: Was it shoreline? Were there swamps? Were there river deposits? Were they on a meander? If you had an incredibly large lake, for example, you might look for different patterns in the archeological sites." Brown notes that the El Molo and the Turkana, both nomadic in lifestyle, don't cross the lake today. "You might have had different cultures on opposite sides of the lake." Or the river. "I think we have times when the Omo went *up* to the Nile, times when it went out the Indian Ocean, and times when it went into Lake Turkana."

Brown intends to hang environments together by drawing up river channels and floodplains at "particular points in time." He describes these as a series of pictures—framing from 100,000- to 200,000-

year intervals over the past four million years. This, he says, will set the stage for telling us habitats.

"Was the habitat," he asks, "like the Karari?" he refers to the region north of Koobi Fora that includes archeological Site 50 and the KBS site; "Or was it like the Omo?" He taps the map in Ethiopia, where a lake figured instead of a river. "If you know where the lake was, and where the river was, then you can start guessing at where other things were. But none of it makes sense until you put it together in little time blocks. And you need the big elements first." The biggest element Brown needed was chronology.

It was a tall order, requiring one widespread clue so that he can "hang everything on it." Because of the scarcity of hominid fossils, "paleoanthropologists try to take collections from everywhere and put them all together." He doesn't complain; the dispersion of facts is a common dilemma to geologists.

To link localities as widely separated as East and West Turkana, Brown needed a common feature on the landscape. A characteristic of rift valleys around the world proved essential. Like many other geologists, Brown uses the products of volcanoes. His approach is unusual because it does not always require lava flows of basalt, or volcanic boulders. He doesn't even need to know where the volcano is, or was. Yet he pursues these sources, as a potential clue.

Brown, like everyone else in this search, must work backward; like the paleontologists addressed by Eldredge & Gould—he must unravel that "peculiar perspective" of the present and invite that element which "enlightens all conclusions—time."

He is not the only good geologist working in the search for human origins, nor does he work alone. But his investigation of the Turkana basin is exceptional, and pertinent to the hominid discoveries mentioned.

While his work represents progress in the search for missing links, there's a catch, one that snags hyperbole and salutes nature's surprises. A few months later, sitting under African skies at a camp erected along one of the former shorelines of this elusive lake, Brown said, "It's important to know the limits of your knowledge." He was addressing the dangers of passionate facts, not discouraging inquiry. Shortly after making this remark he turned his surveyor's scope on the mountains of the moon.

On a blistering Sunday in August 1986 I set out to join Frank Brown on his survey of "this year's hominid" site—an exercise in no way confined to the site itself. Our road will cross alluvial fans, shoreline deposits, big river deposits, small stream deposits, and the odd tephra layer. Tephra, the term used for products of volcanic eruptions, embraces all sizes and forms, from vast boulders that gravity solicits to fine ashes that may float across several geopolitical borders before drifting down to earth. Ashes that ride the winds are called aeolian; they tend to be comprehensive in their range.

Ashes from Yellowstone floated over the Pacific and filtered down through fathoms. The same deep discharge sent identical ashes across the plains of Nebraska and Kansas, across Brown's hometown in California as well as his current one in Utah. Ashes from Mount St. Helens changed the hue of sunsets on New York's Hudson River; ashes from Krakatau gave a golden hue to Turner's seascapes of England. Off the eastern coast of Kenya, an ash found near the island of Lamu was matched to one found at Koobi Fora. The same ash has also been found in Ethiopia's Awash Valley—that's 1,500 miles from Lamu, and another 1,500 miles to Koobi Fora.

A volcano sent its dark billowing cloud over 385,000 square miles. Considering the meticulous nature of Brown's work, you wouldn't think locating a volcano would be a problem.

"We don't know where it is," he sighs, adding a quick, "Yet." He contemplates the Ethiopian highlands, a geological hotspot where the earth's plates collided. Three rift systems converge in the Afar Depression, one from the Gulf of Aden, one from the Red Sea, and one from the Ethiopian Rift Valley. It is the only place on earth where such a triple junction is accessible on land and therefore can be studied in detail. Ethiopia's Guraghe Mountains are thick with lava. Addis Ababa, at 8,000 feet, is higher than Nairobi. With the tremendous rainfall, "nothing lasts up there," says Brown, referring to the Guraghe range. He thinks there were at least two volcanoes, although he would allow a dozen. He has a record of 125 eruptions, based on his samples of ashes.

Consolidated ashes appear in the landscape as volcanic tuffs, and in their most ideal form ripple across an exposure like a gray ribbon. They may occur waist-high, beneath our feet, or require some climbing, some digging, or substantial walking. They may have settled neatly and remained orderly and contained, or they may have been redeposited by rivers that moved them. They may have lost continuity to a fault, or been stretched thin when the Rift expanded, as it still does today. Tuffs may be relatively pure, with shards of glass dazzling like diamonds. They may appear murky, mixed with mud and gravel, and unworthy of the trip back to Utah. They may be altered, weathered, reworked. They may look like mud, sandstone, crystals, or the bottom of a fireplace. They may be a few inches thick or fifty feet thick. They may disappear at length only to reappear elsewhere—so suddenly that Brown is likely to say they "popped up."

Ribbons of ash not only lace through the entire Turkana basin but extend south all the way through Kenya, north to Hadar in Ethiopia's Afar Triangle, and northeast and *down* into the Gulf of Aden. Before we're finished Brown will attempt to stretch his survey to South Africa. He refers to tuffs as "thin slices of time."

In the search for missing links, they appear to win the prize, for they offer the promise of linking a huge number of hominids and hominoids into some chronological order. Other methods for dating, whether potassium/argon, radio carbon, or fission track dating, are more isolated efforts, fixing the age of hominid sites in arenas like Olduvai Gorge. But with tuffs, Brown has a common and comprehensive link between numerous hominid sites all around the Turkana basin. The notion of linking tuffs in East Africa began with geologists Thuré Cerling and Bill Nash during the KBS controversy. "Ian Carmichael—my major professor, a petrologist—really started things in this direction for me," Brown recalls; "Bill Nash and I published a paper in 1976 using mineral chemistry to show that the KBS was not Tuff D. We suggested that glass chemistry might provide links between the two areas." Brown is not the only one seeking these tuffs, but his bold and persistent efforts to correlate them, a monumental project begun ten years ago, put his career on the map.

The initial results, summarized in a paper he delivered at the

"Ancestors" symposium entitled "An Integrated Plio-Pleistocene Chronology for the Turkana Basin," brought the toughest audience in the world (his own colleagues) to attention. "Brown's work is the most important contribution to this search in the past two decades," says paleontologist Todd Olson; another colleague, Ray Bernor, says simply, "Brown's the most inspired geologist in the field."

The method he employs is known as "fingerprinting" the tuffs. Because each volcanic eruption produces a distinctive chemistry, each tuff has a chemical signature that can be discerned from the elements within. The actual eruption date is calculated by using the potassium/argon method (see page 184), and whenever Brown finds that same fingerprint again, he already knows the date of the tuff. The position of the hominid bones in relation to the tuff gives him an estimate of the fossils' age. Bones above the tuff would be younger; bones below the tuff, older.

Brown needs only one ribbon of ash to correlate any particular site on the landscape. "We have a record of at least one hundred and twenty-five eruptions. All you have to do is find out where those fit in time, sequentially, and whenever you find one, you can immediately link the sections above and below it." He of course prefers to find more than one tuff. "It's nice if you find two or three or four, but you deal with what the exposures give you."

We are to begin this particular survey near Kalodirr, including not only the Miocene sites visited by Stephen Jay Gould but sediments ranging from the Cretaceous (100 million years ago) to the Present. Brown's survey, then, includes the time frame for dinosaurs as well as the hominids that make this area famous. He has, in these surveys, stumbled across bones that appear to be those of dinosaurs, and those of hominids. Brown, as mentioned, discovered the new fragments to 1813.

Exploring Area 123 nine years after the original skull was found, Brown's mission was, as he puts it, "pure geology." He returned to confirm the position of 1813 in relationship to the KBS tuff for his ongoing revision of the chronology, a double check he would do for every hominid found in the Turkana basin. Accompanied by two members of the Hominid Gang, Wambua Mungao and Nzubi Mutiwa, "We were just looking around" when Brown seized upon a couple of tiny fragments at the site. "They were covered with carbonate concretions—perhaps's that why these guys didn't see them," he adds modestly. "Because I tell you, these guys don't miss much bone."

"I've found other things here and there, but, it's funny," he says, "paleontologists see a lot less of the landscape than geologists do. They've always got their eyes on the ground. In geology, you're looking to see if some stratigraphic characteristic will carry to the next hill. So you see a lot more animals, a lot more birds, and generally speaking, fewer bones." But geologist J. W. Gregory discovered the stone tools at Olorgesailie. As it turns out, Brown's Search Image is equally comprehensive.

To meet up with Brown, I take a Sunbird charter from Nairobi to Kalokol (Richard Leakey will not fly up in his Cessna until the following weekend). On board there are a couple of French tourists, an American architect who "wanted to get the feel" of the Turkana landscape after hearing one of Leakey's lectures, and a chain-smoking engineer for Amoco who disembarks at Lodwar.

Lodwar: Don't picture an air-control tower, an Avis neon. During the "Mau Mau crises," this dusty outpost was considered sufficiently remote for the incarceration of Jomo Kenyatta. Today, Lodwar is Africa's version of *The Last Picture Show*, rivaling Texas for understated habitat. Perhaps in the not so distant future it will be an exit on the Cape to Cairo Expressway. Perhaps there will be a movie of great local interest, which will open like this:

Bloomsbury, 1934: Couple meet for lunch, brunette with lots of spark, talks of glider flights, hand axes, lights her own. He's taller, older, and bears an uncanny resemblance to Errol Flynn, with a thin mustache and the actor's penchant for stealing a scene. Louis Leakey's scene is Early Man. Mary Nicol's is Stone Tools. She is to illustrate his book.

They encounter a young Kenyan, also tall, with a presence and bearing that would change the way the Western world looked upon emerging Africa. In this thin slice of time, the Kenyan attends the London School of Economics. The two men exchange greetings in Kikuyu; passers-by, overhearing, steal glances, but with no time for recognition they move on.

Nairobi, 1952: Louis Leakey leans into a microphone at the Voice of Kenya Radio Station, broadcasting propaganda against the insurgents. Jomo Kenyatta, having learned his economics well, inspires his people to confront the injustices.

Mary Leakey, still brunette, sleeps with a pistol under her pillow. The very design of the Leakeys' house in Langata was inspired by the Mau Mau "crises," with bars on the windows, a center courtyard for the Dalmatians. Louis, a prime target, employs a bodyguard. A U-bolt is loosened on the family Chevrolet, driven by Mary Leakey, as luck would have it, slowly. A cousin, Grey Leakey, was buried alive, after being forced to watch his wife strangled.

When Kenyatta is brought from Lodwar for his trial, Louis Leakey, because of his knowledge of Kikuyu, is subpoenaed as translator, then subsequently dismissed by the defense for his expertise, which they feel is effusive in a telling sense. Leakey, who has spoken Kikuyu since childhood, is able to enlighten the court on certain buzz words within the revolutionary rhetoric, potentially powerful phrases deemed otherwise innocent. Yet the two men—whose biographies juxtaposed tell the story of Kenya—become confidants as *Mzees*, wise old men. Louis Leakey is welcomed in the State House, though on his first visit, Kenyatta is said to have chided, "You knew my language too well." The Leakeys' youngest son, Philip (the product of an intimate celebration when *Proconsul* was discovered) is elected the only white member of the new Kenya Parliament. Credits roll.

The sequences featuring another view of former Kenya resume but a few miles to the east of Lodwar. The dirt airstrip at Kalokol is attended by a single Land Rover. Frank Brown unfolds his six foot four inch frame and approaches the plane with his legendary stride. (Warning me of Brown's pace in the field, Richard Leakey suggested I take what he called a "keep fit" course. Mind you, I'm relatively fit and substantially long-legged. But when Mary Leakey added, "How will you keep up with Frank Brown?," I stepped up my tennis and switched my bike into low gear a couple of months before, warned not to impede the progress of science.)

Progress wears safari shorts, leather sandals, and has rolled up his shirtsleeves on long tan arms. His canvas hat shades a substantial storehouse of knowledge, including a smattering of the language of the Turkana people, the names of birds and trees. A magnifying lens smaller than a quarter dangles from his neck.

We head north, toward a blue, knuckled mountain ridge of relatively recent origins that shift back and forth across the hood of the Land Rover like target ducks at the penny arcade. The famous Koobi Fora spit lies east, across Lake Turkana. Behind us, to the south, is Teleki's volcano. In the heat haze, the mountains that slide across the hood appear to disappear, which is useful for envisioning Brown's words:

"Prior to about four million years ago, there's no evidence that these mountains were sitting there. About three million years ago we get this big alluvial fan—there seems to have been another big river system, shoving everything out to the east. Even then the mountains probably weren't there yet." His narrative drowns in the whine of the Land Rover to resurface in a general statement: ". . . I know where things are stratigraphically. Structurally, I don't understand how some of the things got where they are."

He lists Teleki's volcano among such features, saying, "It would be nice to know when the southern barrier to the lake formed, but we don't have a clue." Like several areas in Kenya's Northern Frontier, Teleki's volcano is off-limits because of "security reasons," indicating hostile *shifta*, or warring factions.

Without the volcano as a barrier, Brown figures the southern shoreline of the lake must have extended into the Sugutu Depression. He suspects the northern shoreline would have changed along with the southern one. "If the river level was raised by ten feet, in a couple of years it could spread dramatically," he explains. Small vertical changes lead to huge lateral changes.

As we drive north along the west side of Turkana, I'm given an update. In the field, this is the news; there is no inclination to gather around the evening BBC broadcast in "Special English," somehow more curious and remote than a dancing lake or a skull part human, part ape.

Today's headlines: An australopithecine jaw was discovered at a new site last week; a carnivore has been found—a saber tooth cat; and at Nariokotome, "They're just getting down to the bone level" of the Turkana Boy, meaning the original level of deposition reached by inching away the adjacent hill.

These are in addition to what Brown refers to as "this year's hominid site," which delivered a complete *Zinj* skull near the banks of the Naiyena Engol, below the Nariokotome (Nary-ō-cot-ō-me). So are primitive tools made of lava, and dated at 2.3 million years old, the oldest stone tools found in Kenya.

Our sixty-mile journey north to Nariokotome will cross a series of dry riverbeds. These are convenient thoroughfares, for they lead to fossil sites. We bump along in a gray Land Rover issued by the Kenya National Museums, its doors touting a previous project: THIS EXPERIMENTAL VEHICLE RUNS ON CHARCOAL. TREES ARE A RENEWABLE ENERGY RESOURCE. As we roll such sophistry across a land where charcoal is derived from burning precious trees, the faded letters glare absurdly. Embarrassed by countless inquiries ("Does it really run on charcoal?" he mocks nasally), Brown will make several attempts to scrape the lettering off, squeezing the Land Rover between thorn trees, letting the acacias squeak for themselves.

The starkness of the West Turkana terrain does not compare with the golden savannas of the Serengeti, or beautiful lakes like Nakuru, where vast flocks of flamingoes rise like pink clouds, billowing and bunching against a horizon of yellow-barked acacias. These badlands—inanimate, stark, and wizened—clearly fall into the minimalist school. Battles between erosion and deposition resemble nothing if not the results of a frantic search. First-time visitors often assume this is Leakey's work. "Boy!" they turn to him admiringly. "You've really been busy!"

This is not a land in repose. To geologists, who use active verbs to describe what they see, the earth moves.

A hiatus is a missing section. Brown explains: "Suppose you have sediments deposited. Then, even if *you don't erode anything away*, for some reason there's nothing deposited for a half a million years. Then *you start depositing* on top. In that boundary, you've lost a half a million years." A hiatus is to a geologist what a fossil gap is to a paleontologist.

When a gray ridge of volcanic ash crosses the sandy road, Brown calls out: "There's a little tuff trying to outcrop!" What? "It's buried, and it's trying to outcrop," meaning expose itself to the surface. "I know—editors always change it to crop out. But it's trying to *outcrop*—just like trying to lay an egg."

Our tires tread across the Present-Day Lag—lag being gravels the rivers left behind, boulders being the most obvious. As we move north the lag will become, in Brown's words, coarser and coarser. Here rocks are a foot wide; along the rivers Lokalalei and Kokiselei, the superlative "incredible" is invoked. These boulders are messages from upstream, read by geologists in what they call the record (as paleontologists discern the earth's fossil record). "When you find really big boulders in the record, it means you have mountains fairly young." Big boulders imply steep gradients on the slopes that carry them. This, in turn, implies mountains tall, and young.

At 2.5 million years ago, Brown has found no lake deposits at all. He finds only deposits laid down by small streams and a big river. "For a long time, we thought this lake was as it is today for millions of years. There's this vast presence and you think it's always been there, right? At least at Olorgesailie and Olduvai you can tell a lake has been there and gone."

The majority of lakes around the world offer only mirages of their former selves. Among the largest of former lakes in the American West, Lake Bonneville once covered 20,000 square miles and had an extreme depth of 1,000 feet; it is currently known as the Bonneville Salt Flats. Sediments in what is now southeastern California are testimony to a chain of lakes that existed during the Pleistocene. Much of Michigan was once under Lake Agassiz, and not for nothing is Salt Lake City called Salt Lake City.

"They know this because they found fossils right here in the city," my cab driver had told me when I visited Brown earlier in Utah. The erudite Jack Williams, the only cabbie in Salt Lake with a radio telephone ("It's the wave of the future"), provided an update on the flooding that occurred during my visit in April of 1986. Folks were concerned, he said, that the water might run over the road. A local politician quipped, "It's a hell of a way to run a desert"; residents were encouraged to "seek divine assistance" and pray for drought. Three months later the water ran over Interstate 80 and the tracks of the Southern Pacific Railroad. An eleven-foot rise in four years nearly doubled the lake's surface, to 2,600 square miles, larger than the state of Delaware but still not quite as large as Lake Turkana, 3,475 square miles. Small vertical changes lend huge lateral changes.

I pull out the gold paper place mats, saved from our meeting in the Utah Student Union, featuring superimposed lakes in a series of dots, dashes, and question marks. Presently, our Land Rover takes us inside one line of dashes that prevailed four million years ago, a time when we could be observed, at our current level, by Nile perch; by name, testimony to a northern link. The transitory nature of Lake Turkana has so impressed Brown that he refers to it as the Present Lake.

Several days into my stay at the camp erected alongside "this year's hominid site" (a camp where precious water is preserved for tea, brushing teeth, and marginal attempts to advance beef stew from a solid form), Brown suggests a swim in the lake. Had it been an August afternoon ten thousand years ago, I could have simply gone skinny-dipping inside my tent. As it is, it took an hour's journey east by Land Rover to see whitecaps.

The winds blow from east to west; consequently the western side of the lake is sandier, more barren in vegetation, higher energy. "Everything over here is higher energy than it is at Koobi Fora; all the energy coming across the lake is dissipated by the waves smashing onto the western front. As far as we know, that's been the case for an awfully long time."

Brown's exploration of the west side began in 1981. He followed in Kamoya Kimeu's footsteps; Kimeu told Brown "where the bones were," the best exposures along the ephemeral streams. There are twenty-four such streams; drainage is from west to east with one exception, just to keep everyone on their toes.

When Kimeu led him to a new hominid site, Brown took a look around and said, "Tell Richard I think it's around one point seven." Brown waves the hunch aside. "You may think you know where you are, then you must prove it."

This is as good a definition of the science as any. Brown not only needed to prove that he knew where he was, but he would have to survive others insisting that he didn't have the foggiest.

To date, there is no method for determining the age of ancient fossil hominids directly. "There are," Brown observes, "just so many places you can go wrong."

In the field Brown pursues three lines of investigation. The first depends on chemistry, as in analyzing the tuffs; the second on the order of geological events—fixing the strata in sequence. The third relies on correlation, the matching of two events that happened at the same time, "or very nearly so": coincidental tuffs, rocks, fossils, geographical barriers, and the earth's magnetic fields.

While he makes various discoveries and insightful observations in the field, revelations often occur elsewhere. Brown is a collaborator, a reader, and a writer. He devours the literature and he corresponds with colleagues, like Jim Aronson and Bob Walter, who did similar research in Ethiopia. His most admired colleague is geochronologist Ian McDougall, based in Canberra, Australia. McDougall delivers independent analyses that confirm or challenge Brown's initial estimates. Brown's central duty is to gather samples, but during the 1987 season, McDougall joined him in the field, putting his own hands on relevant rocks.

That's the first place you can go wrong. You can grab a rock that's weathered—as implied, altered by subsequent influences. Rocks, like fossils, can be altered by chemicals in rainwater, by sand grains carried by the wind or water, by corrosion and corrasion. Rocks also tend to crack from the heat of the sun; the outer layer may be altered, the inner layer honest. "To some extent you can tell in the field," Brown explains. "But you can never trust what you see. The microscope often tells you that things that look fresh aren't."

Within the crystals of volcanic tuffs, uranium offers a measure of time. It does so by an atomic process of explosion, or fission, that coincidentally inspired the so-called Atom Bomb. One of the isotopes in the zircon crystals of tephra, uranium 238, fissions spontaneously, naturally and slowly. The process etches tracks on the crystals that relate to the half-life of the isotope; the tracks are counted under the microscope. It's not unlike counting tree rings except that the tracks are multiplied times the life span of uranium 238. "In fission track dating, the biggest problem is track fading. If fading occurs, the ages are younger than they should be." Fission track dating, when accurate, can be used to cross-check other methods.

The potassium/argon method was first tested on the hominid sites at Olduvai Gorge thirty years ago. "That technique," Garniss Curtis told me in his lab, "was invented right here in Berkeley." Curtis was Brown's instructor at the University of California, and pivotal to the dating of the *Zinj* site at Olduvai and the KBS site at Koobi Fora. Curtis now works out of the basement of the Institute of Human Origins, at the newly established Berkeley Geochronology Center. The potassium/argon method of dating was developed by Curtis and his colleague Jack Evernden during the fifties. Again, the source is volcanic rock, but within this, potassium. What is measured is the ratio of argon to potassium, because as potassium decays in time, argon accumulates.

Contamination is "a real bugaboo," explains Curtis. The majority of hominid sites in East Africa fall into the Late Miocene and the Plio-Pleistocene—a considerable expanse of nearly twenty million years. But the Precambrian basement rocks of East Africa are one to two *billion* years old. If a single grain of billion-year-old material find its way into a recent sample, it creates a gross distortion toward antiquity.

"In the beginning, huge corrections had to be made," Curtis recalls. "When you activate one element, you activate a whole bunch of others. So you gotta correct for the whole pudding." Curtis is an endearing character who has a tendency to speak at about 90 mph; what's impressive about this articulation is that he appears to be thinking at just over 100 mph. "Air," he moves on, "is a big bug-aboo. Every breath you take has .934 percent argon in it. You gotta get rid of it. Usually you bake it out. But if you do, your specimen has to be clean to begin with."

Extraneous argon can impose itself into the pudding. Volcanic rocks rise from extreme depths in the earth's surface—some find their way up from regions one hundred miles below the surface, about the distance from New York City to Albany. Potassium exists at such depths, just as it exists in the human body, and like potassium everywhere, it's decaying to argon all the time. If any of this argon is captured in a rock as it cools, it leads geologists to ages that are too old.

Pumice, the stone used for buffing heels and toes, is an ideal sample for the potassium/argon method. Whittled to the core, pumice offers a pristine sample of feldspar inside. "If you can't find any pumice, it's real dicey," Brown adds. "You can get numbers all right. But you're better off not producing those numbers if they must be ex-plained away."

Fission track and potassium/argon dating are primary because they allow geologists to arrive at numbers. Secondary methods of dating rely on correlating the "very nearly so," details on the landscape that may influence the numbers. Among these is a record of mag-netism, known as Paleomag, for paleomagnetic. It's often called "fossil" magnetism because it offers a record of the earth's magnetic fields, which tend to wander.

Four hundred million years ago, the north pole was in the western Pacific; this was a time of reversed polarity. One theory suggests the earth's magnetic poles are affected by our moon's gravitational pull, another that the movement of the earth's own magnetic molten material beneath the crusts effects the changes. Whatever the cause, particles in rocks assumed the prevailing pull when the rocks were formed, maintaining a record. So rocks found at hominid sites in-dicate eras when the polarity was in a stance, and therefore time.

These are uneven, natural spans of time, based on several research projects conducted worldwide, including variations among the deep-sea ridges. For example, around 700,000 years ago there was a major polarity change. Within this span are short periods of reversals.

Because they're short, they're not recorded in very many places on earth, so a geologist might not see them in a vertical exposure, or section. "Or you might just be having a bad time in your section," Brown says "Sections are notorious for having pieces of time missing. Only in a simplistic world," he concludes, "do you find things in order."

Within the calendar of paleomagnetic events, with dates assigned to all the transitions, there is revision, as befits any science. Where once there were only divisions of Epochs and Events, now there are subdivisions of Chrons and Sub-Chrons. The splitting that occurs on the branching bush also occurs in the geological record. ("Things are more complicated than we thought.")

Fossils also offer correlations. For example, horses trotted into the geological record of East Africa at around nine million years ago, so if there are any horses on the scene, the assumption is that you're in a slice of time no older than nine million years. Hippos made their appearance at seven million years ago. So if you only had a site with horses and without hippos, its age might be calculated at eight million years old. Rarely does a time frame depend on a single species; that would be as precarious as naming a species based on a fragmentary jaw. In the best analysis, there are a number of species from various sites, even sites quite distant, that provide similarities in the same horizon—everything from elephants to ostracods, tiny shelled crustaceans.

"Fossils are terribly important," says Brown. "They tell you when you're blatantly wrong." While fossil pollen is used to reconstruct the green tones in his paleogeographic picture, plants can't tell Brown time "because plants haven't changed much in the past four million years." However, fossils of mammals that evolved quickly can tell him time. "Pigs are tremendously useful; the elephants, very useful, and to some extent hippos—even snails." Brown doesn't include hominids, since their age is the puzzle to be solved. (Hominids remain independent variables.)

With so many ways to go wrong, there are two ways to be right: accuracy and precision. Yet Brown discerns a difference. "With accuracy, you get a true and correct age. If we could wait around for 100,000 years and date the ash from Mount St. Helens, we would *know* we have an accurate age of 100,000 years. Precision, on the other hand, is *how* you produce a result," featuring a theoretically correct method, and based on theoretically good samples. "If tested over and over, and by other scientists, that age, theoretically, should be true." So you may have a precise formula, and it may be dead wrong.

In 1972, Richard Leakey suggested that skull 1470 was nearly three million years old. As mentioned, the skull was found 147 feet below the KBS tuff, which was dated at 2.6 million years old. "Originally, we were told it was two point six by the Cambridge lab, then that went down to two point four," Leakey recalls. Then, from the work of Garniss Curtis at Berkeley, "It was one point six, then one point nine." Of the first dating range, Leakey says: "It wasn't as if they took one sample and assumed that was all they needed. They did it over and over again, and they were always consistent. But they were consistently wrong—which is not like science." They were precise.

The controversy over the dating of the KBS tuff extended for nearly a decade. Richard Leakey eventually asked Ian McDougall to tackle the problem. (At the time Frank Brown was working with the Omo team, and Garniss Curtis was his graduate supervisor.) In his Australian lab, McDougall fixed the KBS at 1.89 million years old, close to Garniss Curtis's date of 1.83 myo, a difference of 60,000 years that Curtis assigns to "just a calibration factor" between the two labs. But the Berkeley results were much closer to the truth than the dates from the Cambridge Lab, and they were the second hint, on top of the omo fossils, that something was wrong.

Why was the KBS so difficult? "You walk for a long time and see nothing," Brown explains. "Then suddenly you come to an exposure. How do you find a pattern?" Part of the muddle of this notorious controversy had to do with Splitting and Lumping.

"Early workers there relied too heavily on correlations based on the tuffs visible in the field," Brown recalls. "They had no idea of how complicated it was." Originally, six tuffs were identified at East Turkana; as it turns out, there were actually seventy tuffs. When a new tuff was found, it had to be forced into one of the six. "If you've got so many things and you're only classifying them into limited alternatives," explains Brown, "there are bound to be problems."

While the final date of the site was confirmed by an accurate dating of the KBS tuff, the initial doubts were raised by pig fossils, based on the careful research of Basil Cooke in the Omo. Pigs were so plentiful, and their evolution so rapid during the Plio-Pleistocene, they virtually mapped the landscape with points in time. One particular pig, *Metridiochoerus andrewsi*, related to warthogs, had a distinctive third molar that became taller as it evolved. Once this tooth was found in an area with a reliable date, the same tooth found anywhere else could be assigned an age. Working with paleontologist John Harris at Koobi Fora, Brown complained: "Can't you find a pig tooth for me?" Harris was incredulous. "I'd never had a geologist request a fossil before."

Brown has no time for polarity, such as occurred between the Omo and Koobi Fora teams. "I don't see any reason not to exchange information," he says impatiently. "If it's wrong, I'd like to know. Everything you do is just an attempt. Someone will come back and redo this someday."

Of the KBS, he says, "It was a terrible time, a terribly emotional business." Many felt that Richard Leakey and his team defended the date too long and too hard, even though the Cambridge lab kept producing the same precise date. Frank Brown was convinced that the 2.6 myo date was wrong, and made his view known "lots of time in public."

So, in 1980, Brown was surprised to receive an invitation from Leakey and Glynn Isaac, co-directors of the Koobi Fora Research Project, to work on their team. "I was in the Omo bunch, and we were on the other side of the KBS controversy. To have this invitation to come finish the geology at Koobi Fora just floored me." Several years later, Brown raised the lingering Why me? "Richard told me, 'For one thing, your arguments turned out to be right, and that's good. Also, your arguments were never personal. It's fair enough to argue about science, but you never joined the character assassination.'" Leakey confirms this with a handy metaphor: "I never had any bones with Brown about his arguments on the KBS."

"I think it might have been clear to Richard as long ago as the

Omo expedition that hundreds of tuffs in the Omo are at Koobi Fora," Alan Walker suggests. "Frank Brown's work there was incisive. Brown knew the sequences at the Omo; he's the man to sort out the rest." The location of many of the same tuffs at Koobi Fora relied on winds that crossed the Ethiopia/Kenya border, and the meanders of the Omo River, currently north of the border.

Certain thin slices of time at West Turkana embrace the fossil gap between four and eight million years ago. Near Kataboi, Brown stops the Land Rover and leads me on foot to view a series of basalt dykes. This bold, black formation is dramatic, smashed upright by a fault. It looks like Rockefeller Center without windows. Because these dykes "intruded," they're younger than the sediments that surround them. The dykes are four million years old. So this is an invitation to search for fossils at Kataboi.

North of Kataboi, Brown stops to ask a Turkana woman the name of the river. She gives him a smile broad enough to write the name of the river on her teeth: Nasechbun, meaning a good place to sleep. "Sometimes it helps to know," he shrugs. He thanked her and moved on.

Brown likes to say that he can only work with what the exposures tell him. He solicits these conversations. They are, like most, a mixture of tacit signals and the occasional misunderstanding. When a fault or a steppe is out of order, why, he wonders, would it "behave" that way? When a tuff turns its back, he goes for a long walk until it resurfaces. He is wary of sections that appear to be what they seem. He looks for hidden channels, missing sequences, historical causes for the present. He is quite capable of exhibiting the ire of a man betrayed. Once, he stomped up to a section and gave it a disgruntled "I'd like to know what this is doing out here."

From Kataboi to Lomekwi, the sedimentary beds dip gently to the east in the oldest part of the section. Just north of this, the beds dip west and are younger. The rule of dips in geology suggests that younger sediments reside on the higher end of the incline. "The older stuff has to be below in order for the younger stuff to lay on top of it," Brown offers logic. But the rule of dips is made to be broken, as is Steno's Law, written in the late 1600s and assigning stratigraphy the order of stacked newspapers, the most recent edition being on top. For every law in nature there is an outlaw.

We come to a thin slice of time, the four-million-year-old Moiti tuff. The Moiti is not your diminutive ribbon of ash but dominates this section of earth because it was redeposited, building with silt along the former river. Most tuffs are three to four inches wide. The Moiti ripples boldly along this exposed riverbank at eight to twelve feet, top to bottom, like too much chocolate between two slivers of vanilla cake. Brown finds tuffs up to fifty feet thick, especially in former river channels.

To collect a sample, he slices into the ashes with a *panga*, then tips the blade into the mouth of a plastic bag, which he twirls closed like a shopper bagging garlic. One hundred kilos of volcanic ashes will be collected during this stint in the field, featuring two hundred different tuff samples. "Collecting samples is easy," Brown says. "The hard part is knowing where you are in the section: what's above it and what's below it. It's never the analysis. Once you've got it in the bag, you're home free. After a couple of hours in the lab, you've got numbers."

I put it at 90 percent sweat and 10 percent analyses. He seems consummately if quietly inspired, and even in rare cynical moments, when, for example, he acknowledges that others would love to catch him at a mistake ("because I publish with Richard"), he turns the threat into an antidote for dogged precision.

"There's an awful lot of long, boring hours accumulating data. But every once in a while, something clicks. You're in the field, and you think: I've seen this before. If you go through your notebook, sure enough, there it is. I write everything down, even though I hate it at the time."

He slaps his notebook closed. Knees pop; we take a look at older lake sediments. "These little orange bands usually have ostracods." He looks with his lens, and the ostracods are where they ought to be, executing a fine imitation of rice. The tiny crustacean shells tell Brown that the lake chemistry was very different from that of the Present Lake. Thinking of the hominids that lived along these shores, Brown says, "It would be useful to know if the lake was drinkable in the past."

To collect a sample, Frank Brown scrapes away at the surface of the ashes, then picks up less than a handful on the tip of the blade of his panga. Samples are shipped back to his lab at the University of Utah where they undergo the chemical analysis that reveals the distinctive "fingerprint" of a single volcanic eruption.

"Well"—he rises—"this is the older stuff. Just having a good dated section of four-million-year-old fauna, besides Laetoli, would be extraordinary. It'd be nice if they could find some hominids, too." As we walk along, he begins to whistle, then stops. "In a sense, they keep the project going."

Kamoya Kimeu is doing his best. Just west of us, at a site so new it's unnamed, Kimeu has found "a few bits and pieces." This, after only two days of initial survey walking pretty fast with a team of only three or four men, marking the most interesting stuff with cairns, then moving on. "Again," says Brown, "it was Richard's little airplane that found the site."

This Cessna 206 is a crucial implement in the search for missing links. Leakey's observations stretched Brown's survey off the aerial photo number 33 that he holds in his hands, and beyond the mountains to the west. "There are sediments all over there," Leakey told him, "and there are tuffs in them." Brown, who'd spent two years surveying the Koobi Fora and Shungura formations to make a "model of deposition," could only muster, "You're kidding." If Leakey was right about a new, unnamed and unknown formation, Brown's ideas were wrong in the sense that they were incomplete. "Fortunately"—Brown smiles—"I hadn't published yet."

"Now we have to fold those in," he says, less with resignation than regard. "Richard's discovery turned out to be tremendously important, a real extension of our knowledge of this side of the lake." These exposures northeast of Lodwar demonstrated that the four-million-year-old margins of the Turkana basin were far removed from those of the Present Lake. "It proved again that we shouldn't be too influenced by the present topography in our thinking."

Perhaps there was a gigantic floodplain, he offers, like the Chalbi Desert? The Chalbi is south of "Lake" Chew Bahir (*bahir* is Arabic for sea). There are diatomites in the desert to indicate that the Chalbi, like Orlorgesailie, was once under water. Now we traverse a floodplain, the top of the lacustrine section; Brown announces that we are somewhere between 2.5 and 1.8 million years old. He stops at another exposure to demonstrate his point, picking out "a very sharp termination of ostracods," which appears as clearly as the "plankton line" in the deep-sea cores. "They must have stopped"—he tosses a pebble to hit the bedding line—"about there." Brown also notes that a tuff called Lokochot is "missing" here. With these big alluvial fans, the tuff was totally washed away by a river. He knows it's missing because there is a record of the Lokochot tuff at Kataboi.

The integrity of the tuff fingerprint makes such a link possible. "Tuffs are nice lines of time. They may represent only a month or so in the middle of thousands or millions of years. But if you just follow the tuff, you can always find it again, because they go everywhere—into lakes, into the sea. And volcanic ash maintains its distinctive character wherever it goes." As long as a tuff isn't altered, its chemical fingerprint remains distinctive, even in the bottom of the Gulf of Aden, where Brown found a fingerprint that revised the age of major hominid discoveries from Hadar in Ethiopia, including Lucy.

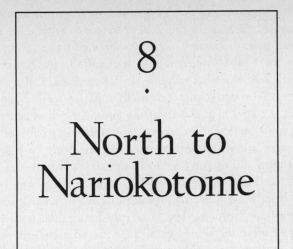

8
.
North to
Nariokotome

Frank Brown, while now associated with the Leakey team, had no particular mission to make younger the fossils from Hadar found by the Johanson team. Discovered roughly four hundred miles to the north, Lucy and the other *afarensis* finds were impressive but unrelated to his paleogeographic picture of the Turkana basin. But once he found a tuff common between them, investigation was unavoidable: Either their date was wrong, or his was.

Lucy was initially referred to as being around four million years old. There were subsequent revisions, all younger. In 1982, geologists James Aronson and Bob Walter of Case Western Reserve University revised the date for the older *afarensis* to around 3.6 million. They based their estimate on samples obtained from volcanic basalt known as the Kadada Moumou, and four tuffs in the Hadar region, the oldest called the Sidi Hakoma. In January 1985, Brown wrote in *Nature*: "The early hominids of East Africa were dated by determining the ages of tuff beds at the sites. Despite much research using paleomagnetic and potassium/argon dating techniques, some of those ages are still controversial." Brown deals with what the rocks tell him, and as the tiny rocks in tuffs told him of a "stratigraphical tie" between Hadar and the Turkana basin, any revision, youthful or otherwise, would prevail in Kenya as well. If the integrity of the fingerprint method was truly honorable, both slices of stratigraphy were the same age because the volcanic eruption they indicated occurred once, that a tuff fell both here and there.

First (to put the story together in "little time blocks"), Brown began to link the tuffs along the Omo River Valley with those of the Turkana basin. The Omo that ran south from the Ethiopian highlands captured volcanic ashes and deposited them en route, a route that included the Turkana basin as marked by meanders in black felt tip. If water carried volcanic tuffs south, why not north as well?

The Omo and Awash rivers have a common drainage divide for roughly sixty miles in the Ethiopian highlands. A fork of the Omo runs through the Guraghe Mountains to a place called Badda Rogghie, where it joins the Awash. Courtesy of these rivers, some of the tuffs at Hadar, located in the Awash River Valley, could be the same—especially if the volcanic sources were the Guraghe range. Where the volcanoes were was merely a potential clue; the trick was to match fingerprints.

Brown had already collected over a thousand ashes in the Turkana basin, but wished for "every ash I came across" in the Shungura Formation. The Shungura, in southwestern Ethiopia, was somewhat familiar from his work during the Omo expedition. "A lot of problems could have already been solved if we'd had that whole series of ashes, knowing the order. I see that now," he sighs. "Hindsight is very keen."

Toward the end of the field season in 1985, Brown set out to rectify this. From Kenya's Northern Frontier, he drove south to Nairobi, flew north to Addis Ababa, then drove south to the Omo River Valley. The formation begins a mere three miles from the Kenya border, but Brown, advised that he could not cross the border, took the long route.

From Addis Ababa, he set out with two students, Bereket Haileab and Tamrat Worku, to assist him. They were told of a new bridge across the Omo. They drove up and down the eastern bank in search of such a feature. Finally they locked up the Land Rover and took a boat to the other side, where local police confirmed there was no bridge. The police agreed to loan Brown a vehicle, but there was no diesel to fuel it. Brown sent the students to buy food, located a trusted worker from the Omo expedition named Atiko, and returned to the eastern shore to ferry across his jerry cans of diesel. From his "pantry" below the passenger seat, he selected two tins of meat and two tins of fruit—"You know those pears in sweet syrup? Just awful"—he grimaces—"but I always like to carry a little something."

The next day they drove into the euphemistic bush, where they camped "under" a lonesome one. The students didn't bring any food; they'd misunderstood. Brown opened one tin of very sweet pears and one tin of meat. Since the police had insisted that a driver and an *askari* (armed guard) escort the expedition, the group now numbered six, none of whom declined the pears.

With such provisions, Brown had one day to collect samples. That was it for the 1985 expedition to the Shungura. When they returned the vehicle, the police asked why he hadn't come across the Kenya border, saying, "That's the best way to get here." In 1986, Brown did so.

He collected enough tuff samples to confirm they matched several in the Turkana basin, including one named the Tulu Bor, after the area in East Turkana where it was originally found.

The Tulu Bor represents more than one tuff—separate eruptions lumped under the same name but distinguished by their fingerprints, and therefore time. In parts of the West Turkana terrain, two tuffs of the Tulu Bor occasionally appear running alongside each other in an exposure, separated by about a yard of sediments. The lower (and therefore the older) of the two is called the alpha, and the upper, the beta. The Tulu Bor presents other complexities, which we encountered on the road to Nariokotome.

Our journey along the west side of the Present Lake began in sediments more than four million years old in the south. We've moved up beyond the Nasechbun River to the Kataboi, where we stand alongside what appears to be sandstone. It's the Tulu Bor. It doesn't look like an ash; it doesn't even look volcanic in origin. "Almost everywhere" Brown finds the Tulu Bor, it's characterized by massive cross beds, running at an angle to the plane surface. Less than two hundred yards away, the Tulu Bor appears again, only this time it's twenty feet wide. The beta Tulu Bor also settled at East Turkana, where it's fifty feet thick. Conversely, the alpha is elusive, or as Brown puts it, "often missing."

For one who spends much of his time tracking down tuffs by putting one foot in front of the other, Brown stumbled across the beta Tulu Bor on a landscape of black on white. In a thesis written by Bob Walter, Brown noticed an analysis of glass shards that looked familiar. Mind you, he's reading a column of percentages, a huge array of numbers relating to the chemical makeup of the glasses in tuffs. The fingerprint was for the Sidi Hakoma tuff of Hadar. "I recognized it as a tuff I'd seen before," Brown says, as if he were remembering a face. A comparison gives you some notion as to how fingerprints are matched:

Comparative Analysis of the Chemical Makeup of the Sidi Hakoma and Tulu Bor Tuff Glasses

	Sidi Hakoma (Range)	Average	Tulu Bor Tuff
Silicon	71.70–73.23	72.54	71.69
Titanium	0.12–0.24	0.16	0.14
Aluminum	12.16–12.60	12.37	11.92
Iron	1.24–1.48	1.33	1.29
Magnesium	0.00–0.06	0.04	0.05
Calcium	0.24–0.33	0.29	0.28

(all elements expressed as oxidized)

By Bob Walter and Jim Aronson's estimate, the Sidi Hakoma was dated at more than 3.6 million years old. But Brown estimated that the same tuff in Kenya was younger: 3.35. Lucy was found one hundred yards above the tuff, which would make her even younger. Estimates as to how much younger depend on the rate of deposition in the area. (At Hadar the *afarensis* fossils spanned about ninety vertical yards, in this instance, a quarter of a million years in estimated time. In a simplified cross section, Lucy appears highest, then the First Family. Lower, and therefore oldest, are the jaws and knee joint found during the 1973–74 field seasons.)

Aronson and Walter "projected" that if Brown's correlation were to be correct, then one should find the tuff in a location in Ethiopia between Hadar and the Turkana basin, which has not turned out to be the case. "There was a good reason for that," Brown explains. "There are no known sedimentary deposits between Hadar and the Turkana basin. I mean, you aren't going to find it on *those* hilltops," he refers to the Guraghe range. "It's blown away; it's not preserved."

One of the characteristics of the winds over Ethiopia is a strong vertical sheer. Low-altitude winds carry ash in one direction, and high-altitude winds move ashes along the jet stream.

The idea to look for the tuff in the Gulf of Aden arose in collaboration with Brown's former roommate from Berkeley, Andrei Sarna-Wojcicki, who works with the U.S. Geological Survey in Menlo Park, California.

Brown had described his tuff problem to Sarna-Wojcicki, who correlates tuffs in the Western United States. "Maybe the suggestion to look at the Gulf of Aden cores was his; I can't take the credit alone." Well, he could, and others would, but the qualification is typical of Brown.

He describes Site 231 in the Gulf of Aden as consisting mainly of calcareous nanofossil ooze. I ask if he might be a bit more general. "It's grainy, not quite white, not quite yellow—if it's really a good ooze." "Ooze" is an apt term for ocean deposits; the literal translation of nanofossils is dwarf fossils—"miserable little creatures," Brown sketches them on a yellow pad, "like miniature Roman chariot wheels." Such tiny fossils were used to correlate elusive volcanic ashes on land. Peter Roth, a fellow faculty member at Utah, checked the cores from the Deep Sea Drilling Program, then at the Scripts Institute of Oceanography at La Jolla, California. He had initially described the nanofossils from these cores in 1974, showing how small the geological community really is.

In the cores taken from the Gulf, the ooze itself was assigned a stratigraphy. Depth indicates time. Horizons are distinguished by LODs and FODs: Last and First Occurrence Datums. For example, just over a million years ago, at a coring depth of 76 meters, it was the end of the line for *Calcidiscus tropicus*. Above this, they disappeared. At a depth of 254 meters, there occurs the first *Ceratolithus acutus* at over five million years ago, which continues to the Present. Highly successful, *C. acutus* made it to the top of the charts.

Within these horizons, there were the occasional tephra horizons. While numbers obtained in the lab granted them integrity, their glassy form was duly noted: "abundant clear colorless angular platy bubble-wall shards and subordinate bubble-wall-junction shards with straight ribs, and some tubular pumice shards having elongated rod-shaped vesicles." These glass shards were attractive in that they were identical in composition to the beta Tulu Bor tuff from East Turkana, to correlative samples that Brown retrieved from the Shungura Formation, and to the Sidi Hakoma tuff of Hadar.

Sarna-Wojcicki's complementary research revealed other fingerprints in the deep-sea cores. For example, the older Moiti tuff that we had seen on the road to Nariokotome was found in a coring horizon of around four million years ago, which matched its stratigraphical position on land. Evidence of a younger fingerprint from the Turkana basin appeared at a higher level in the deep-sea core, which is to say that things were in order: the sequence of the tephra layers from the bottom of the Gulf matched those on land.

Brown not only matched the Tulu Bor in Kenya with the Sidi Hakoma at Hadar, he also came close to estimating its age *without* an actual eruption date on the tuff from East Turkana. He had based his original estimate on the position of the Tula Bor in relationship to another tuff, which had a firm age of 3.35. The correlative tuff in the Gulf of Aden turned out to be 3.2, a little younger.

"This," his *Nature* paper concluded, "has significant implications for the ages of hominid specimens in the Hadar Formation." Brown's younger date was also influenced by the paleomagnetic record for the Hadar site. "If you look at the Paleomag," he says, "it's reasonable to think the hominids are around three million years old, rather than the four million they were being pushed toward."

When the results were published, *The New York Times* ran a report by John Noble Wilford entitled "Age of Man's Oldest Ancestor in Doubt." Paradoxically (and in fairness, Wilford does not write the headlines), many scientists acknowledged that the age of *afarensis* of Hadar was closer to home. In a 1987 lecture at the American Museum of Natural History, Don Johanson referred to Lucy as being three million years old. (To further qualify that headline, the *afarensis* fossils from Laetoli, Tanzania, are 3.75 million years old.)

James Aronson emphasized that the basalt from Kadada Moumou was not ideal for dating. "It had been altered by subsequent heat and weathering. Our best interpretation, 3.6 million years, may be wrong. It's possible." Aronson and Walter had expected their investigations to be challenged; they sent Brown Walter's thesis, along with a sample from Hadar. "We didn't push for an older date," Aronson notes. "We worked completely independent of the anthropologists in our dating."

It should be noted that Brown's work is also open to challenge. He is careful and he is precise, but there are so many ways to go wrong that he fully expects his results to invite revision. The correlating ooze suggests that any revision may not be as great.

This kind of link could not have been done with boulders or basalt, or lava flows, the standard source of dating. Most volcanic products are arrested within the general range of their source. But ashes carried hundreds of miles by wind and water make such a comprehensive link possible. The ooze established an independent source for correlating tuffs on land.

More important than revising the age of the Sidi Hakoma, the productive link between ocean and land data was confirmed once again, as happened with Stan Margolis and the global carbon budget. For Brown, this wasn't enough.

"You know the monsoon goes both ways," he offers. "Half the year the wind blows east, and the other half it blows west. And," he pauses, "it comes back inland over South Africa."

Poor dating in South Africa has frustrated two generations of paleontologists. The efforts are so inconclusive that some do not include the South African hominids in their arguments. Others emphasize the unknown: What if some of the australopithecines from South Africa turn out to be older than those from Hadar? If genetics dictate a single origin for species, as Stephen Gould has emphasized, where did the australopithecines arise? If they arose in one place, did they migrate both north and south?

Hadar, Ethiopia	3 myo
Laetoli, Tanzania	3.75
Baringo, Kenya	5
Makapansgat, South Africa	?

Current estimates on South African sites range between one and two million years old; pig fossils, as analyzed by Basil Cooke, suggest Makapansgat may be at least three million years old. It was Dr. Cooke's analysis that led to the so-called pig clock, creating a stratigraphical tie between the Omo and East Turkana during the KBS controversy. As Brown says, fossils tell geologists when they're blatantly wrong.

Brown wrote colleague C.K. "Bob" Brain in Pretoria in hopes of obtaining samples of ash. (Dr. Brain continues his investigation of the evidence in South African caves, studying charred bones that suggest campfires were used by early hominids in these caves.) "It's not inconceivable that there are some of the bigger volcanic ashes in the South African caves," Brown says. "If you could prove that, if you could link the two chemically, then you could link the South African hominids to the hominids here."

We continue our drive north to Nariokotome. The hominids here include the black skull, which Brown dated at 2.5 million years old based on the tuffs around the Lomekwi River. Along the banks of the Lomekwi, we stopped for lunch under the shade of the local "Tree of Man"—the traditional name assigned by the Turkana men to denote hierarchy of gender and age, having nothing to do with the tree of hominids that paleoanthropologists pursue. At two o'clock, when the temperature edged above 100 degrees, a shade tree along the Lomekwi seemed a good idea.

Brown, gentleman geologist, lifts the passenger seat out of the Land Rover, positioning it in the shade of the acacia. He unfolds a most ingenious toolkit made by modern hominids, using a Swiss Army knife to whittle acacia branches into chopsticks, opening tins of grapefruit and plums, the latter about as sweet as those pears consumed in Ethiopia. As we eat, he lets his mind wander to certain features on the landscape in Utah.

Just before this 1986 field season in Africa, Brown worked with paleontologist Michael Bell in Utah, "trying to correlate a quarry." The landscape was white with tuffs, "beautiful ashes, as white as sandstone. If we can correlate those, it will be a fascinating story of the volcanic history of the western U.S. But the ones I've analyzed so far look incredibly similar." He held a plum aloft on his stick. "You know the story about the pot of gold being hidden under a plant, and the Irish elf told the guy to tie a ribbon around the plant? And he tied ribbons around all the plants that were the same?" He bit into the plum. "I hope these tuffs don't turn out that way."

Another feature on the Utah landscape is Theresa Brown, a tall, thin blonde who is a specialist in data storage. In the summer of 1984 she journeyed to Kenya for the first time, to join her husband, a specialist in unraveling stored data. Theresa envisioned a romantic safari in the famous game parks: "The last thing I wanted to do was go into the field." But in the summer of 1984, Kamoya Kimeu found the first clue to the Turkana Boy, and the excavation was under way. "You must come up and see it," Frank told Theresa at the Nairobi airport. "Thirty years from now you'll look back and be glad you were there."

Brown wipes the Swiss blade and folds it closed. We pack up the restaurant. He pauses before cranking up the engine. "From here on," he said, "it gets harder to explain."

A dove enters a trilling note into the conversation. It sounds like a muted drumroll on my tape. "The exposures are really poor," Brown continues, "but for the next 200,000 years—maybe 300,000—there's the same sort of deposition, a series of river deposits, sand-filled clays with a bunch of tuffs in them. Then you get into a big lake sequence that extends from the Shungura to Koobi Fora, to here." After that, Brown says, there's a return to deposits left by rivers. Following that is "a very odd period of time." It happens to be the time frame for Gould and Leakey's discussion on the point of origins for modern humans.

We've just left the black skull site, dated at 2.5 million years old. The synopsis that Brown rendered embraces a time frame that extends to exposures marked by the Chari tuff, at 700,000 years old. It includes the time frame for the Handy Man, descendants of the black skull, 1813, and the Turkana Boy. Then something really odd happened. At 700,000 years, Brown encounters a substantial hiatus. The record picks up again at 100,000 years. The hiatus covers the transition for *erectus* to *sapiens*. Before I arrived, Brown had gone north toward the Ethiopian border in search of sediments to explain the gap. He didn't find any. He says incredulously, "We've got no deposits—we can't find them. I'm sure they have to be there. *Something* had to happen in those 700,000 years. Maybe there was no deposition, maybe it was all erosion."

Brown is more comfortable with three to four million years ago than he is with 500,000. He knows that four million years ago the southern part of the basin was already a big depression that stretched from Lodwar on the western side to North Horr on the east. He finds lake sediments in between these two outposts, sediments rich in diatomites and ostracods, clays and strange orange sediments, the environment for the older Moiti tuff. Around the edge of the basin he finds pockets of basalt, associated with crustal stretching. The sediments change around the basalt. He thinks this marks the beginning of the Omo's entrance into Kenya. Perhaps the Omo is responsible for the missing deposits. Or perhaps the Nile is. "It may be that the Omo was delivered through the Nile for that period of time." He sighs. "So where did over half a million years go?"

During the hiatus, there were mountains on the west side, and on the east, a broad general rise that contained a lake. "If you do a section over there, you get all shoreline sediments. But if you do a section someplace else, you get alluvial fans," indicating river and stream deposits.

"The sequence of environment depends on place as well as time."

The alpha Tulu Bor at Kataboi appears in big river deposits; here the tuff is associated with alluvial fans. "So it depends on where you are, what story you make about the environment." As thin slices of time, the tuffs tell a story of varied habitats around the Turkana basin at the same time. The simplistic scenario of hominids descending out of the trees, into the savannas, and camping by the lake has been undone, just as the scenario of big brain, upright gait was reversed by australopithecine finds like the Taung child and Lucy, where an upright gait preceded a larger brain. Will the large brain = toolmaker scenario be undone? Tools have been found in East Africa considerably older than the oldest known large-brained *Homo*. The first tool site I encountered at West Turkana was relatively young.

We are now well into the Stone Age, climbing around an imposing fault up to a new site called Kalochoro, strewn with stone tools. Brown picks out a chopper. The site is estimated at around one million years old, and since there are plenty of known tools from this time frame, there's no rush to dig trenches and excavate. "Tell me if you see any obsidian," he says.

In his lab in Utah, Brown had shown me a clear plastic disk with tiny bits of black obsidian inside—suspended meteora in a universe contained. They dangled disorderly within these bounds, an appropriate microcosm for his recent study (with archeologist Harry Merrick) tracing "the movement of obsidian in East Africa," the movement being that of obsidian tools.

The Stone Age is also known as the Flint Age, since the first early tools found in Europe were made of flint, a microcrystalline quartz. Apparently every stone and bone in this search endured a misnomer at one point or another; the miracle is that occasionally they are seen for what they are. In 1915, when Louis Leakey was twelve years old, he received a Christmas gift from a cousin in England. It was a book on the Later Stone Age, *Days Before History* by H. N. Hall, that described tools made of flint. So inspired, young Leakey began to search for arrow and ax heads near Kabete, just to the north of Nairobi, where, unknown to him, there was no flint. There is no flint in all of East Africa.

Yet he found tools along the dirt roads cut through British East

Africa, and kept them "with religious care." His missionary parents were skeptical; whatever these things were, they told him, they weren't flint. To his Kikuyu friends, who laughed at his suggestion that these were the work of men long ago, they were *nyenji cia nqoma*—the discarded razors of spirits of the sky. When a museum expert confirmed their authenticity, Louis Leakey, at thirteen, "embarked upon a study of the Stone Age in East Africa." The ones he found around Kabete were not, as his parents observed, made of flint. They were fashioned from obsidian.

Obsidian is a glassy-textured stone that, sliced thin enough, admits light, revealing an occasional bubble and isolated crystals. All volcanoes do not produce obsidian; it requires a chemical recipe high in silica. The most desirable obsidian, in the hands of a knapper, derives from a volcano's "chill zone" where the process of crystallization was interrupted. Chill zones are manifest in lava tubes like those on Hawaii's Big Island. While the outer lava cools upon contact, the inner molta maintains heat and crystallization takes its time. One can actually see the chill zone at Hell's Gate, northwest of Lake Naivasha, where it appears in flat sheets at the bottom of the lava flow. But Frank Brown needed more than visual clues; he needed fingerprints to link volcanoes to tools. Only one such study had been conducted in East Africa; tools found on the slopes of Mount Kilimanjaro were chemically traced to the obsidian near Kibo crater, Kilimanjaro's larger of two crowns of snow.

Brown was encouraged to investigate a level considerably below this and one hundred and fifty miles to the west, at the most famous archeological site in the world: Olduvai Gorge. The impetus came from Mary Leakey, who challenged Brown to find the source for the obsidian flakes discovered in the Naisiusiu beds, an Upper Pleistocene section at Olduvai. The lack of "flaking debris" suggested to Mary that production occurred elsewhere, that the tools were imported. Such was the case in a section of Bed IV, where hand axes were fashioned from green phonolite, a lava traced to Engelosin, a small volcano seven miles away. Brown went down to Olduvai and showed obsidian tools to a local Masai, who pointed to a certain hill. "So I ran around for an afternoon, and found nothing. Then they said, 'From that hill over there.' Nothing again." When Brown told this to Mary Leakey, she laughed. "I've been through that exercise before." The Masai simply wanted to please, to offer answers, to rest the visitor's mind of quest and inquiry. Brown managed to collect samples, however, by teaming up with archeologist Harry Merrick, who trekked to various volcanic chill zones to collect rocks to compare to the obsidian artifacts in the archives of the Kenya National Museums. These comprised tools not only from Olduvai but from thirty-one other sites in Tanzania and Kenya, including Hyrax Hill and Kariandusi between Lakes Naivasha and Baringo, three sites on the shores of Lake Victoria, three sites at East Turkana, and two along the eastern shoreline of Naivasha—Cartwright's and Wetherall's—named after their discoverers.

Brown told Merrick the tiniest fracture would do. Fine. But obsidian breaks like Coke bottles and splinters penetrate blue jeans. Merrick managed to sever a nerve in one of his fingers. He also prepared fourteen hundred samples from thirty-two sites, placing the tiniest fractures into epoxy-resin disks about the size of two Casino chips pressed together. He sent all the disks to Utah. Brown took a fine sewing needle and etched a number for each of the fourteen hundred samples on the face of each disk, after he'd ground and polished each sample. It took three hours to prepare one disk of thirty-eight samples.

The first stage of study was the same used for fingerprinting the tuffs, to determine the elements within. Various techniques have been used for the next stage, including emission spectrography, neutron activation analysis, and proton-induced X-ray and gamma-ray analysis. Brown prefers to zap obsidian with a microprobe, "probably *the* advance in rock studies of the sixties." For all its zapping finesse, the microprobe on the fifth floor of the Mineral Science Building at Utah was a rather unimposing apparition, a sort of giant microscope wearing an electron gun. The target was about the size of the period at the end of this sentence. "It's easy." Brown popped a disk from Olduvai into the chamber. "Three different spectrometers read three elements in ten seconds off that little tiny spot." After fourteen hundred samples, Brown himself was still amazed. "Instead of taking a rock apart physically, you just pop the beam down on it, and get an analysis in essentially no time."

Brown's fingerprints pinpointed fifty-four volcanic sources for the obsidian tools found at Olduvai; most were around Kenya's Lake Naivasha basin. In 1912, two American archeologists explored Naivasha in search of prehistoric tools, yet went home empty-handed. "I believe they actually stayed at a Naivasha hotel," Louis Leakey wrote in *White African*, "where the whole surface of the ground is covered with obsidian flakes and tools. . . ." Had their Search Image not been fixed on flint, Leakey was convinced they could have preempted his entire career. Yet fragmented obsidian looks like broken bottles; perhaps the archeologists dismissed the shattered glass as a record of target practice.

Brown "zapped" tiny targets from the Early Stone Age, the Middle Stone Age, the Later Stone Age, and then the Pastoral Neolithic. What he and Merrick discovered was that obsidian tools moved. In the Middle Stone Age, they found obsidian had moved thirty-five miles from its original source. For Mary Leakey, they found that the obsidian flakes of the Naisiusiu beds of Olduvai came from two hundred miles to the north, in the central rift, at Sonanchi. "Big deal," one is inclined to scoff, wading through a paper so cautious ("It is our contention that the mechanisms by which obsidian may have moved . . . are certainly not known at present") that you wonder if they would not let themselves ponder how it moved. For the most part, they won't. Then you come to a little curiosity on the Sonanchi obsidian.

Sonanchi, a volcano crater to the west of Lake Naivasha, produced some of the finest obsidian for flaking. Small as volcanoes go, Sonanchi has a crater lake. The crater walls feature chill zones.

Sonanchi's "premier obsidian," as Merrick termed it, was present at all the archeological sites but one, Cartwright's. Cartwright's assemblage came from the east side of the Rift, on the edge of the Kinagop Escarpment, also near Lake Naivasha. Brown and Merrick pondered this distribution anomaly like two Toyota executives wondering why their cars weren't selling in Portugal.

They came up with three potential explanations for its absence: (1) The tools at Cartwright's site were made before the Sonanchi eruption; (2) access to the Sonanchi obsidian was precluded by another group of hominids; (3) the source for the obsidian was buried

ABOVE: The main research camp at Koobi Fora, on the eastern shores of Lake Turkana. Built of flagstone, with thatched roofs, the buildings are designed to take advantage of the breeze.   BELOW LEFT: Richard Leakey examines fossil fragments to skull 1813, found at Area 123, 15 miles southeast of the Koobi Fora camp. The fragments belonged above the left eye, or orbit, and are featured in place on a cast of the newly reconstructed 1813 on the book jacket.   BELOW RIGHT: Taphonomist Rick Potts holds a hand ax in his right hand and a piece of fossilized bone in his left. Both were found in sediments dated at about a million years old, and may have been the work of *Homo erectus*. Potts, who studies scratch marks on bones to determine if they were made by stone tools, continues an investigation at Olorgesailie begun by Louis and Mary Leakey in 1942.

ABOVE: A view of the eastern branch of the Great Rift Valley, seen on the road from Nairobi to Lake Navaisha. To the south on the horizon is Mt. Longonot (10,880 ft.), a volcano with steaming fumaroles, or holes, still active in the crater.   BELOW: One of the excavation sites at Olorgesailie, less than an hour's drive south of Nairobi. The tools are of the Acheulian industry that includes hand axes, cleavers, flakes, and cobbles, and visitors can see them just as they were found. This site is protected by a thatched roof enclosure.

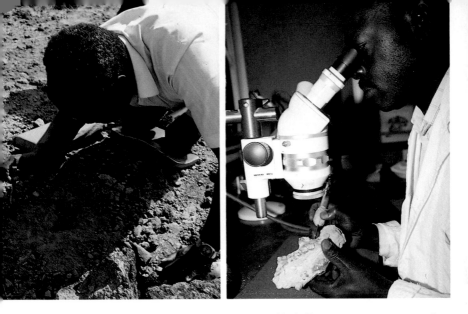

ABOVE LEFT: After carefully excavating a 17-million-year-old skull, Kamoya Kimeu, resting his knees on a green cushion, brushes away at the matrix in search of more pieces to the Miocene hominoid the Leakeys named *Afropithecus*.   ABOVE RIGHT: Joseph Mutaba, a member of the Hominid Gang who also searches for fossils, cleans the *Afropithecus* skull with a sensitive airscribe, viewing his work through a microscope.   BELOW: Tanzania's Olduvai Gorge offered the first evidence of ancient hominids in East Africa. Prior to Mary Leakey's 1959 discovery of *Zinj*, the oldest hominids known were the australopithecines of South Africa.

OPPOSITE: One of the many Miocene fossil sites around Kalodirr, on the west side of Lake Turkana. Stephen Jay Gould watches as a member of the Hominid Gang shows a discovery to Richard and Meave Leakey.   ABOVE: Stephen Jay Gould and Richard Leakey study the KBS site, provenance of the *Homo habilis* skull 1470, dated at just under 2 million years old.   BELOW: The eroding mountains on the west side of Lake Turkana offer numerous unexplored fossil sites. Richard Leakey discovers many fossil-rich exposures from the cockpit of his Cessna 206, and has marked 500 sites on a map of Kenya.

ABOVE: The excavation site of the Turkana Boy in August 1986. The first clue to the skeleton, a skull fragment no larger than a matchbook, was found two years earlier by Kamoya Kimeu. Along with members of the Hominid Gang, Alan Walker, (in pink shirt), works away at a hippo fossil he found on the "bone level," meaning the same level at which most of the *erectus* bones were found.   BELOW: Frank Brown, his *panga* stuck in the soil, makes notes on the position of a volcanic tuff he has just sampled.

ABOVE: Leakey and Gang members Nzube Mutiwa and Wambua Mangao survey a West Turkana site where primitive stone tools made of green lava were discovered during the 1986 field season. Alan Walker (left) bends over to look at tools with Meave Leakey (hidden behind her husband). A trench was dug to confirm the age of the tools at 2.3 million years old, the oldest ever found in Kenya. The search continues for the makers of these tools.   BELOW: At the end of his survey of the hominid site near the Naiyena Engol, West Turkana, Frank Brown adjusts his surveyor scope to show members of the Hominid Gang the mountains on the moon.

LEFT: Mary Leakey on the lawn of her Langata home in Kenya, with one of her many Dalmatians. Dr. Leakey retired from fieldwork in Tanzania in 1984, a few months before this photograph was taken. The Ngong Hills appear in the distance.

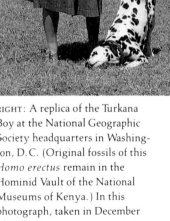

RIGHT: A replica of the Turkana Boy at the National Geographic Society headquarters in Washington, D.C. (Original fossils of this *Homo erectus* remain in the Hominid Vault of the National Museums of Kenya.) In this photograph, taken in December of 1985, green represents missing pieces, gray the parts created by mirror imaging. By the end of the 1988 field season, more bones were found, including those of the hands and feet. *Photo by David L. Brill © National Geographic Society.*

by Lake Naivasha "at a maximum high stand." Brown and Merrick favor the first explanation. Thus spake Sonanchi.

No one is sure of Sonanchi's eruption date. Brown took a sample of obsidian to Ian McDougall, who came up with a ballpark figure that he refused to allow to be published. After all that work McDougall had the integrity to recall his own product. "It would be nice to be able to say that a source was a certain age," says Merrick. "Then we could correlate other sites." But the scientists in this search are becoming more cautious, more mindful of what might be wrong. So they didn't use the estimate.

Yet Brown expanded Mary Leakey's challenge, stretching the survey west to Hyrax Hill, north to Koobi Fora, then hinting that Ethiopia should be next. Knowing I would see Merrick in Nairobi, he gave me a message to deliver: "Tell him I need more obsidian."

He qualifies that the obsidian project is sort of a hobby, "something I do when I have the time."

We come to a beautiful gorge, with sheer red exposures not unlike Olduvai. High in the walls are small caves, "ground" hornbill nests. An Egyptian vulture perches on a limb. At the base of the walls is a textured surface called confetti clay, because after erosion the clay looks like confetti. In sediments like these at Koobi Fora, Brown found fossilized fish nets. The gargantuan nature of his task comes home when one considers that this gorge is but one section of twenty-four riverbeds Brown must describe. Geologist Dick Hay spent fifteen years sorting out the stratigraphy of Olduvai Gorge.

Brown points to a gray stripe about fourteen feet above the riverbed in the wall. "See that thing up there? That's our tuff." By our tuff he means the one that marks the Turkana Boy site as well as "this year's hominid site." Brown explains, "You can follow it all the way back to the Nariokotome camp," which is exactly how he found it, on foot. The survey to determine the age of the newly discovered australopithecine skull would begin after an overnight stay at the Nariokotome camp.

Nariokotome is this season's headquarters for West Turkana; with staff from the Nairobi Museum and an annex camp for visiting scientists, the tents number thirty. Yet the schedule remains the same as Kalodirr and Koobi Fora, with tea at dawn, showers before Sundowners, and priorities (food and fossils) in the work tent—where I find Alan Walker, dressed in tennis pastels. "Oh, hello, Delta," he greets me matter-of-factly, as if we'd encountered each other at the local deli. I hand him a leg of lamb, brought all the way north from Nairobi and thawed, as I figure it, for around four million years.

Walker, British-born, is the consummate deadpan. When he made "the greatest fossil find since Lucy," the black skull, he strolled nonchalantly over a hill to tell his wife he had a hominid to show her. "Great! What part?" Pat Shipman naturally asked. "Oh, skull," said he.

His salt-and-pepper curly hair looks unusually well styled for the field (at the time, it was complemented by a mustache, since relinquished along with ultra-light cigarettes). Now fifty, Walker's interest in fossils began when he was eleven ("I was a museum brat"); to clarify his disposition, he quotes paleontologist A. S. Romer: "I hate to remember names of people; it always makes me forget the name of a fossil."

Walker, like Brown, is one of many U.S.-based scientists who serve as research associates for the National Museums of Kenya. Every "summer" there is a migration to Nairobi, and the lobby of the Boulevard Hotel on Museum Hill Road is thick with professors and graduate students. After consulting with the director of the museum, the migration disperses to points north. In Richard Leakey's absence, Walker is in charge of the Nariokotome camp. While Frank Brown organizes our camping equipment for tomorrow, I corner Walker, whose view of anthropology resembles an alluvial fan left by the Omo.

"Anthropology is too broad for its own good. You've got one scientist studying archeology in Egypt and another one studying prostitution in Hawaii. Then you end up with people influencing paleoanthropology who aren't even trained in anthropology. People like me, for instance."

His focus on primates, he terms "accidental." As a student at Cambridge he wanted to work on fish, "where you have lots of

fossils, tremendous variations." Kenneth Oakley (aforemen-
tioned sleuth on the Piltdown hoax) offered to introduce Walker to
E. I. White, chief of Ichthyology at the British Museum, and Keeper
of Paleontology.

At the appointed hour, Walker stood before the door to White's
office, but in the British Museum of Natural History, like the American one, you can't get very far in paleontology without a key. So
Walker banged on the door, and White shouted, "Come in!" This
exchange went on for half an hour, until a secretary finally let Walker
in. "You're late," White noted. Walker was late for all the fossil
fishes, too, taken up by other researchers. He returned to Dr. Oakley.
As Walker tells it, "Oakley said, 'There aren't many fossil hominids—we've just done away with Piltdown,' " a typical Walker
recapitulation, the John Cleese approach to paleontology. He was
presented with a collection of Madagascan lemurs, assigned a supervisor, and encouraged to learn human anatomy. "On the first
day, they wheeled a body into the lab and said, 'Start learning.
You've got a class to teach this afternoon.' "

From London he set out for University College in Kampala. In
Uganda, Walker found a Miocene site on Mount Elgon, collecting a
few fossils to show Louis Leakey in Nairobi to ask his advice. " 'Oh,'
Louis said. 'We've got plenty of Miocene fossils,' then walked off,"
Walker recalls. "In addition to being bloody rude, I thought how
funny that he wouldn't be interested." Shortly thereafter the Uganda
Antiquities Department received a copy of a letter Leakey had sent
to President Milton Obote, warning of a "young, untrained British
paleontologist raiding Uganda's fossil sites," Walker remembers.
"Now, this wasn't true; I'd gone to the same college in Cambridge
that Louis did. But Louis knew my background—it was just another
person too near to home. So I kept well away from the Leakeys."

But when Walker worked at the University of Nairobi in 1970,
Richard Leakey sought him out for advice. And when Louis "learned
that I was harmless," he too relied on Walker. "He'd call me up at
preposterous hours, like five-thirty in the morning, with crazy ideas,
asking me to sort them out.

"Richard and I get along because we're both naturalists," he explains. "We enjoy being in the field together." Walker volunteers

that he's not interested in power ("I like intellectual things; I'm not an empire builder"). In his opinion, the rivalry between the Leakey and Johanson camp "is all to do with personalities; it's got nothing to do with the science." The public view of it wrongly diminishes the differences that prevail in their own camp (or for that matter the Berkeley camp). "Richard and I argue all the time. We disagree about fossils and other things in life as well." Leakey prefers a slow, methodical approach; Walker is keen to "blitz" the fossil gap, "with hundreds of people searching and sieving, satellite mapping. . . ."

He yearns to develop a high-tech approach to interpreting bones, to spring the search out of the nineteenth century ("We need a lot more brainpower and we need a lot more money. Imagine if NASA said, 'We've got to find hominids!' "). Both affable and self-effacing, he is capable of childlike awe: "What do you think they were thinking?" he asked me when cleaning a hominid skull in the Nairobi lab, adding, "It helps me get through the boring bits." He is occasionally polemic and capable of cynicism: "All our ideas are half-baked. Today's truth is tomorrow's trash."

Thus far, his interpretations of fossils have avoided the trash bin, though they are better known to colleagues than the public. On the papers he co-authors with Richard Leakey, Walker prepares the anatomical descriptions; Leakey reviews, Walker rewrites. When the two discuss ideas, Walker makes notes. The same procedure prevails with Frank Brown and paleontologist John Harris. "They contribute the data from their disciplines, but I put the grant proposals together. It's a team," Walker finishes.

While Leakey takes pleasure in power, the empire that he built is largely in recognition that he could not do all things and do them all well. While he concentrates on administration (and he is best in public forums), anatomical descriptions are generally left to Walker and Meave Leakey. So are reconstructions, which suits Walker. "I'm the sort of person, if someone asks what does a specimen look like, I can reconstruct it, or I can draw it," Walker explains. "Those colleagues of mine that depend on mathematical measurements alone I tend to disagree with, more than those who have a visual memory for shapes, those that know the art."

With Peter Andrews of the British Museum, Walker built a reconstruction of a *Ramapithecus* jaw that helped dethrone this hominoid from its hominid status. His reconstruction of the 1948 *Proconsul* skull was reviewed in the Hominid Vault. To add the new fragments to 1813, he had to take the whole skull apart. Skull 1813, like most hominid skulls, was deformed by the pressures of burial. When piecing together the original bits, he allowed a slight space, less than a millimeter, between some of the fragments, so that the face would fit onto the skull, and in general, 1813 would look less deformed. But they had to be adjusted again in order for the new fragments to fit. If it sounds as if they're forcing together something that doesn't belong, the opposite is true. Grain of bone is matched, and over much of the skull it is difficult to tell where one fragment ends and another begins.

When 1470 was discovered, Walker and Meave Leakey pieced together the famous skull from one hundred and fifty fossil fragments. Their training was the same. Both studied anatomy, but so did a lot of other people. During the "War years" there were few toys in England but jigsaw puzzles. When they became bored, both Meave Epps and Alan Walker turned the puzzle pieces upside down.

The pieces of 1470 fit together to form a large braincase, which Richard Leakey and anatomist Bernard Wood saw as a *Homo habilis*. Skull 1470 has a cranial capacity of 750 ccs; the australopithecine average is 500 ccs. However, Walker felt, as he still does, that 1470 was a large-brained australopithecine, and included this view in his draft of their scientific report. "I'd done all the descriptions and the other guys [Leakey, Wood, and anatomist Michael Day] were checking them." During a session at the Nairobi Museum, the title of the report became an issue. Walker felt that it must be noncommittal, since there was an obvious difference of opinion and "the evidence wasn't straightforward." Leakey and Wood favored "*Homo*" in the title to the point where Walker threatened to take his name off the paper. When it was hastily allowed that this might be a welcome omission, Walker picked up the fossil and left the room.

"*Homo habilis* is a funny business," Walker expands. "Those of us who know anything about it don't agree which specimens are *habilis*." Skull 1470 isn't the only fossil in question; Leakey, in the Hominid Vault, questioned *habilis* specimens from Olduvai. He also describes it as a transitional form—the big question is, transitional from what? If Walker is right, then it appears that *Homo* evolved from the australopithecines. Yet Leakey sees *Homo* affinities in the older fossils from Hadar and Laetoli.

In the end an interesting compromise, devised by Leakey, was reached on the 1470 paper published in 1975; the title mentioned neither *Homo* nor australopithecine, to wit: "New Hominids from East Rudolf,* Kenya." The article began with Leakey "personally" preferring the *Homo* designation, qualifying that the final nomenclature would arise from further study, which he assigned to Bernard Wood rather than Alan Walker.

Walker's opposition was eventually acknowledged in a *Scientific American* article published three years later: "We ourselves cannot agree on a generic assignment for 1470. One of us [Leakey] prefers to place the specimen in the genus *Homo*, the other [Walker] in *Australopithecus*. The disagreement," the article continues, "is merely one of nomenclature. We are in firm agreement on the evolutionary significance of what are now multiple finds." The same analysis might be applied to skull 1813. Both Leakey and Walker think it's like the gracile australopithecines found in South Africa, but not enough to call it that. As Walker likes to say, when sensible people disagree, there's not enough evidence. Whatever his differences with Leakey, their dialogue continues, and with the assistance of the Hominid Gang, they are the most productive team in the field.

At best, other researchers spend six weeks a year in the field; grants are rare, and expeditions expensive. But the field season in Kenya extends throughout both dry seasons, roughly six months of the year, every year. The search for hominids continues while Leakey devotes his time to other projects, with Kamoya Kimeu reporting important finds by radio phone. (Leakey generally flies up on weekends; the trip with Gould was an exception.) And joint research projects with other institutions, like the Harvard University project at Lake Baringo, extend the investigations to several sites at once. There are thirty fossil sites at Nariokotome alone.

* Now Turkana.

That said, research remains a part-time proposition. Walker complains that the better part of his year is spent teaching and scrambling for grants. This is true also for Frank Brown and the bulk of paleontologists and archeologists. "I happen to earn my living teaching at one of the best medical schools in the States," Walker says, meaning Johns Hopkins University. (In 1987 Alan Walker received a Guggenheim grant that allowed a sabbatical; in 1988, he was awarded a MacArthur grant of $300,000 for the next five years to pursue his research interests.)

"The basic reason we lag behind other sciences is that no one's an expert." He contrasts the search for hominid fossils to the biochemical boom: "If you held a research conference on two proteins, you'd get five thousand people. Now where do you even find a thousand people who know about hominid fossils? At the moment (and I'm not puffing this up) we're the only ones coming up with stuff." (At the time he was right; the last expedition by the Berkeley team into Ethiopia was in 1981, and in 1984 Mary Leakey retired from field research in Tanzania at the age of seventy-one.)

In the work tent at Nariokotome, Walker surveys a tabletop of a week's worth of fossils, collected the week before I arrived. A massive antelope skull has a single horn broken short of its potential six-feet span. These oxlike creatures were first discovered on Louis Leakey's 1931 expedition to Olduvai with Hans Reck, who named them *Pelorovis*, or "monstrous sheep." Nearby, a diminutive monkey skull has a tiny hole through its head. "It's not a bullet hole, but a hole made by a carnivore." Walker inserts a saber tooth cat tooth—handy for demonstrations, but not, in the key word required for piecing the puzzle together, associated. The saber tooth skull, the first from these beds, belonged to a baby. It nonetheless appears enormous alongside the monkey. "We're sieving for more teeth," he runs the tip of his finger across little serrations on the incisors, "like steak knives." There's also a fossil impala, a horn from a bush buck, the skull and teeth of a baby pig, another monkey, a gazelle, and "these," Walker says, holding in the palm of his hand some toebones from the Turkana Boy. "You can't tell what they look like until they're cleaned." These *Homo erectus* toes are thick with calcite, as was the entire skeleton found at Nariokotome. I will remember this when sieving for bits of bone, when we wash the soil from the site at the lake, taken to the shore daily like laundry.

Now Walker is holding a hominid skull before me. It's an australopithecine *boisei*, better known as *Zinj*. It doesn't look as bold or hyper-robust as the black skull or the *Zinj* from Olduvai because it was a teenager when it died. Brown sandstone patches fill the eye sockets and shallow regions of the cheek. The fossilized bone itself is purple-gray, weathered by its exposure to the wind. "This has been a pebble sitting on the surface for a long, long time," he says tenderly, "hundreds if not thousands of years." The wind had begun to etch away the sinus area, glossy from blasts of sand.

Because its wisdom teeth had yet to erupt, Walker figures this hominid was between twelve and eighteen years old ("in human terms, probably thirteen"). The specimen is significant, he says, because it's of an age group yet to be seen. Walker runs his finger along the top of the cranium, where you can see lines forming for the sagittal crest. The skull is also quite unusual in that it was found incredibly intact. This young *Zinj* has a fairly complete set of teeth, except for one incisor. "It's downriver somewhere," Walker insists, as if to say, "There's a needle somewhere in that haystack." Kamoya Kimeu and his team sieve for the missing tooth.

I learn that Nzube Mutwiwa, a member of the Hominid Gang— a Kamba with immense presence and piercing eyes—discovered this skull on the banks of the Naiyena Engol earlier in the season. This, then, is the particular hominid whose time Brown has come to fix. One of the first skulls that Richard Leakey found at East Turkana was a fully adult *Zinj*. Known as skull 406, it is about 1.6 million years old, and was the discovery to establish that at least two species lived at East Turkana. If this new skull is dated anywhere around 1.6, the age of the *Homo erectus* Turkana Boy found here, it will mean that the same sort of cohabitation occurred. One small-brained, the other large-brained, at the same time. Frank Brown's paleogeographic picture should indicate whether they both lived along rivers or the lakeshore, whether there were geographical boundaries between them, whether their food sources were the same.

"Come sit by the river"—Walker suggests Sundowners. Campaign chairs are positioned along the banks as if we expected a parade. In due course this expectation is fulfilled. A cloud of dust rises, accompanied by a mechanical rattle akin to a storm in a Chinese opera. Equally surreal (since vehicles are rare) is the sight of a Land Rover leaning briskly around an island of acacias, to pass in review on the dry riverbed in front of us. Craig Black, head of the Los Angeles County Museum, waves on his way to the annex camp. He has come to West Turkana to look for dinosaurs and tiny Cretaceous mammals, pawn and bishop in a very significant event that led to human evolution. Brown thinks he knows where Black might have better luck. He discusses the site with Walker.

"I'll bet you that's the Mesozoic," Brown says, meaning over 175 million years ago. "There's nothing in there you could call an angiosperm leaf," or flowering plant, which appeared about the time that dinosaurs disappeared. "I wouldn't go any further than that now," he says cautiously, adding, "There's sand in there right on top of the limestone."

Walker: Is it indurated sand?
Brown: It's hard as hell.
Walker: What's the cement?
Brown: Silica, I guess.
Walker: Jeepers!
Brown: Right on top of that, there's clay. Under all that stuff would be the place to look. It's a weird little spot.
Walker: Remember, for the mammals, they're looking grain-sized, teeny-tiny, the stuff that comes out when you wash the soil. I keep telling them to look for termite castles. Termites can't build in that really hard stuff. So look where you see the chimneys.
Brown: I think someone should look at the bottom of the section at Koobi Fora—the perfect place to find little mammals. And Loperot! It's a bone basin!

Loperot! A few seasons earlier, a research camp had been set up in this fossil-rich area, roughly eighty miles to the south. When

Walker and Leakey left in the Cessna for Nairobi, "before the sound of the plane had died away," Walker dramatizes, *shifta* with automatic rifles materialized out of the African bush. They demanded blankets, equipment, "anything and everything they saw in the camp." Kamoya Kimeu offered them tea.

They sat for tea, fascinated by the handles on the cups. In the early days of Koobi Fora, *shifta* invaded the camp to steal all the equipment, investigating all items, even the cans of educational films, 16mm frames of time which they unfurled at great length, to mix with glue, ink, varnish, and tape measures similarly unfurled. Even the bed springs were taken, to appear later as earrings on local people. From then on Leakey never left a camp unguarded, which is to say occupied by staff; he refused to maintain even a single weapon, trusting to personal negotiation. The ploy worked well at Buluk, near the Ethiopian border, where he became friends with a *shifta* leader who fascinated Leakey anatomically—Big Foot. (Unfortunately, many *shifta* are involved in poaching, and Leakey has since taken up arms against them, and in self-defense.)

Several areas of this Northern Frontier District, like Teleki's volcano, are off-limits because of *shifta* or warring tribes. In an article for *National Geographic Research*, there was mention of an area called Loruth Kaado: "Exposure is good, and sufficient vertebrate fossils were observed to warrant detailed prospecting in this area," Frank Brown wrote. But "detailed investigations . . . had to be postponed for security reasons." That's the official version.

When Brown stepped out of his Land Rover at Loruth Kaado, the first thing he saw were abundant fossils. Then he looked up to see that he was surrounded by "people pointing their rifles at me. Atiko was with me; he speaks six languages, and started jabbering away. Finally he seemed to hit on the right language. They lowered their rifles. They talked back and forth for a few minutes. Then Atiko turned to me and said, 'I think we should go.' "

Brown adds a complaint that Big Foot once shot at him. "Oh, yeah," Walker confirms offhandedly, "he asked us about the *mzungu* [Caucasian] in the Land Rover. He thought you were the police." Brown didn't find this explanation amusing. Nor did I. Apparently the Land Rover that brought us here was similar to those used by the police.

At Loperot, Kimeu somehow convinced the *shifta* they should return for their bounty at dawn. They finished their tea, rose from their seats, adjusted their hardware, then walked away into the night.

It is difficult to imagine the following scene occurring without a battle cry. But it necessarily occurred with the eerie quiet that prevails when a lioness walks through camp at night, a cunning contained. Kimeu gave a signal: the camp crew grabbed *pangas* and ran through the camp, cutting the guy ropes on every tent. Zing, droop, zing, droop. They quietly threw the entire camp, including the mess tent where dinner had been cooking, into the vehicles, did not slam one door, then drove away in the dark, headlights out. After an hour or so, Kimeu dared turn on the lights. Having been deprived of all the fossils at Loperot, I imagine that Kamoya Kimeu heaved a heavy sigh, as he does now.

It is daily preamble to his report from the field. His presence about camp is both modest and monumental, evoking a Buddha's aura. Kimeu represents 190 pounds of dignity—even his laugh is reserved. Withheld long enough, it emerges from great depths and equally great surroundings as a sigh.

Kimeu's talents are many: he is a wise diplomat, honing his comments to those perfectly suited for the occasion; as often as not this is: "I think we had better wait for Richard to come," a firm hand on the rudder in a camp that easily contains all the conflicts of a ship at sea and the politics of paleoanthropology to boot. (In Walker's absence, Kimeu is in charge of the camp.) He also serves as sommelier, and maitre d' of napkins. Given a little book on the art of napkin folding, he attempted a rabbit. ("But it came out looking like a hyena," Walker says within earshot. Kimeu sighs lightly, like the low of a wildebeest.)

In the fifties, when first recruited to "dig bones" for Louis and Mary Leakey at Olduvai Gorge, Kimeu fully expected to spend his days exhuming human graves—a notion, he explains, quickly undone by the profusion of fossils at Olduvai. In a 100-square-yard site in Bed I, for example, over 3,500 bones of different creatures were found. One of them, a new species of monkey, was named *Cercopithecoides kimeui.* The Leakeys provided food, shelter, salary, and tutelage for a small fleet of fossil finders.

"First they taught us to know fossilized bone—you know, you

might think it is only a stone. They showed us animal bones, then primate bones, and very slowly, hominid bones. It took us some time to know. I would hand them to Mr. Leakey," Kimeu continues. "Some made him very happy, and I wanted to make Mr. Leakey happy." Upon seeing Lucy, Kimeu told Don Johanson, "If you found that, think of what I could find!"

While he doesn't presume to make scientific statements about what he finds, his curiosity emerged early on at Olduvai. "One day I asked why these bones were so important. Mr. Leakey said that only this way could we know our past and how we are here." Evolution was not part of the instruction at his Thomeandu Mission School, and Kimeu's own Kamba tribe have their myths about human origins. Yet he took the evidence in stride. "Well," he concludes simply, "we can see this."

After working at Olduvai, Kimeu moved to Lake Natron with Richard Leakey and Glynn Isaac during the 1963–64 season. From Natron, he accompanied Richard and his first wife Margaret Cropper to Lake Baringo. In 1977 he was named the museum curator for all prehistoric sites in Kenya. So for six months a year he oversees the annex museum sites, and for the other six months, leads surveys during the dry seasons. He led all the major surveys at Koobi Fora, and began to explore West Turkana in 1980. Kimeu has been unearthing fossils for three decades, and working in the field with Richard Leakey for a quarter of a century.

He is the same age as Alan Walker, yet only six of his years were devoted to classroom study. Because his father lived "far away" (a two-day walk when collecting school fees), Kimeu went to work at a dairy farm near Ukambani, in central Kenya. His job was to herd the cows home in the evening. In the dusk of the African bush, he found them by listening for their bells. He now says that the bones speak to him.

He has yet to find the tooth to complete this year's hominid's smile, but he has seen something else, a curiosity he will impart in due course. He sits quietly for some time, joining Alan Walker and me on the banks of the Nariokotome. Kimeu finally imparts, "I've been thinking about this bone I saw."

Kimeu has been thinking about this bone for the last eight hours. When Walker asks him to describe it, he says nothing, but traces an outline on his leg. Walker jumps up to retrieve a handy anatomy book from the work tent, thumbing toward a hominid toe that resembles Kimeu's sketch.

After dinner, Walker does the rundown for tomorrow. "Frank, you're going to measure the sections for the new hominid?" Nod. He points to two grad students. "They'll be sieving at the carnivore site," meaning where the saber tooth cat was found. "Nzube, Kamoya, and I are going to check out this toe. Then I've got a few bovids [antelopes] to collect. Louise is transporting water." Richard and Meave's daughter, Louise Leakey, aged fourteen, has just learned to drive a Land Rover, useful for bringing water to the camp and taking excavated earth from the Turkana Boy site to the lake to be washed. Two young paleontologists, one from the Nairobi Museum, the other from an American university, are joining the Craig Black team, or as Walker puts it: "Isaiah and William are going to the dinosaurs." He continues to outline tomorrow: "The Gang is going to prospect, then later they'll do some brushing at the hominid site. We'll do some washing at the carnivore site. Can we take some more water? Five gallons wasn't enough." He gets a tableful of nods. "Tea at six."

I am assigned the most remote tent. Its normal occupants, Richard and Meave Leakey, are not due until the weekend; simple sandals, hats, and combs await their owners. There is nothing else beyond bunks and blankets, yet I feel intrusive, as if I'd opened the wrong locker. Outside, a mattress floats, framed by the screened window of the tent. It rests atop a sheet of plywood balanced on two aviation-fuel drums. I grab my flashlight and a blanket and climb on board, careful to leave my sneakers near my feet, out of reach of scorpions. I was equally mindful to leave my tape recorder in the tent; there are too many questions, promising a sleepless night.

I have, for the better part of this journey, been anxious to understand. Brown talked of mountains rising and shorelines dancing, missing volcanoes, missing time. Grown men fall to their knees, digging for toes, sifting for teeth. People wash soil. The horns of a *Pelorovis* would not fit across this mattress. I am certain of this and very little else. I do my best to imitate Kimeu's sigh; the setting before me elicits this.

The universe slips behind a tree. There are above me more stars than I have ever seen; the limbs of an acacia wave like a hand across their brightness. This is a formidable tree, its trunk rises from my toes. When I crane my neck I see still more branches, even the thinnest distinctly black against the stars. I think of the branching bush. There is *Homo erectus* near the top, and a new *Zinj* just lower, winking. There is Lucy nearby. There are stars from South Africa, rarely noticed, and constellations of hominoids. Stars from Europe and Asia, stars everywhere, winking. There is nothing simple about this tree. I am mesmerized as with a fire and watch until I sleep.

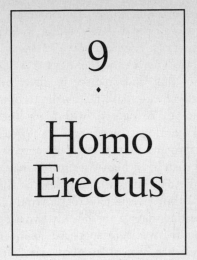

9

Homo Erectus

The next morning, Frank Brown and I set out in the general direction of a bent acacia. From Nariokotome we head south toward the new *Zinj* site, taking a right from the main dirt road, moving upstream on the Naiyena Engol. The dry riverbed is lined with scrub that smells of garlic. *"Acacia nubica,"* Brown tells me. "Elephants eat it." When we come to a fork in the river, Paul Mulinge, the driver, and Mwalali Nganga, man-about-camp, proceed further south to set up a camp near the new site. Brown and I will walk the rest of the way. We are left looking at an aerial photograph. On a scale of 1 to 10,000, you wouldn't see us; trees appear to be poppyseed.

A majestic termite castle, guarded by a lone goat, towers high on a ledge. "Look where you see the chimneys," Walker had said. The heat and aridity of this landscape are in direct proportion to the design of this castle of clay, built tall by the termites to maintain a steady temperature of 78 degrees within its interior. Vents are opened and sealed according to need; eggs are stored in one chamber, termite-sized mushrooms in another. This termite castle is better thermo-regulated than most high-rises in Manhattan.

We follow along ridges thick with pebbles, the shape of dinosaurs slumbering under a thin sheet of pink rocks. From such heights there is substantial indication that we are the only two people in the world. Before heading south, we were supposed to meet up with Alan Walker to explore what Brown described as a "weird little spot." There is no sign of Walker or his Land Rover, though plenty could be hidden in the folds of the land. Used car lots could hide behind every hill, but there is considerable comfort in knowing they don't. To double our chances of seeing Walker, we split up, to meet back at the termite mound.

Now I have the world to myself. I think of Wilfred Thesiger, famous for his treks across Ethiopia when it was Abyssinia. A prolific author and walker, he lives in northern Kenya and treks nearby. Some years ago he wandered into the camp of a research geologist, who invited him to stay for dinner. The octogenarian regaled with stories of his adventures late into the night; his listener brightly suggested he ought to write a book.

Back at the termite castle a student walks by briskly, as if between appointments on a Nairobi street. A relatively new member of the prospecting team, he tells us that Walker has gone further west. Then he moves on. "He's just dying to find a hominid," Brown explains.

Ralph von Koenigswald, who found hominids in Java, said you must love fossils—"If you love them, then they will come to you." Martin Pickford and Alan Walker found *Proconsul* fossils in museum drawers; at Buluk, Walker found fossils at night by ultraviolet light. Mary Leakey, stopping on the road to Olduvai, reached down to pick up a stone to wedge the wheel of her car and picked up a hominid jaw. The Taung child gained notice as a paperweight in an office. The fossilized footprints of Laetoli were found during a lighthearted exchange of elephant dung tossed between men in the field. Richard and Meave Leakey found the *Zinj* skull when his camel became thirsty, sending them on a different route back to camp. George Gaylord Simpson wrote his first monograph on fossils recovered from slate roof tiles in England. Scottish paleontologist Robert Broom often began his search for fossils in formal dress, complete with a top hat, but when the trail became hot, discarded his clothes and continued in the nude.

Fossils are found in strange and mysterious ways. A piece of amber purchased in a Manhattan jewelry store was found to contain a perfectly preserved specimen of a previously unknown species of termite, twenty-six million years old. Chinese pharmacists dispense "dragon bone" powder, composed of ground-up fossils. An investigation of wholesale distributors in the 1920s led to the discovery of Peking Man, *Homo erectus* in form.

If the odds are against finding a hominid, the odds are also against seeing a hominid for what it is. Alan Walker was not the first to "find" the initial clue to the black skull, and Kamoya Kimeu "found" 1470 twice, marking the fossilized fragments both times as an antelope. One day Bernard Ngeneo reported, "I got something to show you," and as they neared the KBS site, Kimeu said, "I bet it's right over here."

The student is right to be keen. In the seasons that followed my visit to Nariokotome, during 1987 and 1988, the work tent at another West Turkana site to the south featured food rather than fossils, with nothing like the past week's bounty surfacing during an entire season. They had gone to search in four-million-year-old sediments, and for some reason the fossils weren't there. ("You told me to search in the fossil gap!" Leakey later complained to Gould. "We didn't find a thing!") Brown has similar sessions in search of tuff samples. They may be missing altogether, or they may be too poorly preserved for analysis.

We encounter the first tuff of the day, a ribbon of light gray that streaks across a vertical exposure of clay. "For some reason, these tuffs are all altered," Brown says, meaning they're no good for his analysis. "I think they were under water, and the lake was slightly alkaline."

For this particular fingerprint, called the Malbe tuff, Brown walked all the way back to the Nariokotome camp until he found a sample that wasn't altered. We saw this tuff in the gorge to the south, and we'll see it again this afternoon at a point betwixt and between.

In some nearby hills we confront the kind of terrain that features in Brown's nightmares. "If that's all you've got to do stratigraphy on . . ." He shakes his head. To me it is simply a well-rounded hill, but it is this perfection in form, lacking exposures, that causes Brown his calamity. "Sure," he responds, "you can slice into it, but do you realize how much rubble is there? You'd have to trench all the way back to the tuff level. It's a gigantic job; one trench would take several days. And there's no assurance the tuff will be there." Once, when confronting a similar lack of exposures, Brown told Leakey, "If you find anything there, I'm quitting." "Well, Frank," came the reply, "we'll stop looking."

Walker arrives by Land Rover. Three members of the sieving team also materialize out of nowhere, ambling like coal miners surfacing. One approaches Walker, pulls a matchbox from his pocket, and saying absolutely nothing, slides the box open to reveal the canine of a saber tooth cat. If the search for teeth seems obsessive, it is not without purpose. Teeth often relate the most demonstrative changes in evolution, reflecting changes in diet. My initial view was that paleoanthropologists emphasized teeth because they comprised the bulk of the hominid inventory. To some extent this is true, but by delving they found evidence of change. They may not always be correct in surmising what the changes in enamel thickness mean, why the number of cusps is different, why the cheek teeth in *Zinj* are larger than those of a *Homo erectus*, but that there have been changes is as evident in hominids as it is in pigs or elephants.

Some *afarensis* had big, apelike incisors and a diastema, or gap, allowing the overbite of big canines. The original *Zinj* was dubbed the Nutcracker Man because of its huge molars and premolars—cheek teeth. They look pretty impressive, but they exerted no more pressure than a modern human's, one quarter of the size. Like gorillas, *Zinj* may have spent a lot of time chewing vegetation. *Habilis* teeth are more narrow, those of *erectus* even smaller. So I look for teeth.

By ten in the morning I am on my knees in the weird little spot, which qualifies as Fish and Mouse Cemetery. "Most of this you could sieve through," Brown says to Walker, who seizes upon a tiny rodent tooth amid all the fish. The tooth is rounded, a result of being rolled in its journey on the river bottom. Its color is the same mahogany brown as a crocodile's tooth, deep and rich, but its surface was finished by sand to a high gloss. "Umpteen fossils," Walker observes, producing a handful of rodent teeth. "How much lag are we looking at?" he asks of the river's postscript.

"Not sure." Brown stands up to gaze south. "About ten thousand years ago the lake was down there, where those trees are on the ridge."

Walker and the rest depart for Nariokotome; Brown and I begin our trek south to the lower tributary of the Naiyena Engol, where the teen-aged *Zinj* surfaced in a setting that is less than distinguished. I do not, for example, stop to take a photograph as I normally prefer to have something in the frame. It is Brown's task to assign this venue distinction.

"See that crooked tree?" He points to a single bent acacia about three hundred yards away. "That's the hominid site." In three days' time, this tree, along with other details—the exact slope, or dip, of the land, the position of dry gulches, the position of the skull, the depth and direction of the Malbe tuff, the color of the sediments, the shape and size of pebbles and ostracods—will feature on a map of such elucidation that a thin layer of sediments atop a hillock will loom like the snows of Kilimanjaro.

Human forms appear behind a gritty cloud of cinnamon. Kimeu and crew sieve for the elusive tooth. Two men pull from cones of excavated soil, spread it onto a sieving screen, which they lift by wooden handles. They shift soil back and forth, and from this gentle music a cumulus rises. Another member of the Gang works alongside Kimeu, brushing up sediment with his left hand, and with his right squeezes larger bits down to—well—about the size of an incisor, rubbing round and round, like coaxing dice in his palm until there's nothing to throw. Kimeu epitomizes woebegone. "He hates not to find something," Brown whispers into his beard, his eyes downcast, as if telling the truth at a funeral.

We walk further south to our camp, two tents set amid tall acacias. After lunch, Brown sets out to put this place on the map. He will work until the sun drops behind the hills he's measuring, and then some. In the evening, sitting at a small table, he studies his notebook and endures the omnipresent reporter, a consumer of chocolate bars during the day in order to keep apace. Paleontologist Ray Bernor, who accompanied Brown in the field one time in Libya, found a new meaning for the term "lost weekend." Afterwards Bernor flew to Rome, checked into a hotel on Friday, went to bed, and woke up Sunday afternoon. Since I am here at my own request, I grab my camera and tape recorder and become Brown's shadow. He carries his surveyor's scope over his shoulder, and begins to whistle.

The first thing Brown must do is create a Level line, to appear on his chart as a red transect across the terrain. For this he squints through a scope perched on a long wooden tripod, and looks for Mwalali. To assist him, Mwalali stands at various points along the terrain, holding a four-yard stick parallel to himself. Brown squints, jots down his reading, then directs Mwalali to a new position. Squint, jot, direct; squint, jot, direct.

We aren't exactly dealing with the Murua Rith range that rises on the western horizon; there are plenty of pilots in this country who could set a Cessna down here and be able to use the plane again. The dip is only 2 degrees, so these hills "won't look very impressive on paper." But if you want to be anywhere near accurate, you have to be precise. To geologists, an undulating airstrip represents low relief.

In this setting the Malbe tuff rests on a bed of silt and clay. Above the tuff is a bed of sandstone. Brown's map will detail a cross section of these features. To do this, he measures the position and depth of every bed, ordering their sequence from the visible tuff over to the northern side of the hominid site, where the tuff does not appear. Where was the hominid in relation to the tuff?

"I *think* it was about seven or nine meters above. But I'll *know* when I'm done." He moves cross hairs across the landscape, seeking the hominid's "absolute distance" above the tuff. Brown figures the hominid might be between 1.6 and 1.8 million years old. But he'll know when he's done.

On the second day the transect moves down a wall—a relatively steep drop of seventy-five yards littered with fossils some distance from the hominid site. As they work their way down, Mwalali picks up a rock and drops it from his end of the measuring tape. This is his plumb line. Where the rock lands, a stake goes. He measures the elevation differences between all these stakes. "Then you can see the topography of this wall, and all the beds dipping down underneath: this one hangs on to this one, and so on. We've essentially laid down these beds."

In laying down these sedimentary beds, Brown must watch for an inverted sequence. "If you have a sequence that deposited and then eroded, and that was filled in by another sequence, you might not recognize the initial channel." Mwalali uses a long hoe to scrape the scree off the wall so Frank can get a clean look.

Things on the surface are not always representative of their surroundings; they may have been "reworked":

"Suppose that hominid skull up there had been found on this side of the hill, and it was washed down to the lakebed. It would be reworked into the deposits of the lakebed, deposits that were younger than the real age of that fossil. If a fossil is very rolled, bashed around, lost all its teeth, your first guess is that it's older than its present setting. It can always be older. It can never be younger." Why is this? "Because it had to roll from upstream." Thank you, Frank.

Volcanic ashes can also be reworked, swept into an older bed of a riverbank following their transport downstream. Uplifts can reposition a tuff, pushing it higher than where it originally fell. But unlike fossils, tuffs have a chemical fingerprint. With regard to the more common usage of the term, ostracods and mollusks tend to present a vast fingerprint, for their shells form a pattern on the landscape, denoting beaches and shoreline.

Brown figures the shoreline of the lake came to points along the wall, with narrow beaches extending up to where the hominid was found. The outlines of this arrangement are distinguished by coarse-grained sand, full of shells, as opposed to fine-grained rock without shells. "It takes a long time to see these things."

I follow them up the wall, stepping around an elephant leg bone, and spy a complete antelope jaw with every tooth in place. A substantially larger jaw is marked by a cairn. "Hippo," Brown suggests. He hands me a smooth pebble: "Fossilized hummingbird egg," and unable to hide his grin, adds, "Fairly common."

A red dot coming over the horizon turns out to be Kimeu in his bright shirt. I report the antelope jaw. Kimeu is familiar with this bovid, as antelopes are called, and politely retreats to his search for a hominid tooth. It wouldn't sound right, "The Bovid Gang."

For the next forty-five minutes, Frank Brown sits down to calculate his position in regard to the universe. Knowing our exact longitude and latitude would help. "It's difficult here," he says "because the only real known point of latitude is at Labur," roughly thirty miles north, on the other side of the Nariokotome. He begins to write up the official description, right down to the pebbles: small, medium, or large. Fossilized hummingbird eggs would come under small. No root casts, indicating lack of vegetation. He describes the limonite, or rusted rock, and the presence of salt: "Could be saline waters, could be secondary and have nothing to do with the section itself." Snails: "They start up higher; these are just washed down. Ostracods come in before the snails do. These ostracods are terribly angular. If they stayed around for very long, they wouldn't be angular; they'd be round." How long? "Another thousand years."

He draws in the Malbe tuff: vvvvvvvvvvvvvvvvvvvvvvvvvvvvvv.

"It's a nice way to make a record. If someone says, 'How on earth do you know this tuff is there?,' well, you've pinpointed the hominid site, and if someone walks along this line I've made, they can find the tuff. It helps if you add landmarks." He draws in a crooked tree.

The *Zinj* skull is between 1.6 and 1.8 million years old. This places it in the same range as the *Zinj* found at East Turkana and at Olduvai. At three sites in East Africa, the small-brained australopithecine lived alongside the large-brained *Homo*. But Brown is hardly done ("The first thing the hominid people want is age"). He wants to know where on earth a half a million years of time went. He wants to know the exact form of the former lake, and the direction of the former river. In the tephra horizons from the Gulf of Aden, Andrei Sarna saw a fingerprint of a 2.3-million-year-old tuff that Brown has yet to find on land.

Apropos of nothing and everything, he offers the single most incisive statement on the state of the art in the search for human origins. Broadcasters refer to this low-key delivery as a throwaway line, meaning it wasn't enunciated to its full potential. Darwin was famous for them, writing in the *Origin of Species* that "light will be thrown on man and his origins." In the second edition, he became truly bold with "much light." Brown says: "There are a number of things we look at now that were more or less ignored before."

He does not imply that they can know it all, and issues a disclaimer that perhaps only someone with crow's feet can appreciate; "My students don't like it. They say, What's the point?"

In his classroom at the University of Utah, Brown likes to show a video segment of Jacob Bronowski's "The Ascent of Man." He seizes upon an episode of the television series entitled "Knowledge or Certainty," in which Bronowski wades into a crematorium pond near Auschwitz and scoops up a handful of ashes, telling viewers: "These are the result of certainty."

"There's a huge lesson," Brown says. "When you become dogmatic about anything, all sorts of bad things follow, whether it's something like Auschwitz, or just screwing up. You need to know the limits of your knowledge." Leakey had issued a similar disclaimer at the very beginning: "You've got to always be careful to indicate to your reader or your viewer the transition from what you know to what you think."

As happens every evening at this camp, yellow-winged bats alight on the branches over our tents. By day you can measure the previous night's success, for they eat beetles with beautiful luminescent wings, and (like the fable of the male preying mantis, certain that its mate's appetite was purely sexual) only their wings remain. Wings appear scattered about camp in the mornings.

Suddenly Brown's face is lit by the light of a full moon. "Oh!" He jumps up. "I promised to show the guys the mountains on the moon." Paul and Mwalali are beckoned from the campfire; Brown tells them about the rifts and volcanic craters that they see. He had done the same thing for other members of the Hominid Gang at dusk, when the full moon appeared on the horizon of the hominid site.

Later, we talk about the "Ancestors" symposium; he says that he was nervous about reading his paper, that he hated wearing a suit and tie. Here he sits in his element, under a sprawling acacia that rains beetle wings, wearing khakis and simple leather sandals that he straps around two impressive tuff-tracking devices. The moonlight reveals a broad smile. "You know what Kamoya said to me the other night? 'Frank, we are going to die in these mountains.' "

Following the survey of this year's hominid site, I am more or less redeposited at the Nariokotome camp. The distance from where the *Zinj* was found to where the *Homo erectus* skeleton of the Turkana Boy was found is less than ten miles. Like scientists in pursuit of the family tree, I tend to move from one tree to another.

A Salvadora laden with berries overhangs the provenance of the Turkana Boy, a locality known as Nariokotome III. Otherwise the excavation site looks much like any other, a rectangular incision into the familiar, and the tree itself does not strike one as spectacular. In a well-manicured garden it could be sacrificed. Yet in mid-afternoon the shadow of the Salvadora extends, providing shade for the Hominid Gang, excavating at the bone level. In early morning, it provides a stage for Turkana children, who sing as they gather the tart-tasting berries, and test gravity by venturing to the furthermost branches, perhaps to gain a better view of the people below on all fours, digging for the toes and finger bones of a young boy long dead. Before the Hominid Gang find what they're looking for, the excavation site will double in size, and this tree will fall.

Trees are a renewable resource; *Homo erectus* is not. It took a full century to find a skeleton of a *Homo erectus*.

In 1887, Dutch anatomist Eugene DuBois set out for Java, announcing that he would return with the Missing Link. In an astonishing display of luck and determination, he more or less did. In deposits along the Solo River, the DuBois team (largely composed of convicts) found hominid fossils—a tooth, a skullcap, a thigh bone—an assortment first described as *Anthropopithecus* (upright manlike ape), then as *Pithecanthropus erectus* (upright apelike man), which finally became known as *Homo erectus*—upright man. As this changing nomenclature reflects, the fossils were viewed differently in time.

Similar transformations affect our view of the australopithecines. Illustrations from only a couple of decades ago emphasize primitive features. Put bluntly, they all seemed a bit near-sighted, such was their squint, and if not engaged in battle, appeared to be looking for a fight, their tool a weapon. Now we see our ancestors as more peaceable, with intelligence in their countenance. They are not aggressive, but share and bond. A monogamous commitment has even been suggested of their sexual unions. Suddenly they were "chaps" in need of a trim and a shave and a tie. Neandertals, once nasty, brutish, and mute, could habituate the New York subway with a modicum of notice. The life-sized model of Lucy displayed at the "Early Man" exhibit in London appeared downright huggable. Her eyes, cleverly programmed to move at different intervals, "put the fear of God into people," enthuses Richard Leakey, who organized the exhibit. One thinks of Woody Allen in his movie *Hannah and Her Sisters*, peering at a picture of Christ in a Times Square window, the Messiah's eyes opening and closing in a bifracted portrait as the Comedian nodded. Thus is our thin slice of time marked; at eight-fifteen, a satellite arches high over the Nariokotome River, as it will every evening.

The broad Nariokotome that separates the excavation site from the camp is bone dry, so to speak. One evening last week the riverbanks lived up to their name. By sunrise there were only trickles, and the team once again walked across the river to what is referred to as the slave pit.

The next day I follow the sieving team along a path taken by Kamoya Kimeu two years earlier, on what has become known as "Kamoya's Day Off."

August 12, 1984, Nariokotome Camp: Frank Brown, paleontologist John Harris, and Kamoya Kimeu "take a meeting" on the banks of the Nariokotome. For two weeks Harris and Kimeu have led a team of six fossil finders along the rocky outcrops north of the Nariokotome, leaving behind relatively few cairns, the symbol of significant fossils, and, as far as they are concerned, a measure of their success. Brown, of course, is in search of telling sediments and tuff samples, of which there are plenty in either direction. But it makes his life easier if there are hominids within this context. The consensus that emerges this evening is that the hominids must be further south.

At dawn the next day a battery is removed from the Land Rover; Kamoya Kimeu attaches the radio telephone, then graciously bellows at the operator, who puts through a call to the museum in Nairobi. Richard Leakey approves the move south. Since they've been surveying fourteen days without a break, this is declared a Rest Day. Their small camp beneath the shade of the acacias emits sounds commonly associated with a lazy summer Sunday or a cease-fire: snores, the tap-tap of a keyboard, gentle flaps of laundry on the line, chortles.

It also emits Kamoya Kimeu, who emerges like a student heading for the library after final exams. He does not meander, but heads directly south. He takes a little stroll across the broad bed of the Nariokotome, then up a hill dotted by Salvadora and acacia trees. Mechanically, he looks for fossils. He is about three hundred yards south of the camp when he spies a bit of fossil that has washed to the surface, a skull fragment less than an inch and a half long and not quite as wide. You could conceal it in your wallet. Not only is this fragment small, but it is the same color as the lava rocks around it, having gained (in microcosm) a sort of lunar surface to it, with pits and scars and tiny bumps of calcite. Kimeu holds the fragment between his big fingers, feeling its curve and its thickness. Then he rubs his thumb on its smooth inner surface, feeling none of the texture found in other animal skulls. Hominid. A few days earlier, John Harris had found a fragment of *Homo habilis*, also south of the Nariokotome.

August 13, 1984, Nariokotome Camp: The radio phone is once again attached to the car battery and Kimeu graciously bellows that two hominid fossils have been found: "ONE LOOKS GOOD! THE OTHER ONE NOT SO GOOD!"

When Leakey and Walker fly up from Nairobi, they naturally pursue the good-looking, which, being a frontal of the skull, has more to it than the fragment Kimeu found. They spend a week "taking the top of that hill off," as Walker puts it. Yet they find nothing else. And the not-so-good bone? "We didn't want to do that one because we'd just spent a week sieving, getting dirty, and getting nothing," Walker recalls. "You rarely do, you know; nine times out of ten you don't even find more of the same bone." Sieving is not anyone's idea of a good time. Leakey points out that many important fossils are found when sieving is required; he is careful to add that such fossils are often discovered elsewhere by someone who will do anything to get out of sieving.

After a week of processing dirt, Walker and Leakey prefer to excavate a baboon jaw, a pig skull, an antelope skull. Only when they run out of mammals do they begin to work on the not-so-good hominid. They start by removing the boulders in "an unprepossessing place," in Walker's view. Then the sieving doesn't look promising. "By mid-afternoon, Richard and I were pretty bored." They regard the odds. In the dozen years of working at Koobi Fora, only once did they find any skeletal remains to eight hominid skulls.

Many *Homo erectus* skulls have been found, but very few with bones that are known as post-cranial, or below the head. Fourteen skulls were discovered near Peking during the early thirties, but of these there were seven fragmentary thigh bones, two upper arm bones, and a wrist bone. (The original fossils were lost during World War II when shipped out of China for "safekeeping" by the U.S. Marines. Only casts of these Peking Men remain, though additional *Homo erectus* skulls have emerged from the same site at Choukoutien.) The Heidelberg Man from West Germany is represented by a lower jaw. A lower jaw of *Homo erectus* was found in Swartkrans, South Africa. In Yingkou (Liaoning Province), China, a skull discovered in 1984 was accompanied by three vertebrae, a rib, some hand and foot bones. One *Homo erectus* skull was discovered at Olduvai Gorge, but the partial leg bones are too eroded for analysis.

Walker and Leakey regarded the odds. Leakey picked out an acacia a few yards from where the fragment was found, to suggest: "If we don't find anything else by the time we reach this tree, let's quit."

Then, for some reason, Leakey chose to focus his investigation on the tree itself, digging carefully around the roots. He plopped down a green cushion, and, sitting in a position normally associated with a small bathtub, used a metal pick with a curved wooden handle, his fingers, and a paintbrush with a four-inch spread. Some time later he stood up, took off his shirt, hung it on a branch of the tree, then lay out flat on his stomach with the cushion beneath his chest, putting his face directly over the roots. He was intimate. He switched to a dental pick, and within a few minutes began to make long, dry scratches against fossilized bones. Eventually he shouted for the others to come over and look. He had found the bones to the face of the Turkana Boy. The roots of the tree had worked their way through facial bones and halved the upper jaw. Now why would a tree pick on a defenseless boy?

Alan Walker suggests the tree was there "because it had found the skull, holding wet soil." In this semi-arid environment, the most subtle cup of moisture would nurture a seed, or, as Walker put it, "The tree grew out of the skull."

Ribs "grew" out of rock, teeth out of a swamp bed. The excavation continued into the side of the hill. Leakey and Walker lay on their sides foot to head of each other, scraping at details with dental picks while the rest of the team "took the top of that hill off," literally step by perpendicular step.

Sieving prevailed; sieving produced. Eyes blinked for reasons other than dust. An unprepossessing place possessed one of the oldest *erectus* specimens ever unearthed. Brown did a survey, collected and correlated, and Ian McDougall fixed the date of the tuff sample. The Boy was deemed 1.6 million years old, based on the relationship of the bone level to the Okote tuff, one of the two hundred tuff fingerprints identified in the Turkana basin. The Okote tuff is 1.65 million years old. The bones, as this age implies, were sitting right on top of the tuff.

The facial bones that emerged from the roots of the tree were found in tuffaceous sediments. The Okote tuff was not only a marker horizon, it was an immediately adjacent bed. They sieved and washed the pebble lag. They picked away at orange root casts. They found ostracods, mollusks, big fish and little fish indicating the former lake had invaded the area. They found the back of the skull, the lower jaw, and much of the skeleton in an area four by five yards. The bones of the Turkana Boy subsequently edged beyond the collection of Lucy and kept on assembling.

To find a more complete ancient hominid, one would need to turn the clock forward by one and a half million years, to the Neandertal, and the first evidence of human interment. In Europe and Asia, skeletons of Neandertals have been found amid what seems deliberate arrangement, alongside tools, surrounded by a circle of stones, and in one case, a pile of flints featured as a "pillow" beneath the head, a stone ax of particular beauty near the hand. In Uzbekistan, a republic of the USSR in Central Asia, at a place called Teshik Tash, the skeleton of a Neandertal child was found amid bones of the ibex, with six pairs of ibex horns encircling its head. A cave in Iraq yielded evidence of dense fossil pollen, including clusters from the wildflowers of hollyhock, grape hyacinth, and St. Barnaby's thistle, testimony that flowers were used in the burial of Neandertals some sixty thousand years ago. Many Neandertals were returned to the earth in the fetal position.

The bones of the Turkana Boy were arranged by water and sand. Early on, during my first visit to Koobi Fora, Leakey allowed that nature does most of the work. In the case of the Turkana Boy, nature played a splendid trick. The notoriously sloppy job of interment could not have been better executed were it attended by gravediggers. Once buried, the sediments of an ancient swamp provided the perfect chemistry for creating fossils out of these bones. Yet nature didn't exactly offer up this skeleton to the surface.

Fossil sites in East Africa rarely reach such depth or width. When I arrived at Nariokotome—two years after the first fragment was found—the Turkana Boy was still being discovered. A twenty- by twenty-four-yard slice into an adjacent hill laterally extends the bone level, six yards down from the top of the hill. Most of the bones were found in a single thin layer of ancient swamp—the bone level—

yet they were dispersed laterally in an area twice the size of the skeleton itself. Because there were no carnivore tooth marks on the bones, this was deemed the river's arrangement.

Many teeth were found some distance from the *erectus* skull. How do they know they belong? "They're from the same time, and the same age," Alan Walker explains, suggesting, "They just got into a little swirl in the river. Kamoya found the first tooth, then I found the P3," or third premolar. "Once we cleaned the calcite off, they fit. So there was no doubt." Also, no bones of a second hominid surfaced; there was no extra arm bone, no extra tooth. The search continues for diminutive details—toes and finger bones. Everything else has been found.

"Listen for the ping," Alan Walker instructed. "Everyone will hear it when you hit a bone; it sounds different." We chip away. There are eight of us: Richard and Meave Leakey, Kamoya Kimeu, Walker, Joseph Mutaba, Wambua Mungao, and Louise Leakey, whose chant of an English song taught in local schools inspires an a cappella chorus from the Salvadora, where Turkana children sing back: "I want, I want . . . To be, To be. . . ." When they stop, we hear a ping.

All heads turn toward Walker's hand. Thirty minutes later, having dug away at this form, he announces: "Hippo." He does so without resignation, for the hippo and fish found here fill in the story of the habitat when this *erectus* lived. Walker stretches a tape measure from a big-headed nail to the hippo bone, making a note that will be added to the excavation grid map and Frank Brown's paleogeographic picture.

Alan Walker instructs Brown: "Don't get too specific. Don't get off into whether the lake is an oxbow or several rivers or this or that. Just give us the general picture, enough to write the paper," meaning their initial scientific report. Brown prefers more details, and more time. "I wish they'd let it weather for a while. With excavation walls, the most apparent thing is pick marks. But if you let the walls alone for a whole year, the wind works them. A year later, you come back and say, 'My God, where did all these structures come from!' "

The soil, for the record, is sandstone, the work tedious, and the African sun intense; hopes for fossils are dashed when hitting upon the hard calcite tree-root casts that snake their way through the floor of the site.

Sandstone is aptly named; the point of the pick goes blunt within an hour, a sharpening session becomes an opportunity to revive what once appeared to be my knees. Even with a sharp pick, a two-inch incision requires muscle; you get leverage by pulling away with the handle, prying loose a bit of earth a couple of inches long and thin enough to hold a tip of a finger bone. (It would be exaggerating to suggest it's like pulling teeth; all the teeth have been found.) This chunk is stabbed into bits, which are squeezed between fingertips in search of fingertips. The resulting dirt is swept to the side, where it is collected for its bath in the lake. The soil is washed on a screen designed to thwart a single mosquito. One thousand tons of soil have been excavated from this site, every ounce of it stabbed, squeezed, swept, sieved, and washed.

Clearly, they wanted these toes and finger bones. A skeleton one hundred percent complete is a nice round figure, but this wasn't the purpose. A few years earlier I would have wondered at this careful devotion—Englishmen without hats in the midday sun? Then you remember the comparative sessions at "Ancestors," the conversation in the Hominid Vault, the details on teeth that tell the difference between an ape and a hominid—or, for that matter, an australopithecine and a *Homo*—that subtle change tells the story of how we came to be what we are today, that not for nothing is the museum at Harvard where Stephen Jay Gould works called the Museum of *Comparative* Zoology, that comparison assigns likenesses and differences. How much can be told from a bone?

The Turkana Boy was not the first *Homo erectus* skeleton found in the Turkana basin, nor was it the first *erectus* ever found by Kamoya Kimeu. A few years earlier, on the other side of the lake, Kimeu discovered a jawbone near the Koobi Fora camp. He found it amid a litter of bones from crocodiles, fish, and antelope. Forty thousand fossils were subsequently collected from this particular site. When they began sorting the *erectus* bones from the others, their discrimination didn't rely on anatomy alone. The hominid bones were abnormal. They had an extra outer layer, like an aberrant ring on a tree trunk. "By Murphy's Law of Paleontology," Walker observes, "the first skeleton of a single *Homo erectus* individual ever found had a bone disease."

Under the microscope he discovered more. Beyond the normal boundary of bone growth, the cells were puffy and irregular, as opposed to being flat. They were dispersed and disorganized, as opposed to a healthy, orderly arrangement. Walker set out to diagnose a disease that struck over a million years ago.

The extra layer was typical of bone that invades a blood clot. While Walker acknowledges this might have been caused by a disease "no longer on earth," he made a hunch based on the known. Perhaps this hominid consumed a near-toxic dose of vitamin A by eating the livers of carnivores (the fate of a couple of Antarctic explorers who consumed their huskies' livers). "Two pounds of carnivore liver would be a fatal dose," Walker notes.

Whatever the source, this female had lived long enough for this second layer to ossify before she had died. Unable to gather food or water on her own, unable to stand and defend herself against lion or hyena, she had been cared for. The extra layer of bone told them something about the "society" of *Homo erectus.*

What did the bones of the Turkana Boy tell them?

Unlike the australopithecine, *Homo erectus* has a face that, as Walker puts it, "is tucked under the brow ridges, rather as our faces are tucked under our foreheads." Part of this came about with the recession of powerful jaws. Teeth became smaller. A general reduction of the face continued to result in the unique human chin, the triangular bit of bone called the mental process.

Walker explains the biomechanics for this: Muscles from both the right and left side work the jaws. Apes gnash, because of their canines, but we chew and bite on one side. This produces a big shear at the midline which requires a bony buttress to resist it—the human chin. The Turkana Boy has no sagittal crest like *Zinj.*

When Walker reconstructed the skull of the Turkana Boy (which emerged in seventy pieces), he had one piece that he couldn't quite connect to the others by virtue of grain or shape. "It had a big hole, a pit so big you could put your thumb in it." It proved to be the bony socket of Broca's area in this young *Homo erectus*. (The frontal lobe of 1470 also has evidence of Broca's area.) Broca's area manages the muscles of the lips, tongue, jaw, and vocal cords during speech. Broca's area, it should be said, has also been found in apes; chimps are vocal, as are gorillas. But it is the smaller, less detectable Wernicke's area that lends comprehension and content to speech; Wernicke's area is not clearly discernible in 1470 or any *Homo erectus* as old (geologically speaking) as the Turkana Boy.

While the initial description of the Turkana Boy noted its "strapping size" (five feet four at a mere twelve years old), both Alan Walker and Stephen Jay Gould seized upon the anatomical detail of the pelvis. (Gould's article, "The Most Compelling Pelvis Since Elvis," was published in *Discover* magazine.) The mental process, in largess, called for a compromise in bipedality.

"The human body is designed by natural selection—if you want to call that design," Walker begins. "The human body can take a hundred years of wear, it can take loads from zero all the way to ten times our body weight, at very slow speeds. Now, if you ask engineers to design a bearing that would do that, they'd laugh. If engineers could figure out the secret of animal joints, they could make a bundle, because if cars ran as well as bodies do," he muses, "we'd save billions in oil."

When Walker taught anatomy at Harvard, "all my students thought the body was a marvelous machine designed by the great engineer in the sky. It took me all my time to get them out of it." Engineers, he explains, can choose their material; animals can't. "If we had teeth of steel, they wouldn't wear out, would they?" But if anything is obvious in the record of evolution, it is that teeth adapt and change in form. The same occurs with bones. Yet working only with the material on hand requires compromise.

To demonstrate this in the Turkana Boy, Walker focuses in on the upper leg bone, or femur, that connects to the pelvis. In the *Homo erectus* the neck of the femur is extremely long, whereas it's short in modern hominids. This affects the way a hominid walks.

The ball and socket of a hip joint keep a hominid balanced on two legs. With each step, as one foot lifts, body weight tends to pull away from the opposite hip joint, disturbing our center of gravity. As Walker explains, "If this weren't counteracted by something, the body would fall sideways. So every time we take a step, the abductor muscles on the side of the standing leg contract, pulling the pelvis toward the femur to balance the body weight."

The long neck of the *Homo erectus* femur meant his abductor muscles were further from the hip joint—requiring less force to balance the body. And because the pelvis of the *Homo erectus* is narrower than in modern hominids, there was less force exerted in turning the hip joint. The upshot? The bipedalism of the *Homo erectus* was more biomechanically efficient than ours. We use much more energy to walk than did this *erectus*. In modern hominid females, the neck of the femur is particularly shortened, "pulled back out of the way, in a sense," Walker explains, for giving birth.

What the most compelling pelvis since Elvis suggested is that the evolving hominid brain inspired a change in hominid anatomy. Even though it was a male, Walker and Leakey concluded that the female *Homo erectus* pelvis was basically the same in dimension. If so, it could not give birth to a modern human baby with its large brain, and thus began a compromised position, in two ways. The first had to do with altering the bipedal efficiency. The second has to do with a change in lifestyle demanded by extensive infant care, known in anthropology as parental investment.

We may be less biomechanically efficient in our ability to walk upright, but that same adjustment in anatomy allows for the birth of big-headed babies. It wasn't enough. Such a large cranium now requires premature passage through a birth canal limited by bipedalism. "Modern humans have a gestation period of twenty-one months," says Walker, confirming what every parent suspects, "nine months *in utero* and a year outside." Or, as Gould puts it, "We are born too early."

That's only one price of bipedalism. Slipped disks are imposed on a spine less perfectly suited for a load on two feet rather than four. Varicose veins develop because upright posture is not ideal for blood circulation. A quadrupedal ape doesn't develop hernias because the intestines are supported by a broader ligament; our upright position created a weakened abdominal wall. Flat feet result when arches collapse from the unusual weight put on two feet. Bunions, backaches. Why be bipedal?

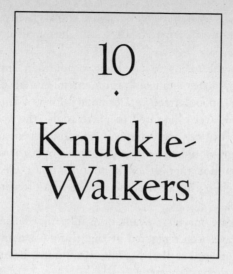

10

·

Knuckle-Walkers

The oldest fossil evidence of bipedalism appears in the hominids known as *afarensis*. The bones suggest a transitional phase in the classic sense of a missing link. The foot bones are exceptionally long, the toes curved, and *afarensis* is often compared to an upright chimpanzee.

How the shape of these bones may have affected the behavior of early hominids like Lucy inspired vigorous debates, for the "moment" of bipedalism has become one of the most pressing questions of the search. Researchers really don't know exactly when it first occurred, or how it occurred. The latter has a history of inspired speculation.

Freeing up the hands to do things other than knuckle-walk or swing from branches is an old argument in human origins, as old as Darwin, and popularized in Desmond Morris's *The Naked Ape*. First the hands were liberated to make tools; the argument drew upon the absence of large canines: hominids seemed defenseless. An upright gait would also allow you to see over the tall grasses, to carry infants—not that other hominoids don't do these things —or even yield a club or a stone. Cause was often confused with effect.

To complicate matters, adaptations like bipedalism (or a large brain) may have been triggered by one thing (or many things) and produced other options that became paramount, having nothing to do with the original trigger(s).

The investigation fell to two schools of observation: behavior and bones. The two became complementary when scientists studied modern articulation (bone and muscle movement) with an eye toward the form of fossils that were being unearthed. Functional studies of primate bones were encouraged by Berkeley anthropologist Sherwood Washburn during the sixties, at the same time that Louis Leakey was encouraging the study of primate behavior in the wild. The two overlapped, as both men were inclined to cross disciplines, with Leakey establishing a Primate Research Centre near Nairobi, and Washburn (with student Irven DeVore) studying baboons in East Africa. Since then, there has been a deluge of data, both from field research and studies of locomotion in captivity. That said, how much can be told?

In the *American Journal of Physical Anthropology* of April 1982, anatomist Owen Lovejoy of Kent State University suggested the hominids from Hadar enjoyed "full and complete bipedality," and "a forelimb not primarily involved in locomotor behavior," meaning the arms were not devoted to moving along. More informally, Lovejoy suggested Lucy might beat a modern human to the nearest McDonald's.

A team of anatomists working at the State University of

New York at Stony Brook expressed a different view. Jack Stern and Randy Susman suggested that any bipedality of *afarensis* "involved less extension at the hip and the knee than in modern humans, and only limited transfer of weight onto the medial part of the ball of the foot." The ball of the human foot absorbs weight during a bipedal stride, just before the toes are lifted from the ground. Part of their studies included videotaping a human and a chimpanzee walking, to compare the position of heels and toes during a stride. The Stony Brook team also found the *afarensis* fossils "indicated a significant adaptation for movement in the trees." The shoulder socket has an angle inclined 15 degrees more upward than a human's. This would be useful for climbing trees or even hanging from branches.

In 1983, Don Johanson invited a group of scientists to Berkeley to debate the locomotion of *afarensis*. Sherwood Washburn began the discussions by suggesting theories be formulated in terms of betting odds. Jack Stern offered 10 to 1 odds that *afarensis* was arboreal—having a preference for tree climbing—and Bruce Latimer, just to make things interesting, bet 9½ to 1 that *afarensis* did not prefer trees. Professor Henry McHenry began the day with 1.5 to 1 odds that the bones implied greater climbing ability than modern hominids. After three days of debates, and two weeks of reflection, McHenry settled on 2 to 1.

During the "Ancestors" symposium, the subject of a foothold in the forest came up again. Stern and Susman emphasized the length of the *afarensis* foot, which is 40 percent longer than a modern hominid's, and the curved toes. *Afarensis* may have been capable of a bipedal gait, they said, but the stride was short (as was *afarensis*, less than four feet tall), the posture bent, and the long, curved toes suggested the ability to accommodate branches.

In humans the toes are shorter and straighter, and therefore less efficient for purchasing a branch—but a better support for the extraordinary weight and novel balancing act imposed by a bipedal stride. Putting one foot in front of the other means that nearly half of the time, all of the body's weight is on one foot. In apes, the big toe is long and diverges from the rest of the toes, much the way our thumb diverges from the rest of our fingers. The toes of most quadruped apes are long and curved. So what do the curved toes of *afarensis* mean?

When I asked Don Johanson about this in his Berkeley office, he rose to the occasion. "Even though the foot bones are curved," he began, then stood up, flipped off a loafer, and demonstrated in a stocking foot what is known as the toe-off position. He slowly pulled his heel up to begin to take a step. His toes were bent up. "You have lots of movement upward, but very limited movement downward." You might grasp a pencil off the floor with your toes, but this has nothing to do with walking. The ability to toe off is refined in modern hominids.

The toe-off propels us along to the next step. "In the big toe of *afarensis*," Johanson continued, "there *is* a human articulation at the base of that toe, but even if the toes were curved doesn't mean they were used for grasping. Owen Lovejoy thinks the curved bones are an example of 'evolutionary baggage'—like an appendix. It may just be one of those things that evolution has simply not refined at this stage of *afarensis*."

There's no reason early hominids couldn't have moved about with a bipedal gait and maintained an ability to climb trees (as we do). The discerning is a matter of degrees, which would shift further back in time, when our ancestors were more hominoid than hominid. Might the hand bones of a four-million-year-old hominid indicate that it walked on its knuckles? If so, would you call it a hominid or a hominoid? The "moment" of bipedalism remains a question of when.

A volcano called Sadiman extended the discussion in an eloquent way. Twenty miles east of Laetoli, Sadiman erupted just over 3.5 million years ago, and the ashes of this particular eruption were air-fallen tuffs, laminated by a series of rain showers that fell in an area known today as the Laetoli Beds.

The site, thirty miles south of Olduvai Gorge, is where Mary Leakey found the oldest *afarensis* fossils. During the 1975–76 field seasons, Dr. Leakey was keen to find more hominid fossils and perhaps even stone tools. At the time the oldest known stone tools were 2.2 myo, from the Omo, and Dr. Leakey hoped they might find tools in the Laetoli sequences, which began at 2.4. What was found instead was the oldest evidence of bipedalism, in the form of footprints. These appeared in the air-fallen tuffs, the Laetoli Beds dated at around 3.5 million years old by Garniss Curtis and Robert Drake.

They were evocative, featuring the long paths of several individuals, and discovered with all the careful detective work and equally careful excavation that followed Kamoya Kimeu's first clue to the Turkana Boy. The first print noticed at Laetoli was that of a rhino, discovered at close range by Andrew Hill, who had fallen while dodging a bit of elephant dung hurled by a friend. ("A friend" is accurate here, as dry elephant dung is inoffensive.) The locality became known as Site A. In time it was extended to include several exposures that became known as the Footprint tuff. Tens of thousands of footprints were discovered, including those of insects, hares, rhino, three-toed horses, and those that appeared to be hominid.

Peter Jones helped prepare casts of the footprints, which were compared to those of modern humans. Impressions of the "heel strike" were evident, and the big toe was already in line with the rest of the foot. A method of photography (photogrammetry) that measures subtle surface contours showed evidence of drag from the toe-off. Why were these hominids on the move?

Andrew Sinclair, Michael Norton-Griffiths, and Mary Leakey suggest bipedalism developed to follow migrations like those of the wildebeest. This time the impetus was diet rather than toolmaking, since no stone tools have been found to match the antiquity of the Laetoli hominids.

Leakey's colleagues are both experts on the ecology of the Serengeti, where the wildebeest roam. They note an advantage that lions to this day do not pursue. By following the herd, the potential diet increases by one carcass per day in an area of twelve square miles, compared with one carcass every fourteen days for a territorial type. To lions that maintain fixed territorial boundaries, the wildebeest are a movable feast. As long as they can hear the nasal low of these white-bearded gnus, prides remain fat and healthy. But the late arrival or early departure of the migration, dictated by weather patterns, may doom a litter of cubs born at the wrong time. Lion cubs often starve to death.

By studying scavenging techniques in the Serengeti, the kind of range thought to have prevailed in Tanzania between two and four million years ago, the three scientists noted "an unfilled niche for a mammalian scavenger," meaning early hominids. Hyena, lion, leopard, and cheetah are contemporary mammals that eat wildebeest, but they do not migrate with the herd on its long journey that today passes very near the Laetoli Beds.

Geologist Dick Hay figured the Laetoli Beds were part of the Serengeti when the footprints were preserved. Around 2.5 million years ago, with the formation of the Rift, the region uplifted, to form Lake Eyasi to the south. But at the time the footprints were formed, Laetoli was savanna with pockets of woodland. The upright gait, then, may have been an opportunity to find a niche, to go where tree climbers couldn't.

Such a habitat was a central feature that enticed Shirley Strum to study baboons in Kenya. She was keen to see how modern primates lived in a habitat like that of early hominids. Her mentor was Sherwood Washburn, who directed her graduate studies at Berkeley. She began to study the troop of olive baboons known as the Pumphouse Gang in 1972, first in a region of central Kenya near a town called Gilgil. Her studies were distracted a few years later when a group of Kikuyu farmers settled in the area. Competition developed between maize harvesters. The baboons quickly learned that a cob of corn was worth half an hour digging for natural foods, like the corms of onion grass. In Kenya, as elsewhere in Africa, baboons are numerous, considered vermin, and often shot.

Strum admits to not only becoming obsessed with baboons but dreaming about them, and at this point, her "friends" pleaded for help in nightmares. She arranged for their translocation to a suitable terrain north of Nanyuki, along the eastern edge of the Laikipia plateau. The area has long patches of savanna grasses, pockets of acacia trees, and even kopje rocks like those of the Serengeti.

In late January of 1987 I set out from Nairobi on a long drive to this area north of Mount Kenya known as the Ndorobo Reserve, named after a vanishing tribe of hunters. Baboons are not as closely related to humans as chimps or gorillas or orangutans; they are not classified among this group of great apes, but are Old World monkeys. "I don't suggest that early hominids were like these baboons," Strum qualifies, "but they had to be at least as complicated. They had to solve these problems which the baboons seem to solve."

Baboons come under study in other parts of Africa, including Ethiopia, where Clifford Jolly became intrigued by the way gelada baboons forage and eat. In 1970, Jolly proposed a theory that influenced how scientists looked at hominid behavior. At first glance, it had nothing to do with tool use, nothing to do with hunting or bipedalism. It had to do with diet. Jolly's paper was entitled "The Seed Eaters." He studied the biomechanics for chewing the small kinds of foods that baboons eat, suggesting the grinding action would get in the way of large canines, and require smaller teeth in general. But in addition to this, perhaps the "precision grip" assigned to the Handy Man might well have been honed by digging for small things like corms. Baboons have opposable thumbs that meet their fingertips. Jolly's paper shifted many people onto thinking about diet, as opposed to culture or tool use, in terms of hominid changes. His influence was reflected in Sinclair's paper, where bipedalism may have been inspired by a dietary niche.

Of all the things that have been proposed as "unique" about hominids—tool use, cooperative hunting—one remains curious. All primates except humans have a visible period of estrus, when the female shows signs of being sexually receptive. Why should human females find some advantage in keeping their fertility a secret? If the key to evolutionary success is reproduction, what was the sexual strategy behind this?

Earlier studies suggested that baboon males dominated such strategies by "brute force." They appeared to monopolize females and prevent other males from mating with them. Now many studies suggest a matriarchal society, with females having a strong say in selecting sexual partners. Strum saw both males and females as engaged in a game of diplomatic finesse. Primatologist Barbara Smuts, also studying a troop of olive baboons in Kenya, noted that old, scruffy-looking males might mate in full view of the younger, higher-ranking males, and suggests that friendship was at the core of the sexual union.

Gross generalizations were being undone by exceptions, and primatologists, like every other discipline in the search for human origins, were saying, "It's more complicated than we thought." Strum once said to me that she was quite certain the baboons read all there was to read on primate behavior, then decided, Let's do the opposite. That baboons might be as unpredictable as humans emerged during my two days in the field.

At sunrise the morning after my arrival I set out to follow the olive baboons in Ndorobo, accompanied by a young field researcher named Thomas Kingwa, one of a team of five that works with Strum. (Because she was expecting her second child at the time, Strum did not come along on this field trip. She regularly employs a team of researchers, as she spends half her year teaching at the University of California at San Diego.)

Thomas Kingwa led me to the peaks of a large kopje formation, and a view which grants surrounding boulders the appearance of elephants kneeling. Mount Kenya was crowned in alpen glow. The baboons were sluggish, just waking up. They yawn, I compare canines. The baboons tend to sleep high on the rocks to elude predators, and it is an observer's task to follow them from dawn until dusk, to know where they're spending the night, in order to find them the next morning. Their daily schedules vary according to the season. During the rainy season, when food is plentiful, they don't travel far for food. But during the dry season, they are moving about shortly after sunrise and may traverse twenty miles during the day. As far as the advantages of bipedalism go, the baboons seem much more agile at descending the rocks than me. Baboons do not walk on their knuckles like gorillas, but extend the palm of the "hand"; their "arms" and legs are about the same length. They greet each other in various ways: some merely grunt, almost low, and others go out of their way and seem enthused. Some embrace.

Strum had devised a chart for field observation. Today's began like this:

An olive baboon stands upright to reach fruit in a tree in the Ndorobo Reserve, north of Mt. Kenya. The baboons are studied by primatologist Shirley Strum and a team of researchers who seek to understand patterns of primate behavior.

Olive baboons are social creatures, with an intricate hierarchy among troop members. Here a young baboon that Strum named "Delta" grooms a mother, while another looks on at the "black infant," so called because of the color of its fur.

An olive baboon bares his canines. Lack of large canines are one of the characteristics that distinguish hominids from hominoids.

January 31, 1987. 8:a.m. Malaika troop Ranging Pattern

Habitat: #3 rocky outcrops [as opposed to scrub brush, grass-land, forest, high ground, whistling thorns, scattered trees and bushes, bare ground].

Observation conditions: Good [as opposed to fair and poor. There is no excellent category].

Movement of troop: Grid 15 [from a grid map of the area].

Type of food: *Sansevieria intermedia*, the tall succulent, fruit from trees, corm.

The chart extends according to a question Strum has posed. Observers in the field have three Search Images. The first is focal sampling—perhaps a study of an individual; the second, scanning; the third is ad-lib, recording important events, like births, or "consorts"—sexual relationships. We're scanning. Kingwa records where the baboons move, what they eat.

"If two things happen at once, you record one event completely," he explains. "You must follow one event from beginning to end." It would seem that researchers miss a lot, and apparently they did until field studies such as this extended beyond a decade. When Jane Goodall first set out to study chimpanzees in Tanzania, she expected to spend a couple of years at it. Hers is the longest field study, now in its third decade.

"What you've got to watch for with the baboons," Strum had warned me, "is the difference between your first impression and the intricacies of their history." She had been following the Pumphouse Gang, now a troop of forty-eight, for fifteen years, and a second smaller troop called the Malaika, which split off from the Pumphouse Gang in 1981. Each baboon has been assigned a rank within the hierarchy of the troop (as Thomas put it, "I know who's afraid of who"), and each has a personal history record. For example:

Delta's life history:

Pumphouse Gang

born: April 24, 1984

Mother is DL; DE female, born on Oct. 3 of 74, is an aunt. DI, male, born April 23, '76, is an uncle. DS female, 12/20/79, is an aunt.

Father: Unknown

Rank: None assigned yet

Promotions: Promoted to Brown infant, October, 1984

Injuries: None

Like many other juveniles (promoted from a brown infant at the age of two), "Delta" appears to be a ball of brown fur with a punk haircut. We found her because it was known that she had established a friendship with the high-ranking male named Norman, and was likely to be near him. After foraging for grass corms, my namesake went over to greet, then groom the mother of a "black" infant. I have precious little idea of what this means beyond what I saw; grooming establishes bonds, and it's smart to hang around with a high-ranking male, for protection. After fifteen years of studying daily behavior, Strum has discerned some overall patterns. She did not find males to be the great dominant forces as had been suggested. At puberty males leave their natal group, to join other troops. They stay longer where they are accepted, moving on after a few years.

Irven DeVore, now head of anthropology at Harvard and self-described as an "old baboonologist," reflected on his early studies with Washburn: "Our view of primates traditionally included a lot of male chauvinism, a lot of puritanical thought. But we're beginning

* "I needed a name beginning with a D," Strum explained.

to unpack these prejudices and examine them, then look back at nature with a clearer view."

When DeVore and Washburn began to study baboons in East Africa, "the males weren't exactly subtle in their ways." So it was easy to overlook the subtle "and much more fundamental" strategies of the females. DeVore, who wears Ben Franklin reading glasses and looks more like a musician than a scientist, or for that matter, the keen poker player that he is, now suggests female primates "are a lot smarter than we've given them credit for," adding an injunction rendered by his father in Texas: "Irv, remember that courtship is a boy chasing a girl until she catches him."

Female strategies were the subject of Sarah Blaffer Hrdy's *The Woman That Never Evolved*. DeVore comments on the analyses offered by Hrdy: "Many of us were forced to realize that not only do males and females have different strategies in species beyond our own but they're often in deep conflict." As the protagonist in Updike's *The Witches of Eastwick* complains of evolutionary strategies for sexual union, "What a bait they set up!"

DeVore asks: "If females are capable of multiple orgasm, continuous or virtually continuous receptivity, and initiative—is it the male's task in this world to circumscribe that female choice as rigidly as possible?" DeVore argues that the most fundamental principle in human society is for males to control female reproduction. "Often this extends to controlling female sexuality as well—I think this is one of our greatest cultural achievements," he adds wryly. "Because if it works, it means you can take the age-old male jealousy and say, 'Wait a minute, fellows, if we can just agree on this and control these women, then we can bond with each other.' And if we do that, then we can raid, we can make war, and do all those things we males love to do." The dynamics of male bonding DeVore deems "the engine that drives" much of human society.

While the majority of researchers do find male bonding among their subjects, Shirley Strum suggests the "transfer" males seem eager to make allies not with other adult males, but first with females, and then with young infants. The male might use a black infant (so-called because of the color of its fur when young) or the mother as a diversion in an aggressive situation with another male.

When DeVore first studied baboons, he described adult males as being protective of the young. "But he didn't know the infants as individuals," Strum points out, "so he wasn't able to see that adult males are not protective of infants per se, but only of certain ones." Strum found that a black infant who was uncomfortable or appeared untrusting with a male didn't prove useful to his plans at all. The infant's screams brought the wrath of the troop onto the male.

Does Strum consider her own behavior with her children when she watches baboons with their infants? "How can you not?" She smiles. "With my own children, it hits home how immature human infants are. With baboons, their physical and mental skills come so quickly." Infant baboons are able to cling to their mothers shortly after birth, riding underbelly. So the mother can continue to move with the rest of the troop, foraging and feeding.

The baboons continue to forage for corm in onion grass; others pop off sansevieria to eat the new, fleshy part of the shoot. They work their way slowly across a ravine, to a cluster of fruit-bearing trees. Several make a deft ascent, and entire trees begin to wave and wiggle with apes aloft.

I move away to take a photograph. (While the baboons allow me to come within a couple of feet of them, my camera's motor drive seems to disturb them.) When I turn around and raise my telephoto, I'm somewhat annoyed to discover what appears to be a man in the shade of the tree. I focus, trying to make out the details within this darkness, an area of high contrast to the rest of the world. A large male baboon is standing perfectly upright, picking berries from the tree. Thomas informs me they do it all the time. If our hominoid ancestors might have done the same, what was the advantage of being upright permanently? Did it have anything to do with reproductive strategies?

The next morning I follow the Pumphouse Gang with Hudson Oyaro, who has been instructed to watch for consorts, meaning sexual relationships. "With consorts, we write down the time, what happened, and who started it, who was involved." His clues include what's known as presenting, when adults offer their rear ends for inspection. The males' are gray, the females' pink, unless they're pregnant. During estrus, which last for two weeks out of a forty-day cycle, the female genital area swells, turning bright pink—what Sarah Hrdy described as a "cosmetic extravagance."

During a 1986 symposium on Primate Reproductive Strategies in Philadelphia, Hrdy was quoted by no less than five other primatologists. (I confess I was impressed by Hrdy before I met her, not only because of an article she'd written, but at a reception before a lecture she was to give at the American Museum of Natural History, I was greeted by the organizer of the event with "Sarah, I'm so glad you're here. Did you bring any slides for your lecture?")

Hrdy's opening slide at the Philadelphia conference featured a sow with a man on its back. He holds an artificial insemination syringe in one hand and a spray container of boar scent in the other. "The answer to that ever-tantalizing question of Will she or won't she," Hrdy began, "turns out to be predictable as long as the timing is right. This sow will stand still as long as she smells the scent of a boar sprayed out of an aerosol can, and feels a boarlike pressure on her back." Hrdy's subject is female receptivity, and the absence of estrus in hominids.

She suggests hominids are "not so unique as we crack ourselves up to be," citing variations in the receptivity of female primates: pygmy chimps are receptive as much as 75 percent of the time. Then she underscores the advantages of promiscuity. She describes these as additional investments from former consorts and protection from males who might otherwise attack their infants, a network of alliance with males. And rather than the old notion of simply breeding with the best male, Hrdy says, "Let's assume that her object is to mate with a range of males, regardless of which inseminates her. Sexual swelling would then be exactly what it appears to be, striking advertisements of sexual receptivity."

Hrdy thinks male care for infants doesn't require certainty of paternity. Certainly male baboons disprove this. As witnessed in the field, male baboons form friendships with infants not their own. Nor are baboons monogamous.

Owen Lovejoy had suggested that bipedalism among *afarensis* may have been a result of females creating a bond with the opposite sex. The theory is this: A female can raise more children if a male brings them food and mother doesn't have to bother with hunting or gathering. The reason the male became so incredibly loyal was that the female no longer limited her "displays" to periods of estrus as most primates do, but was "continuously receptive."

"A pair-bonding system was arising among those early hominids as a way of keeping a male attracted to a female and ensuring that she be impregnated by him through the strategy of fairly continuous mating instead of a frenzy of it at the peak of her ovulatory cycle," Lovejoy is quoted in *Lucy*. "You can't have a tremendous amount of fighting and indiscriminate copulating, and have pair-bonding and food-sharing. They just don't go together."

How does he know what she's doing when he's off foraging, Hrdy and William Bennett ask in an article for *Harvard* magazine entitled "Lucy's Husband, What Did He Stand For?" And if a male is keen for maximum offspring, why doesn't he spend his time with many females? Hrdy and Bennett suggest that male primates become monogamous when there is no other option. Competition among females, they say, keeps males in order. Of the two hundred species of primates living today, only thirty-seven are monogamous. That's 18 percent. Among these are lemurs, gibbons, de Brazza's monkey, tarsiers, and rare colubines. Hrdy and Bennett find no trend for monogamy leading to success in the current populations of primates.

Then they turn to the issue of sexual dimorphism. In monogamous species, the sexes are nearly the same size. In polygamous species, the female is much smaller. In modern hominids, males are 5 to 12 percent larger than females, "a size disparity," note Hrdy and Bennett, "that would place humans among the mildly polyandrous species"—having two or more husbands at the same time.

They note that only 20 percent of the world's cultures are monogamous. The bottom line is that while the nuclear family may be considered ideal in Western civilization, "there is no reason to assume that it was typical in the past; there is even reason to suspect that it was not."

While Lovejoy's theory on monogamy was challenged, his studies were influential in noting that some of our ancestors were more efficient bipeds than we are (confirmed by the Turkana Boy). Lovejoy also emphasized the change in the shape of the pelvis, and how this allowed the birth of larger-brained infants. The pelvis of *afarensis* was small.

If the bones of *afarensis* represent a transitional phase in bipedalism, how long was the transition? From three million years ago (the age of Hadar fossils) to 1.6, there is the transition from an upright chimpanzee sort to the more statuesque Turkana Boy. A clue to what happened in between emerged from Olduvai Gorge, for half a century the domain of Mary Leakey.

Mary Leakey relinquished her fieldwork in Tanzania in 1984. "My field days are over," she told me; but "retired" would be the wrong word. Dr. Leakey accompanied her son to the new West Turkana sites and Rusinga Island, where the "new" *Proconsul* skeletons were discovered, which she helped piece together. Since her move from the simple, tin-roofed hut high on a cliff over Olduvai Gorge, Mary Leakey has concentrated on completing the massive monographs on her discoveries in Tanzania.

In 1985, Don Johanson announced an "exclusive" agreement for scientists from his Berkeley Institute of Human Origins (IHO), in association with Tanzanian scientists, to conduct research at Olduvai. Mary Leakey was not consulted, which many consider to be an error of protocol on Johanson's part.

The initial impetus to pursue research in Tanzania, according to Johanson, arose from a soft-spoken Tanzania grad student, Prosper Ndessokia. On leave from Tanzania's Department of Antiquities, Ndessokia was studying paleontology at Berkeley for his dissertation. Among his fossils was a primate skull from Tanzania. Gerry Eck, from the University of Washington in Seattle, was keen to see the skull, and sought Ndessokia out. Eck was a member of the Omo expedition, and primate skulls were his specialty. The two exchanged data, and talked of the inevitable—getting back into the field to find more. When Eck mentioned the continuing ban in Ethiopia, Ndessokia suggested, "Why not Tanzania?"

On July 15, 1986, the team from Berkeley descended on the road to Olduvai. Gerry Eck arrived first to establish camp, assisted by Ndessokia and geologist Bob Walter, who'd worked on dating the sites at Hadar.

Walter set about gathering volcanic ashes, accompanied by Paul Manega, head geologist with the Tanzanian Department of Antiquuities. The two set up a small lab in a stone hut called the Laetoli Building, where fossils from Laetoli were protected during Dr. Leakey's excavation at that site some thirty miles from the Main Gorge. Within this hut Walter and Manega crush and sieve tuff samples, studying them under a microscope Walter brought along from Boulder, to see if they are worth the trip back to the United States to undergo the "fingerprint" analysis.

Don Johanson and Tim White make the descent to Olduvai a few days later; the team now includes several archeologists and paleoanthropologists. On the afternoon of July 23, Tim White said what everyone wanted to hear: "Whoa. This is a hominid!" White spied a fragment of an elbow in sediments known as Bed I. Johanson, walking alongside him, saw the upper part of an arm bone. Berhane Asfaw, a graduate student from Ethiopia, found a piece of upper jaw. The search at Olduvai was renewed in a section designated as Geological Locality 45c. It was one of the most convenient discoveries ever made, within a few yards of the road that transports tourists to the *Zinj* site. As mini-buses whizzed by, they began to excavate.

First, they marked off the area in grids of two yards square; from the air their geometric slice into the earth looks like a Mayan figure. They dug three trenches into the adjoining hillsides, one called Dik Dik Hill, after the little African antelope. Then they began to sieve. They sieved through thinly laminated beige and brown clays and sands filled with volcanic tuffs.

The date on the find at Olduvai was not difficult to ascertain. Peter Lauwo (the governor of Olduvai, who also worked with Mary Leakey), points out that the new site is firmly dated at about 1.85 million years old. A bold ribbon of volcanic tuff laces an exposure on Dik Dik Hill as neatly as an accompanying plaque at an exhibit. Tuff C1, front and center. Born on the slopes of Kilimanjaro, Lauwo speaks English fluently, breathlessly commenting on the new site like a reporter on the sidelines at the Superbowl. "You can see the tuff over there." Lauwo begins to list the finds: "Part of a femur, several teeth, part of the face, part of the arm."

For five weeks, the IHO team gathered and sieved. From an area forty yards square they recovered fragments of antelope, pig, giraffe, elephant, monkey, reptiles, fish, and hominid. There were eighteen thousand fragments of fossil bone and teeth. From this inventory they sorted out three hundred and two fossil fragments that they could identify as hominid. They based their identification on the color of the bones, dark gray to black, so distinguished from those fragments they found higher in the section, and the inevitable dental comparisons that suggested they were assembling one hominid, of one age.

Of the elbow that Tim White saw, there would be eleven pieces that they glued together. Of the arm bone that Johanson saw, there would be five pieces that they glued together. Of the top of the skull, there would be twenty-one pieces, and of the teeth and roots, one hundred and sixty-one pieces. The upper jaw was discovered in fifteen pieces. Olduvai had given the Berkeley team a hell of a puzzle; nature might as well have been a Cuisinart. All the fossils were shattered as they eroded from their original deposition. All the articular ends of the leg and arm fragments were missing except for a portion of one end of the elbow. The exact length of such limbs was estimated. They called the assemblage OH 62.

News of the discovery drifted north to West Turkana, where the description took on an amazingly familiar ring. "Smaller than Lucy's" was the news in Kenya, where the Hominid Gang had also found post-cranial bones "smaller than Lucy's."

Below the head, the IHO team preferred not to compare these bones to other *habilis* bones, either those from East Turkana or Olduvai. Their comparison relied on a different genus and species, from a different location, from a different age—twice as old. Their comparative data focused on Lucy and the *afarensis* finds from Ethiopia. The IHO team suggested that there was no legitimate *habilis* material to use for comparison, that theirs was the first to be found. Richard Leakey's comment was "Absolute rubbish. We have more." Alan Walker expanded. "We have a *habilis* skeleton 3735 that we published in 1985. It's as much [of a skeleton] as OH 62. We also have two femurs and half a pelvis that are assessed to be of the same type as skull 1470. And we must have more, but associations are poor. IHO may be correct in that much of the Koobi Fora material is not associated with teeth and skulls. 3735 has good skull bones.

"In any case," Walker continues, "Johanson and White say that only one species [habilis] of a non-boisei hominid occurred at two million years ago. Our finds from East Turkana then, by their definition, is a habilis skeleton." Walker and Leakey, with the assistance of the Hominid Gang, have found post-cranial evidence of boisei in association.

The IHO team suggested that this was the smallest hominid ever found; Lucy was three feet six inches tall. Yet when they compared the details of the face, palate, and dentition to other fossil finds, they figured that the name for their puzzle was Handy Man, or Homo habilis. If so, its arms are weird. Their estimates suggested the arms stretched nearly to the knees. Despite its bipedal stance, this habilis appeared to be far more apelike than humanlike. Another appendix?

The Berkeley team began to talk of leaps in evolution, of sudden changes. "The very small body size of the OH 62 individual suggests that views of human evolution posing incremental body size increase through time may be rooted in gradualistic preconceptions rather than fact," they wrote in Nature. Time magazine quoted Johanson as saying, "The new specimen suggests that the body pattern we call modern did not appear until Homo erectus and that it happened fairly rapidly." Tim White added, "The question is, 'Why did they lose those features, and what made them change in just 200,000 years?'" meaning the small stretch of time to erectus. If erectus was fully upright at 1.6 (the date on the Turkana Boy), then the habilis find dated at 1.8 meant a really quick change to the uprightness known to define hominids. On the other hand, the Berkeley team had employed Owen Lovejoy's analyses to argue that afarensis was fully bipedal.

The New York Post, famous for its headlines, printed the news of the discovery under SCIENTISTS GO APE OVER FOSSIL FIND. The Time report was entitled "Lucy Gets a Younger Sister," which indeed suggests extraordinary leaps in generational time.

11

·

Shared
Characters

To reach the paleontology section on the fifth floor of the American Museum of Natural History, you need a key either to the doors within the labyrinth or to the Museum elevator. This is true of all the off-limits areas of the Museum, occupying 130,000 square feet and including much of the fourth floor, and all of the fifth. Niles Eldredge's office is on the fifth floor. Eldredge is chairman and curator of the Department of Invertebrates, and co-author with Stephen Jay Gould of the theory of punctuated equilibria. They are credited with inspiring the most passionate debate in evolution over the last decade.

A Museum employee inserts her key into the brass elevator plate, then gracefully leaps out between closing doors, which reopen on the fifth floor, where I follow the overhead signs to Invertebrates, an area of study that covers creatures without backbones and takes me, in this brief walk, past filing cabinets that store remains of the Devonian era, 400 million years ago, when trilobites were swimming with their skeletons as swimsuits.

Should I smell mothballs, I have gone too far. The hallway beyond Eldredge's door is largely devoted to a vast inventory of insects. There are enough specimens within these halls to document that for every creature living today, nine other species are extinct; the most successful creatures on earth, insects, number 700,000. Only here does the mascot of Manhattan, the cockroach, find honor and preservation, the latter by mothballs designed to deter insects. Like all insects, the cockroach has an outer skeleton and a body divided into three parts: characteristics that it shares with trilobites, now extinct. Trilobites disappeared in the Permian, 230 million years ago.

Eldredge's plant-filled office is a reasonably vast section of Manhattan real estate; a one-bedroom apartment within his view across 77th Street would easily earn $250,000 for the same space. There are several desks, bookcases of burden, and bold on his desk before me, a lead cast of a trilobite the size of my hand. Trilobites vary in size; most are smaller.

Eldredge is taller and slimmer than Gould; he has a trimmed beard, and wears glasses, jacket, and tie. If ever he tired of trilobites he could work on Madison Avenue as a commercial spokesman; his words glide in deep resonance. Yet despite this presence and six books (on this subject, *Time Frames*), he is not as visible as Gould, but voices none of the resentment that some colleagues feel toward their uneven public partnerships.

Paleontologist David Raup writes that Gould has been "Saganized," a reference to Carl Sagan's stardom in the television series "Cosmos," universally criticized among scientists with a fervor equal to its public acclaim. And of their co-authorship, another paleontologist scoffed, "Niles came up with the theory and went to Gould for advice. Gould exploited the situation."

Eldredge recounts it differently. "We've known each other since graduate school," he begins. "Steve was two years ahead of me. I looked up to him. He was a good model for encouraging people to think on their own feet. So," he says affectionately, "he means a lot to me." Eldredge was especially impressed when Gould began to publish scientific papers as a graduate student. "He didn't believe for a moment that you had to wait until you were sixty-five and had seen it all before you wrote about what it might mean. And I thought that was wonderful. He set an example."

Eldredge credits the context for their theory to a group of four. T. H. Waller's studies of Atlantic sea scallops (*Argopecten gibbus*) stretching over eighteen million years and a vast area of Eastern America, gave the concept scope. H. B. "Bud" Rollins, like Gould, was interested in snails. Rollins came from upstate New York, "smack in the middle of the Middle Devonian"; his father-in-law, a former road commissioner, knew where the quarries were for finding fossils.

Eldredge extended the search, driving from New York to Iowa, scouting for exposures in pastures, streambeds, shale quarries, railroad and highway cuts, "some on the vaguest of directions." He dug for trilobites along the shores of Lake Erie and all through the Appalachians. He found especially good samples in the Silica Shale near Sylvania, Ohio, and near Jaycox Run in New York State, and even ventured into Canada, along the Ausable River in Ontario. Most of his trilobites are around 350 million years old. And most seemed nearly identical in form, evidence of little or no change throughout long periods of time according to their position in the stratigraphy, which he compared to similar finds from Germany and northern Africa.

Trilobites, like shrimp or crabs, shed their outer skeletons to grow. They swell up and molt. A single trilobite might shed twenty skeletons during its lifespan, providing a paleontological wealth that would make Kamoya Kimeu sigh. Trilobites are also ideal for study because they're more detailed than most invertebrates, with eyes, a tail, and a series of ridges on the body that can be counted. Eldredge also measured length of the head, distance between the eyes, height of the eyes, and length of the tail by looking through a microscope. On the way home from work at the Museum, he saw New York street life double through the bus window, an unexpected bonus.

It was along U.S. Route 20 near Morrisville, New York, that Eldredge found the sudden change in trilobites that served as pivotal data for his and Gould's theory. (Eldredge refers to the site as a "transitional cow pasture.") Gould's work on Bahamian land snails provided two examples used in the paper. Snails go back as far as trilobites, and *Cerion* shells preserve a complete record of growth from egg to adult. Their variety in form is exceptional. Some are tall and pencil thin, others round like golf balls. When a colleague suggested "square snails" as an example of an impossible animal, Gould promptly presented him with the impossible.

According to Eldredge, Gould "co-developed" the theory, and coined the phrase, "punctuated equilibria" (Gould winces at the trendy abbreviation "punk eek"). As mentioned, the traditional view of evolution is that changes occur gradually, but Eldredge and Gould suggest that punctuational change dominates the history of life on earth. Gradualism they flay as a preconceived notion that reigned as a falsehood from the very beginning of attempts to draw up the family tree (their references stretch back to Aristotle). They even suggest that gradual changes were never "seen" in the fossil record, but were merely an expression of nineteenth-century liberalism. When reviewing political influences on nature, they cite the official Soviet handbook of Marxism-Leninism: "The evolutionary development of society is inevitably consummated by leaplike qualitative transformation, by revolutions." Typically, Gould confides his bias outright: "It may also not be irrelevant to our personal preferences that one of us learned his Marxism literally at his daddy's knee."

Karl Marx felt that Darwin's *The Origin of Species* contained "the basis in natural history for all our views"; in a famous letter to Friedrich Engels, he commented: "It is remarkable how Darwin recognizes among beasts and plants his English society with its division of labor, competition, opening up of new markets, 'invention,' and the Malthusian 'struggle for existence,' " which was promptly translated to the survival of the fittest—like Social Darwinism, an idea not promoted by Darwin himself. (Darwin politely responded to Marx by suggesting that persuasion lay not in agitation, but in "increasing the storehouse of knowledge.") As Bernard Shaw said of Darwin, "He had the luck to please everybody who had an axe to grind."

Gould and Eldredge expanded the storehouse of knowledge in the manner of Sears, Roebuck, with wide distribution and what amounts in scientific circles to an advertising campaign. At the same time they honored good value and tradition, they promoted their washing machines as revolutionary.

A 1977 paper ("Punctuated Equilibria: The Tempo and Mode of Evolution Reconsidered") begins with a historical quote, Gould's format. They cite a letter Thomas Huxley wrote to Darwin the day before the publication of *The Origin of Species*, in which Huxley advised Darwin to eschew gradualism as an "unneccessary difficulty."

On the same subject, Eldredge subtitles his book, *Time Frames*, "The Rethinking of Darwinian Evolution and the Theory of Punctuated Equilibria." Their refinement of Darwin's tenets was misconstrued in headlines singing Darwin Was Wrong. Yet they did not refute Darwin's theory of natural selection, but the pace (tempo) and way (mode) in which it occurs. Gould and Eldredge emphasize stasis—long periods of little or no change—the equilibria of their title. The punctuation denotes rapid events of change—so rapid, that within the vast history of life on earth, missing links occurred too quickly to be maintained in the fossil record. Yet their boldest statement was that gradualism was "an empirical fallacy," a confrontation to the majority of papers written on the subject of evolution, from Darwin to dinosaurs to diaprotons. "We chose to be deliberately provocative"; Eldredge explains that they wrote the paper in "a no-compromise style."

"You read that and come away impressed that although everybody thinks everything's gradual, there's no evidence for it. In a sense we overstated the case." He adds philosophically, "The worse thing that can happen to you in this world is not to have any attention paid to you." He thinks twice about this. "That's not literally true but it's the way one looks at it."

One of their contentions was there is no evidence for gradualism within any hominid species, from the australopithecines to *Homo sapiens sapiens*. Since gradualism implies slow, progressive change, this is why Gould was excited that the cranial capacity of the Turkana Boy at 1.6 was on a mean with that of the Peking Man, at 200,000 years ago, an example of stasis, or no change. If one considers *habilis* a transitional form, if it can be proved that the changes in brain size and bipedalism were sudden, there's punctuation. The hominid record remains anecdotal when compared to other fossil records, but already they see proof for their contention. The sudden change inferred from the long arm bones of *habilis* OH 62 was discovered fourteen years after Gould and Eldredge wrote their initial paper, the same year the large skull of 1470 was officially described.

Paleoanthropologists were not silent. In July of 1981, J. E. Cronin, Noel Boaz, Chris Stringer, and Yoel Rak argued point for point against Gould & Eldredge when it came to hominids. They dismissed an argument for stasis among *afarensis*, based on lack of diagnostic skull evidence, and a short time frame. (The time frame for *afarensis* has since been extended by Frank Brown's work, from 3 to 3.75 million years, a span connecting the finds from Hadar to those of Laetoli.) Based on similarities between *afarensis* and the *africanus* of South Africa, they saw no evidence of sudden change. They argued against *habilis* being viewed as a sudden change from the australopithecines, and against stasis in the *erectus* cranial capacity. (Their paper was written before the Turkana Boy was discovered.)

While several of their arguments have been altered by new discoveries, some are sustained, and the jury is still out on proof of punctuation among hominids. The analysis of OH 62 from Olduvai remains preliminary; 1813 remains in limbo. Most scientists now think that both gradual changes and sudden ones figure in the evolution of all things.

Eldredge expected the 1972 paper to have a great impact among paleontologists ("I just had a feeling in my bones"). Gould didn't.

In 1976, Gould suggested they do a follow-up to their original paper, "Keep fanning the flames." Eldredge resisted, "Oh, I think it's peaked." But, he adds, "Steve was right."

With the second paper in 1977 (which Eldredge calls "Son of Punk Eek"), Eldredge did the bibliographic "spade" work. Gould wrote the paper. They met in a motel room in Denver to refine it, featuring in their title "tempo and mode." At the time, the two were thinking differently. "Steve thought it was strictly about patterns of change in morphology—not so much about the pattern of species change. At least that's the impression I got, by his preference for tempo. I made him put in mode every time he put in tempo."

Tempo might indicate a sudden change in one species; it could also indicate different tempo among species, which may evolve at different rates according to their generational time. Humans, reaching reproductivity in their teens, have less chance to make changes than *Drosophila*, the fruit fly that reaches sexual maturity within twenty-four hours. How fast is fast? And natural selection may operate at many different levels—genes, organisms, local populations and species—mode.

Eldredge enjoys being identified with their theory. "This whole punk eek thing—it's like having a skull you've found. Very few people get to find a hominid skull, but the recognition goes beyond the general public—people within the field are cognizant of it. Everyone knows who Tim White is, but somehow there's a real aura around Don Johanson because he found Lucy. This affects the way other anthropologists think about them—though they might not want to admit it. These guys associated with the actual specimens also happen to have personalities that allow them to take advantage of this. When you think of Richard Leakey, you don't think of ideas so much as all those specimens!

"And when they think of us (although they think of Stephen Jay Gould in many ways) they think of punk eek." He suggests their theory gave Gould scientific credibility. "People would love to lay him off as a popularizer. He's not; he's a good scientist, but his work on *Cerion* is not well known. We were fortunate to publish something that caught on."

Did it catch on because they were so provocative? Some critics deem it a mere revision of ideas that have been kicking around for a while. For example, in the mid-1800s, Hugh Falconer, a Scottish surgeon digging for mammoth bones in India, found exception to gradual change. But Gould & Eldredge gave previous suggestions synthesis, visibility, a spunky title, and new data. They were joined in this by two erudite observers, Steve Stanley of Johns Hopkins and Elisabeth Vrba (who presented the idea of "pulses" in evolutionary change during the "Ancestors" symposium). Though the four of them disagree on fine points, they proceed within what Eldredge terms "a matrix of agreement, a climate more likely to produce results." Their dialogue is not unlike that between Walker and Leakey (who disagree on 1470) or Johanson and White (who disagreed about a single species at Hadar).

Once, with Gould in his office, Eldredge contemplated this, his back to us as he stood on a chair watering his plants. "I wonder why we don't disagree more?"

"Well," Gould said matter-of-factly, "we do have a few disagreements we should confront." Like cladistics, for example.

In classifying all things on earth, there are three major schools of thought (for the record: evolutionary taxonomy, numerical taxonomy, and phylogenetic systematics). Each seeks similarities in organisms, similarities as basic as backbones, as refined as opposable thumbs. Similarities are key; genealogical descent casts similarities, which is how the family tree should be constructed. Yet differences surface within each school's definition of such, to the point where similarities become dissimilar. For example, two scientists studying the same hominid skull came up with a different count of similarities; both employed the method of cladistics, the simpler term for that third school listed above, and now enjoying a cult status.

"Clade" means branch, and cladists determine branching order by seeking sister groups—two species that share a more recent common ancestor than either does with anything else. Since everything on earth is related, they must discern levels of similarities.

Similarities derived from a recent ancestry are called a synapomorphy. The second level concerns symplesiomorphies, similarities derived from more distant legacy, and therefore deemed primitive. (Primitive does not always imply early; in a sense it is more basic, or common, rather than specialized.)

For example: Hominids share with chimps warm-bloodedness, fur or hair, milk-producing glands, nails instead of claws, eight incisors, and an opposable thumb. All mammals share warm-bloodedness (a primitive similarity), but when it gets down to hair, not all mammals (like warm-blooded whales, for example) qualify. But eight incisors qualify as derived features shared by chimps and hominids.

In looking at creatures, you also see similarities based not on descent, but function. Butterflies and birds fly, but their wings are not derived from a common ancestor. These are analogous similarities. Birds do not belong in the family of butterflies; catfish and their whiskers do not belong with cats. To establish branching order on the family tree, you need to sort the levels of the homologous.

Cladists study the anatomical details of creatures, discard those similarities they deem analogous, like wings, and look for "nested" groups of homologies.

The process is complicated, the result a picture of simplicity. A cladogram is a V-shaped geometric chart which denotes parallel branches by the apex of the V's; it looks like a detailed section of the Big Branching Bush, but it should not be confused with that. The more familiar charts of a family tree denote branches tracing lineages in time, branches of unequal length, based on history. In a cladogram, the branches are of equal length. Longevity is not at issue, relationships are. Nor do some cladists seek ancestors—the apex. To classify things, they simply seek sister groups, the two most closely related. The view is strict.

"Cladism is a perfectly consistent philosophy of branching order," Gould says, "but it doesn't give you any magic. You still have to determine what's derived." Gould doesn't like it that the functional similarities are swept from view. "I appreciate some of the methods they use, but then they make this god-awful mistake of thinking that when they have a cladogram, they've got the biology of the animal. To me, to be a disciple of this is to give up half of what's interesting about biology"—the "particulars that fascinate" like a panda's thumb or the human chin, not derived from an ancestor, but an adaptation inspired by function.

In evolutionary taxonomy, which Gould prefers, both primitive and derived characteristics are combined to determine a creature's classification. "Take a concept like Fish," he begins; I hand him a three- by five-inch index card, on which he draws the "proper" branching order of salmon, lungfish, and horse, which features the two fish as closest relations, with the horse on a more distant branch.

"But if you were classifying by cladistics, you would unite lungfish with horses into a group." Lungfish are deemed to have more in common with horses (or elephants or cows), since they diverged from other fish to come ashore. The characteristics that tie fish together are deemed primitive.

Gould finishes the cladogram with salmon out on a limb. "It violates every notion of functional order we have," he complains, "because the lungfish lineage leading to horses diverged enormously: it went out on land, it adapted in wonderfully different ways. Functionally, lungfish and salmon do a lot of things that are similar, like swim." So do hominids and retrievers, but the similarity here is a pair of fins. Gould deems this part of the biology of a creature, and thinks this view should be maintained in classification. On the other hand, to group salmon with lungfish is to say nothing of their branching order. Sister groups are meant to denote this.

He flips the card over and makes a cladogram for hominoids. According to some cladists, he says, the chimp and gorilla are sister groups; hominids are sisters of the orangutan. "In principle, this is a true report of branching order," Gould allows, "and I follow them up to a point." He values the work of Willi Hennig, who developed the cladistic method in the fifties, but feels the merits of Hennig's work have been distorted by the so-called transformed cladists—referred to as "rabid" cladists by their critics. "It's just another example of taking a system that has interesting things to offer, and making a dogma out of it. In their system, there's no such thing as Fish. The category doesn't exist. Technically, it's called a paraphyletic group."

Later Eldredge says, "Steve just doesn't get the point. I think it's one of his failings. He's expressed admiration for Hennig—that if you really want to just get genealogy, Hennig was the first put down the analytic steps. But then Steve says, 'So what? I still don't want to classify by cladistics. To me a fish is a fish.' "

Eldredge recalls the origins of the cladistic movement in the United States. "The Museum was known as a hotbed" because for a while it was the only source of the method in the country. The method was introduced by Museum paleontologist Gareth Nelson, who learned of it while studying in Sweden; Hennig's work gained popularity when it was translated into English in the sixties. When Nelson returned to the United States, "he began to proselytize these ideas in a very confrontational, Angry-Young-Man style," Eldredge recalls. "So he got a lot of people upset, but he also got a number of us to rethink our approach."

Nelson, chairman and curator of Ichthyology (Fish/Paraphyletic), slowly built a fire under a group of systematists, who felt they'd lost their voice in the search. "Systematists had been in the basement of biology for a long time," one observer notes. From the basement surfaced resentment against the widely published evolutionary views of doyens like Ernst Mayr and George Gaylord Simpson, both giants in the world of paleontology (and not incidentally, influential to punk eek: In 1942 Mayr suggested that "jumps" occur in evolutionary change; one of Simpson's most influential books was *Tempo and Mode in Evolution*).

Cladistics offered an alternative to a statement by Simpson, that "Classification is more of an art than a science." "That did tick a number of people off," Eldredge allows. Some cladists prefer the philosophy of Karl Popper. To satisfy the Popperian philosophy of scientific inquiry, a hypothesis must employ rigorous deduction and be "falsifiable." In other words, a theory must withstand tests that attempt to prove it wrong, and classification as an "art" was out. Of the exaltation of Popper, Eldredge explains, "Well, scientists use philosophers for their own specific political purposes. The purpose of using Popper was to say, Look: this can be done with rigor and precision, and by God, you can even call it a science! This cladistic stuff can be taken seriously, we're not out here stamp collecting!" Such is a common criticism, loudly voiced by Luis Alvarez, who dismissed taxonomists as mere stamp collectors. Alvarez wasn't the first.

Yet with the rigor of cladistics, sister groups do not denote an ancestor. "According to this view, it is impossible to recognize ancestors, whether fossil or living," notes anthropologist Stephen Zegura, who found "a certain irony" in many "Ancestors" papers, "unabashedly cladistic in approach, preoccupied with listing synapomorphies, yet often desirous of determining ancestral-descendant relationships." Zegura also finds that many cladists show a strong bias for dichotomous branching; what if descendants of *Proconsul* (or anything else) branched into three new species, rather than two?

"Taxonomic statements will always be subjective," Owen Lovejoy points out, because no two creatures will have identical genetic backgrounds or be subjected to exactly the same pressures. In reviewing the papers from the "Ancestors" symposium, Lovejoy noted that many "reflect a stubborn refusal to face this difficult reality."

When paleontologist Peter Andrews asked Alan Walker which characters of *Proconsul* might be shared with the great apes, Walker replied, "I understand this method of analysis, but I don't agree with it. I like to see things as animals, not as a collection of traits."

Milford Wolpoff considered the focus on taxonomy "unfortunate," writing in the book *Ancestors*: "Evolution is a description of what happens to populations over time . . . the characteristics of populations can no more be derived directly from descriptions of an individual than the characteristics of a house can be derived from the description of a brick with which it was built."

The same rigor throws out evolution itself. Eldredge finds this a defensible position: "Transformed cladists suggest you don't need any precise theory of how evolutionary change occurs—you don't even need the notion—in order to use these techniques to reconstruct the relationships." Obviously, as co-author of a theory on how evolution occurs, penciling in mode at every opportunity, Eldredge is intrigued with how evolution creates these changes. "Why you should then conclude not to worry about evolution, I don't know." He expresses admiration for Theodosius Dobzhansky, who said, "Nothing in biology makes sense except in the light of evolution."

Two passionate debates involving cladistics swept Eldredge and Gould into them; critics suggested they'd "fanned the flames" for both. The first featured the British Museum of Natural History, and the second, the American one.

The first revolved around "sinister implications" to do with new exhibits on dinosaurs and hominids at the British Museum. In 1978, Dr. L. B. Halstead, of the Department of Zoology and Geology at the University of Reading, began his protest in the prestigious science journal *Nature*. Feeling that his initial warning ("to ensure the survival of the [British] museum's reputation for scholarship in its public galleries") was ignored, he wrote again in 1980. Halstead claimed that both exhibits were vehicles for the promotion of cladistics, as favored by the Museum staff who had prepared the exhibit.

The two exhibits are among the most prominent in the British Museum. Entering the main, triple-story hall facing Cromwell Road in South Kensington, you encounter an enormous dinosaur in the center of the room. A majestic marble staircase leads up to the Fossil Man exhibit, modern in its presentation, with video monitors activated by pushbutton, life-sized models of hominids (a female Neandertal is featured), along with furry hominoids and casts of skulls and leg bones, with charts and diagrams. There are interesting sections on bipedalism ("How did the australopithecines walk?"), with comparative drawings of hip joints and muscle structure. It's colorful, and instructive.

A large standing book introduces the exhibit. It features vast pages, like those frames that hold posters, allowing one to flip through and read. Lesson Number One: Man is an Animal. ("Man" meaning humans.) What Sort of Animal? it then asks. "There are countless different kinds of animals alive today, of many different shapes and sizes. In order to make sense of this bewildering variety, we *classify* animals. We sort them into groups on the basis of characteristics that they share with one another."

Next chart: "Working Out Relationships. How Do We Begin?"

"*First*, we assume that new species arise when one species splits into two, like this." Three tomato-red balls are pictured, with two arrows indicating the two newcomers springing from one.

"*Second*, we assume that none of the species we are considering is the ancestor of any of the others."

Well, this got Dr. Halstead's dander up. "It is axiomatic, therefore, that no species in the fossil record can be considered ancestral to any other, nor can one species evolve directly into another," he wrote. "The well attested sequence of human fossils representing samples of succeding populations has, until the Natural History Museum's latest exercise, been taken as a classic example of the gradual evolution of a single gene pool."

A book entitled *Man's Place in Evolution* was published as a companion to the exhibit. The introduction notes that "it makes no attempt to reconstruct the history of human evolution. Instead, it looks more closely at man's unique characteristics, and then examines the fossil remains for evidence of these characteristics."

Halstead raises the question, "Why is there such a fanatical insistence that data should be presented within such a framework?" He suspected propaganda, and indicted the notion of sudden change, or punk eek, and its authors, by seeing the exhibit as a Marxist plot. Gould finally responded, after letting a great deal of correspondence spend in *Nature*, to suggest that there was no link between the two notions of cladistics and punk eek, "unless I am an inconsistent fool, for I am not a cladist, and Eldredge is not a Marxist."

As for the presentation of hominid evolution, anatomist Bernard Wood (who described both 1470 and 1813) supported Halstead's objections to the cladistic approach. Wood began, "The broader implications of cladism are not my special concern, but human evolution is." Wood suggests that "The strengths of the method are its simplistic rigour, but therein also lie its weaknesses." He points to some confusion in the exhibit: 1470 is called an australopithicine, 1813, a habiline—exactly the opposite of Wood's studies. He points out the difference in cranial capacity, and while he notes that 1813 "has yet been formally assigned to a taxon . . . its position is sufficiently enigmatic for it to have been compared by some authors, to *A. africanus*, and by others to early *Homo*." Wood joins Halstead in protesting a statement in the exhibit that *erectus* is not ancestral to *Homo sapiens*, citing "well known discoveries in Europe and Africa" which "strongly suggest a continuous gradation of morphology from *erectus* to *sapiens*." The Museum staff who'd prepared the exhibit preferred to designate the Neandertal as our direct ancestor, based on two "important" characteristics: its large brain, and the ceremonial burying of the dead—neither a symplesiomorphy nor a synapomorphy.

The second battle with cladistics involved another discipline. It occurred on the very same stage at the American Museum that was the setting for the "Ancestors" symposium, and it might be seen as part of the Bones vs. Blood War, in which scientists who study bones often disagree with biochemists who devise branching order based on molecular evidence. The "Blood" contingency is so named because the initial research involved blood proteins. Now DNA, the blueprint of life, is also used to determine family trees. The second debate was inspired by Gould's enthusiasm for the work of Charles Sibley.

For more than half a century, Charles Sibley has been interested in birds. He has delved into the whites of their eggs, the protein in their blood, their growth and form, both muscular and anatomical. He's studied natural populations in the field, with a special interest in species that hybridize, which so intrigued him that he attempted to breed them in captivity, (but "I guess I didn't have a feathered thumb"). In recent years he has used a technique that compares the genetic message in the DNAs of birds. If he's right, what works for birds can work for primates, and may provide the branching order for hominoids.

I first heard Sibley speak on the subject during a meeting of the American Association for the Advancement of Science in New York in 1984. The AAAS symposium was entitled "Fossils, Genes and Time," and underscored the impact of the molecular clock on paleontology. At the time Sibley was based at Yale, where he worked with ornithologist Jon Ahlquist. The two began their experiments in a second-floor laboratory in Yale's Peabody Museum.

The method they favor is known as DNA hybridization and it features a peculiar dance of the famous double helix. In short, the DNAs of different species are encouraged to bond together to create hybrid DNA molecules. Only matching units within their strands bond. Heat tests are used to melt the bonds, and their resistance to separation is thought to be a measure of their kinship. The notion of charting kinship by molecules, however, has been around since 1902.

At the turn of the century, British biologist George Nuttall conducted experiments comparing immune reactions that were incisive and stunning. Antibodies had just been discovered in 1890.

Nuttall compared the production of antibodies of rabbits and humans, then monkeys and humans. The second reaction was much more subtle. In 1902, Nuttall suggested immunology could determine "degrees of blood relationships." In 1962, Morris Goodman, working at the Wayne State University School of Medicine in Detroit, repeated Nuttall's experiments using modern techniques on oxygen-carrying red blood cells. Human and chimp hemoglobins contained exactly the same sequence of 287 amino acids. (Gorilla hemoglobin differs only by two amino acids.) Emile Zuckerkandl and Nobel laureate Linus Pauling suggested differences in the chain were proportionate to the time elapsed since those two species diverged from a common ancestor. So began the notion of a molecular clock.

A sheared strand of DNA contains many genomes (a complete set of genes), and within this, smaller units known as nucleotides; a sheared strand features five hundred nucleotides. There are roughly two billion pairs of nucleotides in the genome of a bird, and three billion in a modern hominid; much of DNA is redundant information. So such a tiny sample maintains a telling genetic blueprint for a species.

The composition of a nucleotide is key. Nucleotides differ only in four chemical bases: adenine (A), thymine (T), cytosine (C), and guanine (G). All genetic information for every plant and animal on earth is coded by the sequence of these four bases—the color of your eyes, your hair, the shape of your nose, your toes, your height— the same goes for an American Beauty rose and the aphids that feed upon it.

An abnormality within a single gene can cause any one of thirty thousand genetic diseases, including cystic fibrosis, muscular distrophy, and Huntington's disease. The source of some can be pinpointed to just one DNA "letter" among the three billion.

Sibley boils the strands of DNA in a solution of salty water. At a certain point, the strands unwind, their bonds of hydrogen melt. Then he creates conditions for reassociation. (He lets the solution cool.) Related species "recognize" the similarities in their kin. They do so only if the sequence of the alphabetic code from the bases A, T, C, and G, matches in perfect order. The hydrogen bonds re-form, and two strands spiral to create a hybrid DNA molecule.

"Strands reassociate in about twelve hours," he offers between bites of a chicken salad sandwich; "We usually give them the weekend." The process can be speeded up by increasing the salt in the solution. Sibley compares the reassociation to a big dance in Kansas.

"Suppose you had five hundred men and five hundred women on a dance floor that was the size of the state of Kansas," he begins. "The probability of finding a partner is much higher if you take the same thousand people and put them on one acre." He increases the odds by adding salt, which occupies space in the solution. Fragments are pushed closer together; the rate of reassociation goes up, until the remaining fragments have few potential partners left. "Those are the wallflowers."

Sibley then records the amount of heat it takes to create the separation of hybrid molecules. The results are plotted in a melting curve, indicating the status at each degree of temperature change. There are curves for every separation, and the data that make up these curves are often adjusted by using formulas known as Tm, Tmode, and T50H. Each formula addresses a different temperature range of the status of DNA at the time (Tmode, for example, is the temperature at which most tracer is melting), and different biochemists prefer different formulas. Like cladists, some biochemists naturally view their formula as more exacting than others.

"Only homologous sequences contain enough complementary information to form stable hybrids at sixty degrees Celsius," Sibley notes. Otherwise there is a mismatch between the alphabetic bases, "because the species have incorporated mutations since they last shared a common ancestor. Thus an A may be opposite a C or a G may be opposite a T, and no bond will form between the bases." The number of mismatches is thought to be proportional to the time the lineages have been diverging.

Sibley and Ahlquist began their work on the passerines, as in the Latin *passer* for sparrow. Over half the birds in the world are passerines; mockingbirds and mynas, thrashers and thrushes, waxwings and warblers, weaverbirds, finches, crows, catbirds, honeyeaters and woodcreepers among them. DNA samples from over 1,700 species were used. Their study involve 2,700 hybridizations.

"Then we got into the non-passerines: birds of prey, herons, cranes, penguins, albatrosses," and in several instances, the tracers were less than discriminating. "Whenever we made a tracer [a DNA strand marked with iodine] out of a condor or a crane or a big penguin, that particular tracer wanted to be close to everybody," he recalls. Suddenly they had short branches connecting birds known to be distant relatives.

The DNA branches should be of equal length, as established by a relative rate test. Within any trio of species where two are more closely related, the genetic change between each and the third species should be identical. Either they had an experimental error, or the rate of DNA evolution wasn't relative among some of the non-passerines. That all things evolved at an equal rate was generally referred to as the Uniform Average Rate, but now it appeared to be less than uniform.

Sibley was not discouraged, but intrigued. It was hardly the time to retire. When the rules of Yale University's mandatory retirement were imposed, he moved to San Francisco State University, where he continues his research at the Romberg Center for Environmental Studies in Tiburon. Charles Sibley, age seventy-one, published his first paper in 1939. For his Ph.D. thesis at Berkeley, he studied the geographic variation of a group of birds known as towhees, which led him to Mexico. "It was a remarkable situation, because these birds had hybridized."

Sibley is an especially good profile for the debate between molecules and bones, or the Blood vs. Bones War, because he's been involved in both disciplines. In 1956, he was attracted to the biochemical methods that had begun to surface. "I tried electrophoresis." The technique didn't produce the results he wanted. Then he tried serum proteins. "That didn't work too well, either." Then he tried egg-white protein. That looked a little better. "Here and there we worked through problems, but I think ninety percent of it was finding out it wasn't the thing to do."

In 1963 Sibley learned about DNA hybridization, but at the time he was at Cornell "working in a very poor arrangement. The study didn't really go. I gave it up for several years." By 1973 the technique was on the road to refinement by Roy Britten, who discovered what's called repeated DNA, sorting out the redundant portion of the genome. Sibley went back to work in DNA hybridization, and that's what he's done for the past sixteen years, "to exploit this technique which we believe can help us to understand phylogenetic histories."

Sibley's white hair is trim and combed neat; he looks comfortable in a dark jacket and a tie; he has a sense of humor and decorum and speaks of his fiercest critics only off the record. The best criticism of the molecular clock is that it may not be clocklike.

The Sibley and Ahlquist report on passerines and non-passerines was published in *Scientific American* in 1986. The authors made several points as to the clocklike nature of their investigation. One, that the differences between the DNA of two species can indicate their genealogical distance *only* if DNA evolves at the same rate. Two, in all their tests, the clock seemed to tick at the same UAR (Uniform Average Rate) in all lineages of birds. "This apparent constancy may seem to be magic (or nonsense) at first glance," they qualified. They also said they thought it "highly probable in mammals," but they needed more evidence.

"We've done more with it than anybody else," Sibley noted in 1986. "We have obtained DNA from representative species of one hundred and sixty-eight of the bird families usually recognized." There are 171. Branching diagrams extend across thirty-two sheets of 8½-by-11-inch paper, end to end. In many cases their branches matched those that had been drawn up indicating subfamilies, families, and most orders. The evidence from the study of bones, as judged by the human eye, agrees well with the DNA data. But surprises arose in the older levels, the way orders are linked together. Sibley found this understandable, because with the older branches, there had been more time for evolution to make complex changes that would be difficult to sort out by studying the morphology of present forms. Often there are similarities in present forms that do not necessarily indicate a sister group derived from a common ancestor. For example, evolutionary changes can be convergent or divergent.

Convergence is the development of similar forms in different groups at different places at different times. Divergence involves a new population of organisms that diverged from an earlier one. Additionally, there are anatomical similarities that occur in parallel, for example, the upright gait of hominids. Was knuckle-walking a similarity that our early ancestors derived from gorillas?

Sibley and Ahlquist's success with birds led them to delve the branching order for hominoids. Within the past few years five different trees have been offered for the branching order among hominids, chimps, gorillas, orangutans, and gibbons. As recently as 1984, the date for divergence between hominids and apes varied from 3.7 to thirty million years ago. The oldest was temporarily reinforced by the notion that *Ramapithecus* was a hominid ancestor.

In the sixties, biochemists Vincent Sarich and Allan Wilson provided molecular evidence that hominids split from the chimp and gorilla lineages around four million years ago. This was a radical departure from the traditional ideas that hominids went back thirty million years. They proposed a trichotomy of branches—that all these lineages diverged at around the same time.

Sibley and Ahlquist took it one step further, and to their surprise, found chimps genetically closer to human beings than to gorillas. This would make chimps and humans a sister group in cladistic terms, and put gorillas on a slightly older branch. Many anthropologists had thought hominids had split from gorillas.

Sibley says, "Maybe we're making mistakes in some of this; we don't know yet. We learn as we go along. You do the best you can, and science improves by progressive discoveries."

Paleontologists and ornithologists are generally confined to the anatomical view. So it was easy to confuse a parallel result (like a long beak) to one that was inherited. But with the DNA match of homologies, there was less chance of being confused by functional similarities that "looked" the same. "Assuming the DNA is giving us the truth," Sibley qualifies, "we believe it's closer to the truth than we had before." That said, there was still the intriguing problem with the UAR.

During their study of the non-passerines, the collection of short and long branches made a very strange-looking tree. "It made no sense. For example, if we used a big albatross as a tracer, and we also used a small petrel, when we compared them to each other they were closely related." But then Sibley compared them to an outgroup—a sample from a species *known* to be distantly related, like an ostrich. "For some reason, the big albatross wanted to be closer to the outgroup than did the petrel. Do you follow me?"

I said I followed him but I didn't understand it. "We're not sure we understand it either," he replied, "but it's consistent enough to believe." Sibley ponders the causes. "Maybe it's generation time."

For example, small rodents evolve ten times as fast as the hominids, which means their genomes are incorporating mutations ten times as fast as hominids'. When people first suggested five times as fast, Sibley didn't believe it. "I thought they were using a date from the fossils that wasn't accurate. But just within the past few years, we now have good dates for fossils of rodents, dates so dense that you no longer doubt them."

They began to doubt the Uniform Average Rate. "How shall I say this?" he begins. "We were both surprised and delighted when it appeared that the branch lengths were close to equal." Now the branch lengths appear uneven, suggesting that there is no Uniform Average Rate.

By 1985, Sibley and Ahlquist began to find evidence that birds, rodents, and hominoids evolve at different rates, proof that there is not a single global clock. "I've been accused," Sibley allows, "of suggesting a universal clock." He reminds, "I said 'perhaps' and 'might be' and 'maybe,' but of course when people look at these things they omit all the weasel words. What I said was it looks like we have it in birds. Now we don't even have it in birds."

"Well," he sighs, "that was a disappointment to find out that things evolve at different rates." If all things were evolving at the same rate, "there would be something terribly satisfying about that," Sibley says. "Then the mechanisms would be pure statistics. That's what I'd hoped for."

Once convinced there was not a Uniform Average Rate among all creatures on the globe, he set about establishing other time frames for each group. To do this, he relies on calibration points based on fossils or geological events causing divergence. For example, when studying the origins of the ostrich and the rhea, similar birds located on different continents—the ostrich in Africa, the rhea in South America—Sibley used as a calibration point the opening of the Atlantic Ocean between the two continents, an effective form of divergence between flightless birds. Naturally, there are not dates for all calibrations, but just as Frank Brown may have a few missing tuffs, some of the other dates can fall into place when he has at least one tuff positioned.

While Sibley's present position is to "tread lightly for a while and accumulate more information," his initial statements were bold. By stressing the superiority of his own method, Sibley pointed up the fallibilities of devising branching order by looking at anatomy only, the trade of cladists and fossil finders. He struck out at the functional similarities that frequently confuse. For example, swifts and swallows look alike because both birds are specialized to feed on flying insects. In early classification by anatomists, these two bird groups were placed together. Later studies showed differences in their anatomy. Eventually they weren't sitting anywhere near each other on the tree. Swifts turned out to be relatives of hummingbirds, and swallows related to songbirds. Sibley suggested that many such cases of analogous similarities "are so subtle that they defy solution by anatomical comparison."

In April of 1985 Stephen Jay Gould wrote an enthusiastic article in *Natural History* praising Sibley's work. Entitled "The Clock of Evolution," Gould suggested that DNA offered homologies so rich that "the problem of phylogeny has been solved." The implication was clear. Branching order would be determined by biochemists, not by cladists. Gould had some gall; his column, after all, is published in the "house organ" of the "hotbed of cladism."

"Gould claims that 'the problem of phylogeny has been solved,' " wrote Norman Platnick of the Museum scientific staff, "and that he does not fully understand why we are not 'proclaiming the message from the housetops.' The explanation is simple: any such proclamation would be at best premature and at worst fallacious. Gould states that 'the decoding of phylogeny requires no more than a method for recognizing homology and eliminating analogy.' More is, in fact, required: primitive homologous similarities must be distinguished from recent ones." In his letter to the editor of *Natural History*, Platnick suggests this cannot be done by the method Sibley employs, "much less the panacea Gould envisions."

Gould was invited to defend his position at a debate. Explaining that he was not a biochemist, Gould suggested they invite Sibley along. Sibley set about assembling what he called the "A Team for the Shootout at the AMNH Corral," scheduled for the regular meeting of systematists at the Museum in February of 1986.

The Sibley team met to prepare for the debate. They decided not to counterattack, not to raise any points about the fallibilities of cladistics, but simply "to respond."

"We went over all the places where there were doubts in our own minds, where we figured the weaknesses to be. We evaluated those and decided who would deal with it," says Sibley. They expected certain points to be raised by J. S. "Steve" Farris of the Department of Ecology and Evolution at SUNY, Stony Brook, who had already challenged the clocklike nature of their work in several publications. Sibley saw some validity to Farris's argument.

The lack of a UAR had arisen when the hominoids of the Old World were compared to a sample of DNA from the New World. The changes in all the New World monkeys should have indicated the same amount of change since they split from Old World monkeys. Most of the branches were equal; the gibbons were an exception. This was based on a study of 495 hominoid DNA samples. "The gibbon branch may be short because the gibbons have slowed down in their evolution," Sibley says. "But I think it's because we have a lousy sample of gibbon DNA."

The Sibley team also expected some arguments from Joel Cracraft, whose trees differed from theirs. Niles Eldredge, Gould's co-author, admirer and "non-rabid" cladist, would chair the event.

The meeting was to take place a mere four blocks from my home in Manhattan. I crossed eight time zones to be there on time, setting out from Nairobi on February 6, 1986. It proved to be a day of inordinate clock-watching.

With eight extra time zones, my day was thirty-two hours long (there is every suggestion that it seemed longer for the participants). I decided to take my time to put hominids into context, calibrating my journey with epochs and eras. The Present was fixed at midnight in a thirty-two-hour day, and my time of departure, to the end of the Cambrian, 500 million years ago.

Long before the Cambrian, all living things on earth shared certain similarities, like cells. All their descendants, from hominids to spinach, are composed of cells. The protein in all cells is based twenty amino acid units; all these cells have nucleotides in their genes. Even

MILLIONS OF YEARS BEFORE THE PRESENT	GEOLOGICAL TIME SCALE ☺			

GEOLOGICAL TIME SCALE ☺

MILLIONS OF YEARS BEFORE THE PRESENT	PERIOD		CENOZOIC ERA 65 million years ☺	
0.01	QUATERNARY	EPOCHS	HOLOCENE	HOMINIDS — Neandertal 70,000 yrs. ago / H. erectus 1.6 M.Y.A.
2			PLEISTOCENE 2 MILLION YRS. AGO	H. habilis / A. africanus / A. robustus A. boisei
5	TERTIARY		PLIOCENE	A. afarensis 3.–3.5 m.y.a
24			MIOCENE	
38			OLIGOCENE	
55			EOCENE	
			PALAEOCENE	

65	PERIOD	MESOZOIC ERA 175 million years ☺
140		C R E T A C E O U S
205		J U R A S S I C
240		T R I A S S I C

240	PERIOD	PALEOZOIC ERA 330 million years ☺	
290		P E R M I A N	
330		C A R B O N I F E R O U S	PENNSYLVANIAN
360			MISSISSIPPIAN
410		D E V O N I A N	
435		S I L U R I A N	
500		O R D O V I C I A N	
		C A M B R I A N	

570	PRE CAMBRIAN TIME About 400 million years ☺

Bob Gale

the smallest and simplest single-cell organism, the prokaryotes, the dominant life form over two billion years ago, had DNA. (They gain their name, Greek *pro* or before, *karyon* or nucleus, from the fact that their DNA was outside a nucleus. Prokaryotes, in their current form, create fermentation for beer and yeast for bread.) With the exception of a few viruses, all living things on earth share cells, DNA, and nucleotides.

Sibley and Ahlquist found that the difference between human and chimp DNA is a mere 1.6 percent. Yet this 1.6 percent corresponds to 600,000 nucleotide substitutions in the genome samples that were sheared. As biochemist Temple Smith notes, "Basically the genomes are being chopped up into pieces five hundred nucleotides long, and a word spelled with four letters five hundred nucleotides long can say many things. That is a complex character with a space 4 to the 500th big, exceeding the number of known particles in the universe." Sibley adds, "If you go beyond the samples, and consider the whole DNA, there may be thirty-two million substitutions different between humans and chimps. Surely that's quite a bit of information."

It was this bulk of comparative information that had inspired Gould's enthusiasm for DNA hybridization, and the potential to discern relative kinship this way. The title of his column, however, was "The Clock of Evolution," and that issue would distort this evening's debate: How clocklike is the molecular clock?

As I crossed time zones, my wristwatch reminded me of Salvador Dali's soft clock, jet lag personified. Was evolution capable of similar warping? A slowdown among hominids was suggested by biochemist Morris Goodman two decades ago. But Goodman's calibration points for the clock were based on assumptions of hominid antiquity, like those about *Ramapithecus*, which put our split from apes before seventeen million years ago. As mentioned, this time of divergence was challenged in 1967 by Allan Wilson and Vincent Sarich.

"This is how we determine a clock," Sarich explained to me in his Berkeley office. His clues were a protein called albumin. "Let's say I want to know how much rhesus monkey and human albumin have changed since they had a common ancestor. Now when they had a common ancestor, they had only one albumin. But since that time the two lineages have split. After they split the albumin can accumulate mutations, amino acid substitutions. We compare the number of substitutions."

To make this comparison, he selects a third species more distantly related; the outgroup in this instance is a New World monkey. "If you get the same distances from the outgroup, it says the amounts of change have been the same in the human line and the rhesus line." After many tests a certain consistency emerged "across the board," with similar amounts of change in different lineages from the time when they had a common ancestor. "We don't find situations where one accumulates ten substitutions and another zero." Just as Sibley had tried to discern a Uniform Average Rate, biochemists first seek internal consistency. Then they hope their results might match those of the paleontologists. When there was a discrepancy, they had to imagine the potential source of error.

Sarich was encouraged to investigate the molecular evidence by Berkeley anthropologist Sherwood Washburn, mentor to Shirley Strum, and influential in functional studies of fossil bones. Recently retired, "Sherry" Washburn genuinely qualifies as an unsung hero in this search, a professor who (like the late Glynn Isaac) inspired a fleet of students, and has an uncanny knack for combining disciplines to find answers.

"For many years he was alone in suggesting a recent ancestry for hominids," Sarich notes. "Clearly he was influential in alerting me to the problem." The problem was a discrepancy between the molecular results and the fossil results—or the way the two were interpreted. Washburn encouraged Sarich in his postgraduate studies, and "he got me a job here."

During the sixties Sarich joined forces with biochemist Allan Wilson, who now devotes his study to mitochrondrial DNA, and was pivotal to the investigation that resulted in the Theory of Eve. Sarich continues to work with protein.

"I just happen to have. . . ." He locates a clear plastic vial from things on his desk. The vial is not dissimilar to the one in which Frank Brown positioned his samples of obsidian, about the size of a casino chip. The experiment features a comparison of protein based on the reaction of the immune systems of three species. "It's just done in a gel so it doesn't diffuse all over the place," Sarich explains. The result, appropriately enough for the Bay area, is varying degrees of foggy precipitation, for within this vial I see three tiny images, like bubbles, surrounded by wisps and a halo. The bubbles themselves are protein samples, the wisps and halo the reaction, or precipitation. "We have three lemurs arrayed in those little wells," Sarich points out. "This is an aye-aye; those are two mouse types down here. Note the little spurs pointing toward the middle well—those spurs tend to point toward the most distantly related species."

This is step one. Step two: "After we infer clocklike behavior, how do you calibrate the clock?" To put years on the clock relies on the geological record and the fossil record, or the prevailing interpretations. "You can't just willy-nilly take a divergence time, no matter how well founded somebody thinks it is. You always have to put it in constants—What does this calibration tell me about the big picture? The more things we include in that picture, the less likely we are to be wrong." This correlation is no different from adjusting the age of a hominid site according to the paleomagnetic record, but of course honing by correlation requires that all elements be accurate.

"Goodman's slowdown existed only if you believed the paleontologists," notes Sarich, who has little faith in the paleontological data—or at least the way the paleontologists interpret them. He's famous for saying, "I don't care what kind of fossil you find." ("I told Vince not to say that," laments Washburn.)

"The quote is not really accurate," Sarich insists, "I would never say anything quite so sweeping. What I did say was, in effect, that a fossil older than six to eight million years couldn't be a hominid, *no matter what it looked like*, because the hominid line wasn't in existence then. Obviously I would not generalize such a comment, given that all calibrations must ultimately derive from the fossil record."

"But until we came along fossil evidence was only challenged by other fossil evidence—comparative anatomy, the morphology of the organism," Sarich sums up. "Basically things went round in circles. Success depended a lot on reputation, who could yell the loudest.

The evidence wasn't necessarily the controlling factor. The molecular stuff provided an entirely independent challenge. That continues to be its major contribution."

At first, the molecular biologists, making enemies (and inevitable mistakes in new terrain) prompted hooting among paleontologists. "Pseudo-science" was a common slur; Sibley's early work on proteins was described as "reading tea leaves."

Sarich was also present at the 1984 AAAS symposium. "That meeting impressed me that our work had such an effect. I don't really remember this too well—that was really a full room in the [New York] Hilton, and when I give a talk I'm not really in the room; my mind is on something else. But this audience applauded me before I began to speak! That would not have happened a few years ago."

I check my wristwatch. My experiment was simple when compared to that of the biochemists, and the sort of exercise that should occur in ninth-grade science. But the earth had aged remarkably since I was a teenager, when it was my impression that all life on earth had been created in six days. Contemplating such vast stretches of time was not solely an intellectual exercise; it allowed me to think of myself in the third person. Or as a friend once said of her discovery of our kinship with apes, "I like to think about it when I'm hassled, because it sort of takes the rub off." I'd given humans an edge by fixing the point of departure to the end of the Cambrian, when the tree at issue this evening had already established roots.

The world's oceans (I am on the runway) featured a primitive recipe for bouillabaisse: shelled brachiopods and mollusks, worms, trilobites and snails, floating plants. There were no vertebrates. The climate over much of the earth was mild. Africa belonged to the supercontinent of Gondwanaland, as did London, New York, and Tierra del Fuego. Eventually, South America would separate from Africa, dividing the ostrich from the rhea. Dawn began over Alexandria, Egypt, by my calculations, Devonian time: lungfishes made their debut.

In London, I showered at the airport, during the Carboniferous, when the first flyers evolved—insects with wings spanning nearly three feet. My flight for New York left from London at eleven in the morning, what Americans refer to as the Pennsylvanian of the Carboniferous. Had these clocks been synchronized, I could have walked home, because the eastern seaboard of North America had yet to pull away from Europe and the British Isles.

I arrive at JFK at 1:30 EST. Time for the dinosaurs. By the time I reach Manhattan island, there are still one hundred and forty million years to go before the Present, marked at midnight in a thirty-two-hour day. On the fifth floor of the Museum of Natural History, one level above the *Tyrannosaurus rex* recovered from this time frame, Charles Sibley and his team were meeting.

At a quarter to seven, when I began my walk to the Museum, I wore my heavy coat; a light snowfall was predicted during the Quaternary.

The American Museum of Natural History is officially closed, the exhibit halls dark and quiet. Normally I can make my way around this Museum by sound, and have done so in the early dark off-hours, when music for exhibits is turned on before the lights are. So I know when I'm in "Agricultural Africa" as opposed to "The Peoples of Pakistan." And a good nose can tell not only the day of week but the time of day. Early in the morning, before the exhibit halls are open to the public, they smell sweetly of Windex; uniformed staffers wipe the glass display cases clean of fingerprints and the occasional noseprint. Shortly after ten on a school day, there is the whiff of children, a distinct blend of the sweet and pungent (bubble gum and wet mittens). On weekends, there's the odd juxtaposition of garlic and perfume—the former representing samplings from restaurants on gentrified Columbus Avenue, where many "eat ethnic" before contemplating anthropology. Applied fragrances prevail in the Hall of Gems.

Mammals emerge. From the maze of the Museum, scientists, grad students, Museum staffers, and one jet-lagged journalist converge on the regular monthly meeting of systematists, which on a good night draws twenty people. Last month's meeting was on the Systematics and Biogeography of the New World Crotalid Snakes; next month's, Catfish Biogeography.

Systematics meetings are normally held in Room 419 of the Roosevelt Building of the Museum. This one has been moved. I am guided by Alan Ternes, editor of *Natural History* magazine, to the Kaufman Theater, which seats three hundred people.

The room is familiar. The same auditorium hosted the "Ancestors" symposium. Every seat is taken except for one on the stage. Stephen Jay Gould is missing.

Niles Eldredge taps the microphone, ordering silence. He inadvertently creates another kind of order, two fields of opposing polarities.

The meeting, Eldredge begins, was inspired by Gould's column in the *Natural History* issue of April 1985. Alan Ternes sits on my left, hands clasped. Ternes infuses *Natural History* magazine with his own fine blend of integrity and inquiry, seeking out scientists who can turn a phrase. Over fifteen years ago, he seized upon Gould as a potential columnist by noting the flair in his scientific papers.

During the last ten months, Ternes has been caught in the crossfire of memos, letters, and comments from colleagues who would be happy if Gould's column became extinct. Eldredge begins to read the offending lines from the last paragraph of Gould's article:

Sibley's work, and other efforts of molecular phylogeny, have received a fair slug of press lately, but I do not fully understand why we are not proclaiming the message from the housetops. Biology and common culture have struggled to portray the relationships of organisms for thousands of years. We finally have a method that can sort homology from analogy; the answer oozed up on us over many years, it also emerged from a profession with low public recognition and no designated Nobel prize, so most outsiders to the club haven't noticed.

A distracting peripheral blur moves down the left aisle. Eldredge, eyes down, continues to read:

Perhaps we should mount the parapets and shout: "the problem of phylogeny. . . ."

"WHY NOT?" Gould bounds onto the stage, plops his briefcase down, and sits to laughter. Eldredge smiles and shakes his head. "I will continue to read despite the entrance of the author." Gould gives his "non-rabid buddy" an open palm to continue:

. . . "the problem of phylogeny has been solved. But then we must descend and get to work"—for the solution is only a beginning, a calibration and context for all the interesting questions. For starters, would you believe (as Sibley now claims) that chimps are closer to humans than to gorillas?

"What better way to start the show," Eldredge intones: "What is this DNA Hybridization? Has it really solved the age-old problems of systematics?"

The cladistic team is thin (Norm Platnick, the author of the letter challenging Gould's stance, was out of the country; Gareth Nelson, founder of the cladistic movement at the Museum, preferred to remain in the audience). It's composed of Steve Farris, from Stony Brook, and Joel Cracraft, from the Department of Anatomy and Cell Biology at the University of Illinois, Chicago. Sibley has strengthened his team by five, not counting Gould.

Sibley begins with wry courtesy. "I want to thank the American Museum for this interesting opportunity to present our wares, and however it comes out, I suspect most of us will leave by the same door through which we entered."

He runs through the basic techniques. He reviews their work on passerines, then hominoids. He shows five cladograms. Each features a different branching order. "These are the members of the cast," he says, taking a pointer to tick the gibbon, orang, gorilla, chimp. "The only one missing is all of us."

For his DNA tests on hominoids, Sibley selected as his outgroup the Old World monkeys known as cercopithecoids, which include baboons. When Sibley says, "These monkeys are the sister group of the hominoids," he adds, "We all agree on that," as if to say at least we agree on something. He then suggests that chimps are closer to hominids than they are to gorillas. Sarich and Wilson had found a different arrangement of branches, a trichotomy with hominids/ chimps and gorillas branching about the same time.

Sibley explains that he and his team *assume* that the rates of evolution are equal along the branches between humans and chimps.

Steve Farris responds: "The paradox addressed in my first paper is still there." He then refers to an article Sibley and Ahlquist wrote in 1984. "They make two assertions worthy of comment: DNA Hybridization distances are clocklike, and these data give a correct indication of phylogenetic relationships."

Farris emphasizes that differing rates of evolution occur in different species. Gould's essay was entitled "The Clock of Evolution." (He originally called it "Australia's Song and Signature." Ternes, as editor, revised the title.)

"The essay in fact says that the clocklike assumption is of little interest to me," Gould says quickly, "if you read it."

"Now why would I do that?" Farris raises his brows, then resumes his attack on the accuracy of the clock. "To that extent Sibley and Ahlquist's argument was in error. The condition of the data does not tell how to root those trees." He suggests that shared derived characters in bones would. "That calls for something beyond DNA. It must rely on morphological analyses."

Farris also challenges their "relative rate test," seizing upon three different set of figures that he terms "peculiar."

"The changes in the figures are said to be allowed by improved techniques." Farris refers to several different tests over a period of time with different results. "The conclusion I would draw from these little historical sketches on birds and primates is: Well, the data keep changing"—a low whistle rises from the audience—"regardless of which tree they settle on, although they somehow seem to settle on the right tree.

"Don't misunderstand me," Farris adds, "I don't object to the idea that chimps are the sister group of humans. That idea has been around a long time." Farris pulls up the enemy flag: "George [Gaylord] Simpson said this was established beyond any reasonable doubt based on morphological evidence. It was unfortunate that he didn't say what the morphological evidence was." He gathers an easy laugh. "It's been suggested that these data have settled the question of primate relationships. I suggest they have not."

Next, Sibley's team, including Jon Ahlquist, Joseph Felsenstein, Maryellen Ruvulo, Temple Smith, and Roy Britten, address more technical aspects of the methodology; their general tone is to impart information, and even in hostile terrain, expose vulnerabilities. Felsenstein, for example, points up potential places for error.

Joel Cracraft, like Sibley, studies albatrosses, penguins, grebes, petrels, and shoebills. The DNA results challenged cladograms Cracraft had published. In the *Scientific American* article, Sibley and Ahlquist wrote: "It's unlikely that the DNA-based evidence will be accepted soon. Nevertheless, we predict that appropriate comparisons will reveal morphological evidence that is . . . consistent with the DNA data." They implied Cracraft's studies were inadequate. He was about to do the same to theirs, addressing a specific tree shown on a slide:

"How those labeled species are known to be at the top of the tree is never explained. Of twenty papers on avian taxa, only two," he complains, "included full data matrix," meaning all the back-up numbers for every branch on the tree. "And it is repeatedly claimed that DNA trees represent the true history of the groups being analyzed. If morphological data are congruent with the data, well and good. If they are incongruent, then the morphological data are pronounced incorrect.

"To my knowledge Sibley and Ahlquist have never expressed a position in print that the DNA data, assuming that they are relatively complete (though they seldom are), *might* be mistaken about relationships. For proponents of DNA Hybridization, an arbiter of truth has been found. As Gould has stated: 'The problem of phylogeny has been solved.' "

It's Gould's turn. "I want to make a general statement about why those who favor cladistical methods should recognize that there's apt to be complete congruence with the method of DNA Hybridization, since the arguments presented by Farris and Cracraft are the type that I would deem negative." He adds, "It doesn't mean they're wrong."

Gould continues, "Why should we have a basic preference for the DNA data which would lead us to perhaps accept it? There's a very good reason. It doesn't mean there might not be technical problems. The reason has to do with homology itself." Gould figures DNA is "the largest conceivable sample of complex independent characters" that would give you a sum of homologies. "In principle, that's what single copy DNA ought to represent. I believe that it does."

But the cladistic approach offers the ability to distinguish primitive from derived homologies, which DNA hybridization doesn't. This was the strongest argument the cladists could have made, and during the Q and A, a scientist in the audience named Mary McKitrick attempted to rescue this, but only received a response to the last part of her question: "Are we expected to accept this as fact or a hypothesis to be tested?"

Gould lobs back, "What science is not for testing?"

Niles Eldredge tries to rescue the inquiry. "This may have been inferred from the single paragraph of your column I read." Eldredge is trapped in his role; he has his own questions, and felt the cladists weren't raising the right ones. Also, as he allowed later, "I didn't want to turn on Steve [Gould]."

Sibley begins to respond, "All we're doing is testing . . . ," but while he's speaking, Roy Britten stands up. He is lanky and relaxed. "Where there is a contradiction you should consider yourself fortunate. Where you have two methods that come to different conclusions, the balance of those two against each other is likely to lead to the source of the contradiction, and answers."

He sits down. It was worth the trip.

The contradictions within the trees presented in this battle of the Bones and Blood were not mistakes, but opportunities. As Vince Sarich had pointed out, biochemists hoped their results might match those of paleontologists, but when they didn't, they had to find the potential source of error. The same analogy applies within disciplines. This is the way science works, but that it sometimes works with personal and territorial animosity provided a troubling footnote to the debate.

In 1988 and 1989 two papers were written by biochemists Jon Marks, Vincent Sarich, and Carl Schmid that featured unpublished data from Sibley and Ahlquist's work. The data had been given to Roy Britten as background for the meeting at the Museum, and with Sibley's permission, Britten handed over the data to Marks.

Jon Marks had been critical of the DNA hybridization process, suggesting that it might not be all that it seems. His own work in chromosome banding had produced results suggesting a closer kinship of gorilla and chimps, contrary to Sibley and Ahlquist's. Marks's data agreed with that of Sarich and Wilson. Sarich is also critical of the method employed by Sibley and Ahlquist, as is Carl Schmid. With the raw data from Britten, they found a potential source of error.

As mentioned, when the melting curves for DNA hybridization are drawn up, three different statistical formulas can be applied. The formulas relate to the amount of DNA involved at certain temperature points; different scientists prefer different formulas based on their own belief of which is the most appropriate. Until 1980, Sibley and Ahlquist used one formula known as the Tmode; afterwards they switched to another, the T50H, because they felt it gave them better results. A combination of the two in their overall results was slightly misleading, and that they did not mention this in their papers was considered an error by everyone. "We were too casual about all this," Sibley was quoted in *Science*; "we should have indicated that we'd corrected the figures."

The issue will go before a review panel, and Sibley and Ahlquist have begun reassessing their data. The error is an unfortunate one, but with all their tests and methodology being exposed to such scrutiny, the potential of DNA hybridization may be honed the same way the age of the KBS tuff was. Now, the controversy has overwhelmed the value of Sibley/Ahlquist contributions, the same way the KBS controversy overwhelmed debates about 1470. Meanwhile, other scientists have achieved the same results as Sibley/Ahlquist, indicating chimps are more closely related to humans.

The debate at the Museum ended in the Mesozoic, during the late Eocene, forty-six million years before the Present. It's ten o'clock in New York. Alan Ternes and I decide to have a nightcap at a restaurant a block north of the Museum. It took the entire fossil gap, from eight to four million years ago, to get the check.

Whether we split from gorillas or chimps, the molecular evidence does tend to agree on one point: hominids began during this time frame. That's a great deal more than was known twenty-five years ago, which amounts to a small fraction of a second according to my watch.

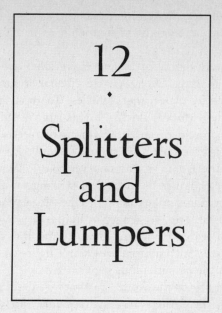

12
·
Splitters
and
Lumpers

From a note on *Stegosaurus stenops*, a dinosaur with curious triangular plates along its back:

> For over 100 years, the position of the armored plates has been an unresolved mystery that has been a continual source of debate centering upon two opposing theories:
>
> (1) that the two rows of plates were paired, and
> (2) that the two rows of plates were alternating.

In all that time it would seem that some paleontologist might suggest the plates were organized in a different fashion. They did, but the either/or refrain dominated, and what was good enough for dinosaurs was good enough for hominids, as if the world of ideas came in pairs:

Hominids were described as aggressive killer apes, then as co-operative and sharing. Changes were gradual or sudden. Primates were dominated by males, then females. Tooth enamel was either thick or thin (how thick is thick?), brains large or small (relative to what?), crests present or absent. Savanna or forests. Species were lumped into sister groups, the hominid family tree looked like a two-pronged fork. *Homo* vs. australopithecine, Johanson vs. Leakey. Lucy was a tree climber *or* capable of striding toward a Big Mac. 1813 was either *Homo* or australopithecine. Vegetarian or carnivore, power or precision grip, scavenger or hunter. It was easy to forget that this was a search for intermediary forms, that snails were oc-casionally square. Such alternatives didn't figure in what's known in the trade as the parsimonious view.

The effusive use of the word "parsimony" first came to my at-tention during the "Ancestors" symposium. Surely the speakers meant to be facetious; parsimony denotes the stingy and to some extent the simplistic.

The word continued to arise like elephant grass, suggesting a new theory for bipedalism, that an upright ape might find advantage in seeing over the parsimony. The concept they meant to employ arose with the monk William of Ockham: *"Entia non sunt multiplicanda praeter necessitatem,"* meaning, "Don't multiply the problem un-necessarily," and is referred to as Ockham's razor—meant for a clean shave, not to cut off an ear. Some scientists draw straight lines linking one species to another, saying this is the most parsimonious view, when they, if anyone, should be leery of what's missing. Some lump specimens together into one species, saying this is the simple solution, and sure enough, it is.

When it comes to splitting and lumping species, "you don't have to listen long before you hear the sound of Ockham's razor swishing through the air," notes Andrew Hill, who finds the concept blunted by abuse, "an indiscriminate weapon in the hands of those who wish to ignore the complexity of the problem."

"Ockham didn't say anything about numerical entities," Alan

Walker expands. "Ecologically we have no such rules. If you worked on beetles or bovids, parsimony would be the most foolish assumption." In the case of hominids, what began as a fiercely parsimonious view embraced by the single-species hypothesis has expanded to include many options. The news is that it's more complicated than they thought. But scientists often present only the dichotomies to non-scientists—what Walter Cronkite referred to as "the great unwashed American public."

In April of 1981, Richard Leakey's New York publisher for *The Making of Mankind* received a letter from Jonathan Ward, executive producer for Walter Cronkite's Universe program. Ward was extending an invitation to Leakey to appear on the new half-hour television series hosted by the highly respected commentator, whose sign-off, "And that's the way it is," on the *CBS Evening News* had for decades lent great comfort to the news accounts on modern hominids around the globe.

Ward envisioned a segment dealing with human origins "bringing together Donald Johanson and Richard Leakey for a discussion with Mr. Cronkite, recorded on videotape at the American Museum of Natural History. The conversation would center on the process of anthropology and *how* we know *what* we know about our earliest ancestors" (his emphasis). "We would expect some disagreement from the world's two foremost anthropologists, but we expect the disagreements to be about concrete scientific issues and techniques. . . . We don't intend that there be a winner, as in a debate, just a clear exposition of the facts and artifacts, or lack of facts and artifacts, to tell us about man's beginnings. We would also hope to be able to discuss the current revival of creationism in the U.S. and U.K. The disagreements among anthropologists are often cited as reasons to disbelieve in the 'theory' of evolution, and the insights of two practicing scientists may help to illuminate the nature of the scientific process."

After reading an advance copy of *Lucy*, Leakey preferred to avoid debates with Johanson about the designation of *afarensis* as the common ancestor. In this instance, he recalled, "I don't think it helps the public understand evolution to focus on a disagreement. The search has nothing to do with Johanson vs. Leakey; there are many people involved. There's a school of thought that thinks it's parsimonious to have a common ancestor at three point million years ago, and another that thinks it's not. It's according to how you look at the fossils. But it's not an issue fundamental to understanding evolution."

Understanding evolution is a problem. In the May 1988 issue of *Current Anthropology*, a survey of twenty-one hundred college students at forty-one campuses across the United States found that 38 percent of the students adhered to the biblical account of human origins. The survey, by John Cronin of the University of California, San Francisco, and Alan Almquist of California State University, Hayward, found that scientific illiteracy extended to a subject so popular as dinosaurs. Many students believed that cavemen battled these creatures that disappeared sixty million years before hominids emerged.

Also in 1988, at a convention of the nation's largest Protestant organization, the literal translation of Genesis was reinforced. Belief that the Bible is without error was central to a meeting of Southern Baptists, with 14.7 million members nationwide; those favoring different interpretations were routed from office and policymaking in favor of "avowed inerrantists."

During the same decade that these leaders lobbied for a denial of error, many engaged in the search for human origins acknowledged theirs with refreshing candor. It was this candor that inspired my inquiry, for there were occasions when they stepped from behind the podium, to distinguish between what was known and what was conjecture.

The supernatural, by definition, is unknowable in the sense that biology can be known. The scientific survey of the ancestral zone generally concerns theories applied to physical facts—the shape of bones, the similarities between hominids and apes, the geological context documenting changes in time. Ideally, these theories are not presumed true, for with inquiry, facts change. With the wrong theory (as in, a large brain emerged before bipedalism) facts like the Taung child and Lucy reversed that theory.

Science embraces the possibility of change by holding that a theory is never proven true, but must be falsifiable. The gist is that theories remain theories, to endure unending tests that do not deny them. So every autumn, the theory of gravity is summarily entertained, and regardless of the accumulation of leaves, gravity remains Newton's theory.

Gravity is demonstrated on a daily basis, starting with the mirror in the morning if you're over forty. We rarely see fossils, though there are thousands that demonstrate descent by modification, which is what is meant by evolution, and these are facts of change. Many of these fossils support the theory of natural selection, but an unknown suite of fossils retain the capability of altering that theory. If natural selection is "just a theory," why shouldn't the "theory" of Genesis be presented alongside it? That "God created man in his own image" is not falsifiable. There's no way to test it.

Einstein, who maintained a large regard for the powers of the deity, once chided his agnostic uncle on his way to synagogue. "Ah, but you never know," his uncle replied. These are different pursuits, but the public want a science they can have faith in. Institutions that fund research projects want results. So scientists are leery of emphasizing doubts, seized upon by creationists who see them as loopholes and often by competition who see them as delicacies to be devoured.

Consequently, Niles Eldredge finds the evangelical arises from behind the podium as well as the pulpit. "Both systems are presented as authoritarian, and here lies the real tragedy of American science education: the public is depressingly willing to see merit in the 'fair play, equal time' argument precisely because it views science almost wholly in this authoritarian vein. The public is bombarded with a constant stream of oracular pronouncements of new discoveries, new truths, and medical and technological innovations. . . . Scientists themselves promote an Olympian status for their profession; it's small wonder that the public has a tough time deciding which set of authoritarian pronouncements to heed."

Leakey was assured "by several people, including my publisher," that the CBS program was not to be a debate with Johanson, but a discussion about the issue of creation science, in which Leakey would be "one of a panel of scientists."

When he arrived at the Museum for the taping, he was surprised to see a group of scientists in the audience rather than on stage, a television set in the Hall of Man. "I looked left, and there was Don." Leakey asked Johanson what the format was to be. "I said I didn't know specifically," Johanson recalls, "but I knew we would be asked about our research. Richard asked about creationism, and said we should make a strong, joint effort to emphasize the evidence for evolution."

The subject of creation science did not come up in the program. Nor did *how* they know *what* they know. After an introduction of the two men and their discoveries, Cronkite began: "We brought Donald Johanson and Richard Leakey together in the American Museum of Natural History to discuss their different ideas of man's ancestry. . . ." As he spoke, Leakey became incensed. "I realized that I'd been absolutely set up." Cronkite's script framed the confrontation as a contest to find the oldest ancestor: "Before the discovery of Lucy made Donald Johanson a celebrity, the king of the mountain of paleoanthropology was Richard Leakey."

Johanson began: "There has been a controversy going on now for nearly three years between Richard and myself, and it specifically focuses on the family tree. We presented our family tree, let's see, it must have been in January 1979, and very shortly thereafter I know that Richard and others, but particularly Richard, had said that it does not fit the evidence of the fossil record."

Leakey epitomizes anger barely contained, his posture bent, his sentences broken: "I'm not . . . I'm not willing to discuss specifics of why I think a bone means this or doesn't mean this. I've been around thirty-five years in a family that has seen lots of controversy. I've seen fossils in favor, out of favor. Let us be . . . let us stand back from it. Of course, it's important, Don; I wouldn't minimize it. But I'm not interested in whether you're right or wrong." Then Leakey adds quickly, "But I think you're wrong!" and laughs.

It was the perfect cue for Johanson, who reached behind his chair to produce a chart of the family tree, with a blank space left for Leakey's version. "I brought along a portrayal of how I look at the family tree, and I've left a spot . . . "

"For me!" Leakey chimes. At first he resists, but when Johanson begins, "Essentially the major difference . . . ," Leakey borrows Johanson's pen, then strikes a huge X across the tree featuring *afarensis* as ancestral to *Homo*.

"And what would you draw in its place?" Johanson asks.

"I think in probability I would do this," Leakey replies, and draws in a big question mark.

When Cronkite asked, "What does it matter to any of us in the great unwashed American public which of you is right?" Johanson replied that it really didn't; then both he and Leakey spoke of the hominid niche in very general terms—even on this, they did not seem to agree.

Leakey: "It's very important for humans today to see themselves in the perspective of time, to realize that we're a part of life. We're not the inevitable consequence of evolution, we are successful as we are, but also the chimpanzee, the gorillas and the giraffe and the sloth are also successful . . ."

Johanson interjects, "Maybe more successful."

Leakey finishes, ". . . in their niche."

"Leakey made a nice recovery with that chart," one of the Museum scientists in the audience reflected later. Johanson said simply, "I won."

Most creation scientists felt they had won. Leakey had implied human evolution was a big question mark. Neither explained how they knew 1470 or Lucy were human ancestors. As one paleontologist complained, "You might have thought there was a dramatic change in the family tree—like we were related to hyenas instead of apes!"

Leakey denies any special allegiance to the so-called Leakey Line—that *Homo* is ancestral and existed much older than has been found. "All I have said is that there is no reason to suggest that *A. africanus*, *robustus*, or *boisei* was our ancestor, because there is evidence that they were contemporary with early *Homo*. However the main issue is whether we can justify presenting all of these and *Homo* as separate genera. Clearly a three-million-year-old skull will not have a large brain, even though it may be directly on line to *Homo habilis*. Should this be called *Australopithecus 'x'* or *Homo 'x'*—therein is the rub."

Now, the above couldn't be inserted earlier in this book, say in chapter 2, when the subject of the "Leakey Line" was first discussed, for readers weren't informed yet about all those different australopithecines. But this is the complex issue that was brought up on the Cronkite program, when many viewers were wondering when and if these two experts were going to prove that we were indeed akin to apes.

CBS producers did film a second episode covering the issues in the 1981 trial in Arkansas, where federal courts overruled the law demanding that creation science be taught alongside the theory of evolution. The second episode, informally catalogued as "Lucy II" because it featured Don Johanson on the road promoting his book, was never broadcast.

In the first segment ("Lucy I"), Johanson had described his chart as "the family tree that Dr. White and I have established." The tree was altered four years later with the discovery of the black skull. The black skull didn't send a bold X across the entire tree, but it did surface as a little reminder that the search belongs in a file marked Unfinished Business.

Cronkite's script had portrayed the science as a race to find the Oldest Man, and his guests were inclined to oblige. Nature wasn't. Neither the black skull from Turkana nor OH 62, the long-armed *habilis* from Olduvai, qualified as the Oldest Man, but they were described, respectively, as older than thought, and older-looking than thought.

When Alan Walker discovered the black skull in August of 1985, he wasn't looking for a hominid. He was looking for a hippo. Walker returned to an exposure near the Lomekwi River at West Turkana to collect a hippo skull he'd seen earlier. The site is not far from the "Tree of Man" where Frank Brown and I stopped for lunch; the terrain is typical of West Turkana overbanks—hills thick with pebbles, boulders, and in this case, ancient river sediments that suggest the Omo River once came this way. On this August morning Walker noticed another fossil en route to the hippo. He picked it up, then put it back down. Then he picked it up again.

Richard E. Leakey, © National Museums of Kenya

Alan Walker, Nzube Mutiwa and Kamoya Kimeu carefully excavate part of the black skull that Walker discovered near Lomekwi, West Turkana. The skull, dated at 2.5 million years old, forced paleontologists to revise the hominid family tree.

The fragment belonged to an australopithecine skull that is hyper-robust-looking, with tremendously broad cheekbones, bold brow ridges, a concave face, and a massive sagittal crest. It looked like an older version of *Zinj*, from Olduvai.

"If we'd found only the back part of that skull in Cameroon or Zaire instead of Kenya," Walker said to me shortly after its discovery, "we would have called it an ape." But attached to this skull is a hyper-robust face. "People didn't expect to find an ancestor of *Zinj* looking like that." Mary Leakey's discovery at Olduvai is nearly a million years younger, so is skull 406 from East Turkana, the skull Richard and Meave Leakey found courtesy of a thirsty camel.

"Kamoya's boy was very easy for the public to understand," Walker says of the Turkana Boy. "All you had to say is: See, here's a skeleton. But the black skull—it's nitty-gritty taxonomy and science." The nitty-gritty involved splitting and lumping—whether the black skull should be lumped in with *Zinj*, or whether it represents a different species, requiring another branch on the family tree. The nitty-gritty had to do with whether some characteristics of the skull were (in the lingo of cladistics), derived, primitive, or exclusively shared.

Walker and Leakey listed forty characteristics shared between the black skull and *Zinj*. It worked no magic. Other scientists disagreed on whether these characteristics were derived, primitive, or exclusively shared.

When the discovery of the black skull was announced, paleontologists were thrown by its age, at 2.5, extending the lineage for *Zinj* back in time. Frank Brown dated the site, finding the skull was a few meters below Tuff D, a fingerprint known from both the Shungura Formation and the Koobi Fora Formation. There was another tuff beneath it, known as the C9 from Shungura. He estimated the age of the skull by correlating three different sites in addition to the Shungura: Lokalalei South; Kangatukuseo; and the Lomekwi site where the skull was found. Brown's assessment did not leave the normal flurry of doubts about a hominid's age. When asked about the accuracy of the date, Don Johanson replied simply, "Knowing Frank Brown, I would say the dating is firm."

"New Skull Finding Challenges Views," was *The New York Times* headline. The *Times* account noted the discovery "may shake some old branches on the family tree." The cover for *Discover* magazine put the revelation in the past tense: "An extraordinary 2.5 million year old skull found in Kenya has overturned all previous notions of the course of early hominid evolution," a bit of an exaggeration. The notions had to do with the two branches attached to the stem of *afarensis*. Johanson's chart on the Cronkite program had featured one branch with three australopithecines in a row: gracile, robust, and *Zinj* as the end of the line.

The black skull suggested *A. robustus* could not have been the ancestor of *Zinj*, since it lived at the same time. And since it lived at the same time, two branches may belong in parallel where there had been only one.

"Bill Kimbel, one of the scientists most knowledgeable about *A. afarensis* and one of the first to see the new skull, acted for all of us the other day," Pat Shipman wrote in *Discover*. "At the end of a lecture on australopithecine evolution, he erased all the tidy, alternative diagrams and stared at the blackboard for a moment. Then he turned to the class and threw up his hands."

"Whichever way you look at it," commented Fred Grine in *Science*, "it's back to the drawing board."

As a potential alternative name for the black skull, Walker and Leakey listed a find from the Omo, a single lower jaw found by Camille Arambourg and Yves Coppens in 1967, *aethiopicus*. They were saying it was a possibility, but holding out for more evidence. Several other scientists resist the *aethiopicus* link because the jaw from the Omo is in poor condition, nor does it have any skull to go along with it. Johanson saw the black skull as a "clear confirmation" of *aethiopicus*.

He also contends that the black skull was no great surprise. "The new cranium has been heralded as forcing a redrawing of the hominid family tree," Johanson qualifies. "As hypotheses about hominid relationships, these diagrams, or trees, are continuously tested and sometimes adjusted as each fossil comes to light. Our 1979 tree had only one branch of 'robust' australopithecine. So our 1979 hypothesis is now, on the basis of the new evidence, wrong."

When it comes to drawing up a new tree, Johanson says of his partners Tim White and Bill Kimbel, "Well, we don't agree. In fact, based on the current evidence, we can't decide unambiguously which

American paleoanthropologist Donald Johanson at a press reception at the Institute of Human Origins, Berkeley. On the table is a cast of the partial skeleton of "Lucy," and at the head of the table, a cast of the reconstructed skull of A. afarensis. The light areas of the skull represent bones known from twelve different individuals of the so-called First Family; the dark areas filled in by latex, unknown portions of the composite skull. Other casts are of skulls from East and South Africa.

of these trees is correct." Their disagreement goes beyond this section of the tree. It extends to the ancestral line.

Bill Kimbel thinks that the line leading to *Homo* may stem not
from *afarensis*, but from the *africanus* best known from South Africa. Kimbel's view is also supported by Phillip Tobias and Henry
McHenry. That Kimbel is president of the Institute of Human
Origins should put to rest the notion that it's the Leakey camp vs.
the Johanson camp, since Kimbel's office is only a few feet down the
hall from Don Johanson's. On an office bulletin board there is a
quote from Sherlock Holmes: "Insensibly, one begins to twist facts
to suit theories instead of theories to suit facts."

But scientists don't always work in terms of theories; some prefer
to develop a consensus, as defined by Webster's, unanimity or general agreement. Others are leery of such agreement. As Vincent
Sarich remarked, "I begin to worry when an idea becomes dogma,
or when everyone agrees with me. I worry that I might be doing
something wrong." His colleague, Sherry Washburn, reinforced
this: "When everyone agrees, you know you're in trouble."

"You're going to hear about a consensus," Dean Falk says quickly,
"but I just want to warn you that this is not necessarily shared by
all of us." Falk adds her remarks to the end of a program she chairs
at the annual meeting of American Physical Anthropologists held
in Manhattan in April of 1987. She refers to a conference that
preceded this one, a conference by invitation only, from which
journalists and the public were barred. Sure enough, we would
hear about not one consensus, but two. The first concerned the
black skull, the second *afarensis*. Falk was concerned with the
latter.

She cites a couple of scientists (Phil Tobias, Brigette Senut) who
also held opposing views but could not attend, leaving the impression
that she felt outnumbered. She then quickly left a roomful of people
with raised brows. What was that all about?

The conference, focusing on robust australopithecines, was directed by Frederick Grine of the State University of New York at
Stony Brook, Long Island. It embraced a broad spectrum, including

papers delivered by Frank Brown on geology, Elisabeth Vrba on environmental "pulses," and discussions on hominid teeth, coincidentally the focus of Grine's study. But the spotlight was on the newest member of the family tree—the black skull.

"A Consensus Emerges That the New [Black] Skull Represents a New Species," a subheadline runs in a report in *The New York Times*. Yet in addition to Johanson, Tim White also suggests that the black skull could be an old species, *aethiopicus*. Walker and Leakey favor the black skull as an old *Zinj*. Eric Delson favors calling the black skull a common ancestor to *Zinj* and the *robust* australopithecines. That's three trees.

The second item of an agreeable nature at Stony Brook was presented in a lecture to the physical anthropologists by Don Johanson: "At the meeting there was a consensus that there was only one taxon [species] represented at Hadar," adding quickly, "There are still some holding out."

In the Hominid Vault, Leakey had suggested to Gould that there may be more than one species at Hadar, that the reconstruction of *afarensis* itself involved two species. If there was only evidence of one species at Hadar, the latter, at least, would be impossible. Johanson offers additional refutation. Another specimen was found during the 1981 Berkeley expedition; ironically, it was found in the museum at Addis Ababa. The fragment belonged to a connecting section that was missing in the reconstruction, "and does not conflict in any way with the reconstruction," Johanson says.

He and Tim White also studied the back of *afarensis* skull fragments from Hadar, and found that there was no similarity "exclusively derived" with the robust or *Zinj*. This is not to say that there are no similarities between the two. Johanson views the black skull as a "perfect intermediary" between *afarensis* and later forms, and lists many similarities. In a more general argument about one species at Hadar, Johanson adds, "It is our contention that there are two types—one is big, and one is small." Different sexes or different species? If it were the latter, he argues, "Where are the small individuals of the large group, and where are the large individuals of the small group?"

At "Ancestors," Todd Olson suggested there were two species at

Hadar; his areas of study included the back of the skull, the nasal area, the teeth. First he cited all the relevant literature before proceeding with his own arguments. An excerpt of the opposing views:

> The homogeneity of Hadar hominids has been questioned by Coppens (1977, 1983), Olson (1981), Stern and Susman (1983), Senut (1983), Schmid (1983), Tardieu (1983), and Senut and Tardieu (1985). That the Hadar and Laetoli fossils should be included in the same taxon has been questioned on morphological grounds by Tobias (1980, a.b.).

"Todd." Glenn Conroy stands up in the audience. "There is an impression that you were locked in a room and tortured for five days to admit to a crime that you never committed." Conroy, from the Department of Anatomy and Neurobiology at Washington Medical Center, St. Louis, addresses not only Olson, but a panel of six others on stage.

The panel includes the organizer of the conference, Fred Grine; Bill Kimbel, president of the Institute of Human Origins; Henry McHenry, head of Anthropology at the University of California, Davis; Eric Delson, from the American Museum of Natural History; Pat Shipman from Johns Hopkins; Jack Harris, the archeologist, from the University of Wisconsin, Milwaukee; and Olson, now at Albert Einstein College of Medicine, New York.

The purpose of the panel was to review the Stony Brook conference for the physical anthropologists who did not attend. Dean Falk had entered her view beforehand. During the panel discussions, two efforts to question are squashed. Pat Shipman, in the minority, is cut short with, "Let's not have a rehash of the conference." When a member of the audience rises to say that he has not a question but a comment, yet again, a voice from the stage intones, "Let's not repeat the workshop."

In responding to Conroy, Olson reconsidered his earlier study of the Hadar hominids that included details of various parts of the skull. "Having considered recent publications on the subject, I do not think we can use the available present material to demonstrate conclusively that there are two dental morphotypes there." Olson was impressed by a new analysis of teeth that suggested only one species. Privately he allows that his argument for two species "failed for lack of support." At one point during the meeting, he remembers being told to sit down, with the words "We've heard it all before, Todd."

Conroy is incredulous at Olson's response. "That's what's so typical about these exercises! The fossils themselves haven't changed. It's just like the *Ramapithecus* argument. One day a jaw in a drawer is a hominid, the next day it's the ancestor of the orangutan!"

Bill Kimbel addresses Conroy's complaint. "I would agree with you that the fossils don't change," he began. "What does change is the nature of the data we can get from them based on new discoveries and more detailed analyses." He suggests the same repose be granted the black skull.

"The discovery of the black skull has caused a lot of us to rethink our ideas about hominid phylogeny," Kimbel says. "The hypothesis initially put forward by Johanson and White in seventy-nine and later by myself does not seem to fit the available evidence. The three of us are not sure how the geometry of this phylogeny is going to work out. To resolve this," Kimbel continues, "I think we have to figure out what *A. africanus* is. Ron Clarke has made the intriguing proposition that the *africanus* from Sterkfontein [the site in South Africa] may actually contain more than one species."

Kimbel stresses the need for more evidence, "something we always seem to say," but if Sterkfontein does indeed have more than one species, the family tree will change yet again.

Several trees remained in pencil after the conference. Several scientists (Grine, Delson, and Olson) prefer to put *africanus* on the other Y-branch of the tree, the branch leading to *Homo* and ourselves. If so, this might explain 1813, which seems to combine features of *africanus* and *Homo*.

Walker thinks 1813 is the northern population of "the original, early little australopithecine which itself has undergone some evolution. But," he adds, "there's not enough evidence to convince skeptics. So we need more fossils. The time period from two to two point five is going to be very critical, I think, and the west side of Turkana is helping." During the 1988 season they attempted to search for more evidence in sediments they knew were two million years old. "But you know it poured," Walker lamented, "and we couldn't cross the Kerio River."

So they looked in the other direction, returning to an area that Leakey initially explored in 1968, during the very first field season at Koobi Fora. The sediments may be around 4 to 4.2 million years old. They found several teeth that they identified as hominid. Kamoya Kimeu also found an armbone nearby, which indicates the sediments were being cooperative; they had a potentially fertile site within the fossil gap, a time frame that could impart much about how bipedalism evolved. Two things have to happen first. Frank Brown has yet to confirm the exact age of the strata. It's fine to have hundreds of fingerprints on file, but Brown must actually trek to the site and fix the position of these bones in relationship to the tuffs. Also, the winds have to reveal bones *in association* with these ancient hominid teeth.

The news of this discovery made me long to return to Koobi Fora, and Area 123. There was a sense of humility to it all. The winds at work were a none too gentle reminder that if humans really cared to know about it, nature was offering up these clues to our past. The same sense of revelation occurred at Olduvai where I could see that the site of OH 62 had already been eroded by the rains. Those who know Ethiopia must feel the same sense of promise.

This nice sense of promise danced with one of reality. East Turkana had inspired me to toss many givens into the Suspense Account. The first to go were certain myths about the search.

Gone are the days of the lone discoverer, if ever they existed. Gone is the steadfast adherence to the "Leakey Line" of old *Homo*, if ever it was steadfast with Richard Leakey. Slipping away with discernible speed is the notion that paleoanthropologists make their discoveries amid fossil-rich horizons. They, or the Hominid Gang, may find them there, but discoveries often arise in the lab, years later. What is sliding at a less discernible speed, on the order of the Great Rift, is the notion that these fossils are properly divided by the names assigned them, or that efforts to fix this are neatly divided between two opposing camps.

Dichotomies forgive context, which, if you're studying the history of life on earth, is an odd thing to lose. An ornithologist who knows only bird beaks knows nothing at all—beneficial are the studies on worms and insects and the material of nests, along with the surface constitution of lakes and ponds, and the deeper record of ooze (what were flamingoes eating a million years ago?). Such dialogue between disciplines is unlikely to occur in a hostile environment.

Certainly this was part of the problem with the Cronkite program, as it is with the Bones vs. Blood War. As Charles Sibley had predicted of the debate with cladists, most left by the same door they entered. There was considerable glee among some cladists when the controversy arose regarding Sibley and Ahlquist's data. But in 1989, the non-rabid Niles Eldredge announced the formation of a new biochemical research lab at the American Museum, to delve into molecular taxonomy. Eldredge, a paleontologist by trade, was intrigued by the potential. Roy Britten, an expert on DNA, noted that the Sibley team of biochemists had learned something about morphological changes in evolution as a result of their meeting with the cladists.

These are the footnotes that attracted my attention, because the more sensational accounts of polarity are somewhat predictable. During the Leakey-Johanson rivalry, the opposing camps seemed to go tit for tat in scientific papers and forums, as if every discovery neatly refuted the others' claims. Now, with much of the tension in hindsight, the tyranny of dichotomies unravels: disagreements among members of many camps give a truer picture of the evidence. Jack Stern and Randy Susman often challenge the "Berkeley camp" as fiercely as Leakey and Walker, but you don't hear much about it, largely because it's not an issue of personalities.

Two major avenues of dialogue reopened during the recent field seasons. The first concerns the South African material, which is often ignored. In 1988, Fred Grine, who knows the South African material well, studied the specimens in Nairobi's Hominid Vault. In 1989, Bill Kimbel, who knows the *afarensis* material well, went to South Africa to compare the specimens.

And while Ethiopian officials did not formally lift the ban, they did allow some foreign researchers in to conduct surveys under their auspices. In 1987, Jack Harris returned to Hadar in a joint effort with officials of the Ethiopian Antiquities Department. Harris was accompanied by one of his grad students at Rutgers, an Ethiopian, Sileshi Semau, as well as the director of the Ethiopian Antiquities Department. Thirty armed soldiers escorted the expedition, largely archeological, but Harris reported finding a hominid arm bone at the Hadar site. In December of 1988, Tim White and Berhane Asfaw conducted a survey of paleontological sites in the Ethiopian Rift. Both White and Asfaw, who is Ethiopian, are with the Department of Anthropology at Berkeley, and both had participated in the 1981 expedition to the Middle Awash region, as had Jack Harris.

While some of the original Berkeley team has returned to research in Ethiopia, as of February 1989, Don Johanson advised that the Institute of Human Origins had not applied for a research permit in Ethiopia. IHO continues to research in Tanzania, though their plans for the 1989 season, according to IHO president Bill Kimbel, are confined to archeological work.

Ethiopia offers many things. There are ranges of exposures, producing hominid discoveries as young as the Bodo skull, as old as four million years. Oldowan and Acheulian stone tools have been found in the Middle Awash Valley. It's rather ironic that neither Johanson nor Leakey is searching there.

The rivalry between Johanson and Leakey was portrayed as a "Battle of the Bones" between "Young Turks." Were the search for human origins actually a contest to discover the "Oldest Man," neither Richard Leakey's nor Donald Johanson's discoveries would have qualified.

The oldest known ancestors come from Laetoli, Tanzania, where they were discovered by Mary Leakey. She did not name these hominids, but in a statement of such diplomacy that it did not inspire headlines, expressed her "deep regret that the fellows from Laetoli" would be known as *afarensis*. Nor did Mary Leakey name *Zinj*. She is known not for her version of the family tree, but for her discoveries. *Proconsul*. The footprints of Laetoli. The tools of Olorgesailie, the developed Oldowan. As it happened, Mary Leakey discovered the "Oldest Man" twice—*Zinj* was the oldest hominid at the time, just as *afarensis* is today.

Mary Leakey's tenure in the field has allowed her to see the family tree change many times. The branches for *Zinj* and the Handy Man didn't exist when she began; the stem for *Homo erectus* was incredibly short, and the cluster of dryopithecines did not exist until she and Louis unearthed more evidence from the Miocene, like *Proconsul*. The bush branches quietly, behind the scenes.

During the meeting of physical anthropologists in Manhattan, the true concept of parsimony was demonstrated by a distant source. Kamoya Kimeu had written from Kenya. "Much greetings," his letter began. "I am well but very busy. At the moment I am away in the fields at West Turkana with my group—working hard as usual finding for fossil hominids. So far, I have not found anything but hope to find something soon."

Unlike many involved in this search for roots, Kimeu had no particular desire to become famous. But he did—in the fifteen minutes allotted for everyone by Andy Warhol. In a thin slice of time from 1986, Kimeu saw his own image on an American television screen, and was awarded a medal given to Amelia Earhart and Jacques Cousteau, to Commander Peary for his discovery of the north pole, to Admiral Byrd and Captain Amundsen for the polar explorations, a medal that the National Geographic Society has bestowed only seven times in its history. Kimeu was presented his award by Ronald Reagan in the Oval Office. Kimeu was pleased and gracious and flattered, but happy to return to the field in Kenya. In Washington, Kimeu endured his first press conference ("Some good questions, some bad"); he allowed that he does not study bones, he only finds them. "Mostly it's a jaw here, and piece of skull there." Of the Turkana Boy, he says, "That was the big one."

Its veracity endures, as does Kimeu's adept use of Ockham's razor. When he told of asking Louis Leakey what these bones meant, "He said they help tell us about our past, and how it is that we are here," to which Kimeu added, "Well, we can see this."

His is a privileged view. The discoveries of the Hominid Gang do not feature in American textbooks. Nor do Lucy or 1470 or 1813. The paleogeographic picture of the Turkana basin does not appear. There was a time when it seemed it might never be completed.

In January of 1989, Richard Leakey resigned as director of the National Museums of Kenya. His resignation was invited by other officials of the Kenya government over an earlier statement by

Leakey, who in September 1988 had gone on record as saying that government officials were involved in the poaching of elephants. Leakey made the statement as chairman of the East African Wildlife Society. His stance was not new; he has always been involved in conservation. To a remarkable degree he is more passionate about wildlife than bones.

This time his protest was direct. In four months poachers had killed at least ninety elephants in Kenya; at the current rate of slaughter, there will be no elephants in Kenya by the year 2000. The poachers had also shot people who had the misfortune to cross their paths. Poachers are equipped with automatic rifles and chain saws, the latter for a quick removal of tusks, transported over the remote badlands of Kenya, through the Northern Frontier, for loading onto dhow boats north of Lamu. The ivory moves north on the seas according to the monsoon; on land, it moves by a network of profit to those who protect the scheme. Naturally such a network requires security; whole elephant tusks are more difficult to conceal than cocaine. In the past, the network has included "game wardens" and vehicles run by an official of the game department. A list of those currently involved had been submitted to the Kenya government and filed. Leakey did not submit the list, but was suggesting that they ought to do something with the data in hand.

The authenticity of the data was known to others in and about Nairobi, as well as American trustees for various wildlife organizations; all were too fearful to say anything. Journalists who pointed fingers have been banned from the country. It is unlikely that Leakey thought himself immune when he prepared to make such a statement.

Leakey's battles with some factions within the current Kenya regime were not new. They were ironic considering his own dedication to education and Africanization. Twenty years ago, when he first became administrative director of the museum, he had battled with his father to have Kenyans trained at casting fossils, not to send away specimens to England. The antiquities laws that he pushed were to guarantee Kenyans their treasures, and their own scholarship. Any foreign researcher, like Frank Brown for example, must employ and therefore tutor a Kenyan scholar.

Yet for years Leakey had been criticized by government officials for having any foreign researchers in the country. A sensational attack in the July 1988 issue of Kenya's *Financial Review* charged Leakey with condoning racist policies at the museum, and portrayed the institution as mismanaged, the two most vacuous charges possible. Leakey makes bureaucracy look interesting. His policies at the museum include a graduate program for Kenyans.

Attempts to displace Leakey as director of the museums go back to 1979, when he was away in London for several months for his kidney transplant. Ironically, he initially envisioned the Louis Leakey Institute as an international organization, independent of the Kenya government or the museum organization. But "it became a monster, one that turned on its own parent," Leakey recalls, and to regain control, he arranged for the institute to become part of the museum.

It was Leakey's Kenyan passport that allowed him to become the director of the museum. Who would replace him? Would they have the same regard for the specimens in the Hominid Vault? Would they trim the budget for research, or trim the number of permits?

By the laws that Leakey himself devised, the director of the museum counsels the government minister who approves all permits for research in Kenya. Did this mean that Leakey would have to apply for a permit to research at any site? Would things be more difficult for Frank Brown, Alan Walker, Rick Potts, or Andrew Hill, since they are foreigners?

In 1982 Leakey had described the antiquities laws as "part of the game plan." His critics saw him as an empire builder. If so, Leakey relinquished his empire in favor of elephants, and in favor of a principle. He could build a new organization, a fund-raising one like FROM, quite distinct from the Kenya government. The conflicts he might encounter, based on the laws that he himself devised, are numerous but negotiable. He could research in Ethiopia, in Tanzania. Perhaps he meant to extend the terrain for the search? Meanwhile, he was no longer the keeper of the keys to the Hominid Vault, and the Hominid Gang, employees of the Kenya Museums, did not know where to look.

Less than two weeks after his resignation, Leakey was reinstated. The hand-wringing that went on in the interim was not just a tribute to Leakey's genius at organizing research. It meant that the "doing of science" could be halted by conditions far more insidious than heavy rains. It meant that these people who search for these clues do so by unwritten laws both precious and precarious, no different from the laws of nature which permitted such a novel form as us.

The novel form of the African elephant and rhino now appear to be Leakey's concern. In April of 1989 he was appointed Kenya's Director of Wildlife, with the challenge of halting rampant poaching. Leakey suddenly appeared on network news programs as Paleontologist Dr. Richard Leakey, campaigning for a different sort of awareness of what Nabokov called "our position with regard to the Universe." He didn't mention any coveted theory on the humans that encroached these creatures; it was hardly necessary. Americans had spilled oil in their own backyard, and the greenhouse effect had become a household word. Conservation, long eschewed as an esoteric concern of the rich and privileged, suddenly concerned all modern hominids. How can modern Africans view wildlife as anything but competition or vermin?

Leakey proposed a plan where the wildlife should pay for itself, and pay Africans in turn. Profits from tourism were central. Maybe even hunting (banned in Kenya in 1978) should be reconsidered, for hunters not only paid a steep price for a shot at trophies, but they also serve as watchdogs on poachers. None of this was new.

My transcript from the 1982 interview with Leakey included his comments on conservation, which I had solicited. "If you look at humankind as a species, and the world population, then the idiosyncracies of America, Japan, Africa, Europe or Russia and China remain relatively insignificant in a biological sense. The trend is for everyone to go in their own direction, and that's what's worrying, because on a larger scale it could have very serious consequences for our species. I think what we've got to do is use the knowledge that we have and try to make sure we don't go in the wrong direction. With regard to conservation, I think that the knowledge exists to conserve everything. We can conserve the soil and the forests and the water. We know how to do it, we know why we should do it, but we haven't got the political will. Conservation means management, and the management of our own species is as important as management of elephant and rhino." In May of 1989, several Western nations adopted this position, admitting that international cooperation on natural resources rival national defense as priority.

Leakey also suggests that only radical steps can save Africa's wildlife, and proposes a grim if inevitable solution—building fences around the major national parks, creating vast zoos. At the same time, as a result of his directing the Museums' research, the Hominid Gang continue to unearth evidence of saber tooth cats, gargantuan antelope, and giraffe more curious than the present form, while other scientists contemplate a potentially diminishing mosaic, a true-blue savanna, then a terrible desert, where all the horizons of life are buried, and there are no shadows on the surface. "We're going to destroy it for sure," a stranger felt compelled to impart to me recently, as we walked amid a rain forest aviary recreated in Manhattan's Central Park Zoo. It was unusual for one New Yorker just to bark out something thoughtful to another, but when I showed him my attention, he stabbed his cane onto the walkway. "Then," the old man smiled, "the whole mess will start over again."

Acknowledgments

In many ways this book was inspired long before I set foot in Africa, by people who engendered a special regard for natural history. Among the "Survival" filmmakers, I am indebted to Alan and Joan Root, Des and Jen Bartlett, Dr. John Cooke, executive producer Aubrey Buxton, and writers James T. deKay, Colin Willock, and John Heminway, who first suggested I visit Olorgesailie.

Several authors influenced me by their example; I'm not certain I would have come up with the idea of following Frank Brown in the field had John McPhee not demonstrated the potential of this, though my habit of getting in people's way while they were trying to work was well established. The value of low flights over African terrain was a tonic I shared in Kenya with my neighbor, the late Beryl Markham, author of *West With the Night*.

Because there are several comprehensive, academic works on this subject, I chose to focus on recent research in East Africa. Many individuals and discoveries mentioned in passing deserve books of their own. For a historical view of hominid discoveries in Europe, China, and South Africa, I recommend John Reader's *Missing Links*. Other references are listed in the Notes on Sources and Further Reading.

I am especially grateful to Andrew Hill, who reviewed the entire manuscript, and to many of the sources listed on page 327, who were consulted for fact-checking as the work progressed. This was as telling as any aspect of researching the book; some "facts" had changed since I first began, testimony to the way science works (or as was noted on one version of the geological time scale, the dates listed were like a train schedule—subject to change without notice). That said, every attempt was made to be as accurate as possible, and their additional comments helped clarify certain issues, and no doubt improved the book. Their patience is much appreciated.

Shep Abbott offered comments on the first draft; Richard Milner, compiling an encyclopedia of evolution, was an invaluable source of historical references, and Rebecca Araya, a student of anthropology at NYU, a dedicated researcher. My literary agent, Dominick Abel, instilled confidence and offered invaluable counsel.

I owe special thanks to the director and staff at the National Museums of Kenya, and the Government of Kenya, for permission to accompany research teams in the field, and in Tanzania, to Peter Lauwo at Olduvai Gorge, and Pelaji Kyauka, Principal Curator of the Tanzanian Natural History Museum, Arusha.

Many at the American Museum of Natural History assisted my research: Malcolm Arth, Paul Beelitz, Eric Delson, Mary Genett, Nina Root, Henry Schulson, Alan Ternes. Professor Terry Harrison of New York University kindly loaned casts of fossil specimens.

I am indebted to Captain Doug Morey and Sandy Price for sharing their homes (and their keyboards) in Kenya, to Paul and Natasha

Weld-Dixon, Frank and Theresa Brown, Alan Walker and Pat Shipman, Henry and Linda McHenry for their hospitality. Alistair Ballantine and Sandy Evans of Abercrombie & Kent, and John Lampl of British Airways, helped with special arrangements for my visits to Olduvai Gorge and Darwin's Down House in England. I am grateful to the staff and scientists at the Institute of Human Origins, Berkeley; the Departments of Anthropology and Geology, University of California, Davis; the National Geographic Society, the Wenner-Gren Foundation, and the L. S. B. Leakey Foundation.

Special thanks are due the members of the Hominid Gang, who graciously allowed me to accompany them at work, as well as the individuals and organizations listed below.

Dr. Jim Aronson
Dr. Kay Behrensmeyer
Dr. Ray Bernor
Dr. Raymonde Bonnefille
Dr. Roy Britten
Dr. Frank Brown
CBS News
Professor J. Desmond Clark
Dr. Glenn Conroy
Dr. Joel Cracraft
Professor Garniss Curtis
Professor Irven DeVore
Dr. Niles Eldredge
Dr. Dean Falk
Professor Steve Farris
Dr. Jane Goodall
Professor Stephen Jay Gould
Professor Jack Harris
Dr. John Harris
Professor Terry Harrison
Dr. Andrew Hill
Professor F. Clark Howell
Dr. Barbara Isaac
Dr. Don Johanson

Peter Jones
Professor Clifford Jolly
Dr. Jon Kalb
Dr. Bill Kimbel
Kamoya Kimeu
Dr. Mary Leakey
Dr. Meave Leakey
Dr. Richard Leakey
Roger Lewin
Professor Dan Livingstone
Emma Mbua
Professor Henry McHenry
Jack Macrae III
Dr. Stan Margolis
Dr. Harry Merrick
Joseph Mutabu
Natural History
Nature
Isaiah Odhiambo
Professor Todd Olson
Lita Osmundsen
Jody Perkins
Dr. Martin Pickford
Dr. Rick Potts

Harvey & Sharon Rosen
Maurice Rosenblatt
Nalyn Russo
Professor Vincent Sarich
Science
Dr. Pat Shipman
Dr. Charles Sibley
Professor Elwyn Simons
Mary Griswold Smith
Dr. Frank Spencer
Professor Jack Stern
Dr. Shirley Strum

Professor Randy Susman
Dr. Ian Tattersall
Professor Phillip Tobias
Dr. John Van Couvering
Dr. Elisabeth Vrba
Dr. Alan Walker
Jonathan Ward
Professor Sherry Washburn
Anna Lee Wilson
Professor Milford Wolpoff
Dr. Stephen Zegura

Notes on Sources
and Further Reading

Introduction and Prologue

Ronald W. Clark, *The Survival of Charles Darwin*. New York: Random House, 1985.

James B. Watson, *The Double Helix*. New York: Atheneum, 1968.

John McPhee, *Basin and Range*. New York: Farrar, Straus, Giroux, 1981.

Andrew Hill, "Hominid Heroes Through the Kaleidoscope," *Nature*, vol. 291, June 18, 1981, p. 599.

Richard Leakey and Alan Walker, "Homo Erectus Unearthed," *National Geographic*, vol. 168, no. 5 (November 1985).

1: The Past and Mr. Leakey

R. E. F. and M. G. Leakey, eds., "The Fossil Hominids and an Introduction to Their Context," G. Isaac, *Koobi Fora Research Project Monograph*, vol. 1 (Oxford, 1978).

Richard Leakey, interview with author, Nairobi, September 1982.

Richard Leakey, "In Search of Man's Past at Lake Rudolf," *National Geographic*, vol. 137, no. 5 (May 1970).

John Reader, *Missing Links*. Penguin, 1989.

"How Old Is Man?" *The New York Times*, Editorial Notebook by Nicholas Wade, October 4, 1982.

D. Willis, "Cradle of Mankind," *Omni* (August 1983).

John Noble Wilford, "The Leakeys: A Towering Reputation," *The New York Times*, October 30, 1984.

2: The Legacy of the Omo

Richard Leakey, *One Life*. New York: Doubleday, 1983.

"Puzzling Out Man's Ascent," *Time*, November 7, 1977, pp. 53–54.

Eric Robins, "Anthropologist Richard Leakey Tracks the Grandfather of Man in African Boneyard," *People*, January 8, 1979.

Lucy. The Beginnings of Humankind, Donald Johanson and Maitland Edey, Simon & Schuster, 1981.

Mary Leakey, *Disclosing the Past*. Doubleday, 1984.

"Battle of the Bones," *Life*, December 1981.

Eliot Marshall, "Gossip and Peer Review at NSF," *Science*, vol. 238, December 11, 1987, p. 1502.

Roger Lewin, "Ethiopia Halts Prehistory Research," *Science*, vol. 219, January 14, 1983, pp. 147–149.

Alan Walker and R. E. F. Leakey, "The Hominids of East Turkana," *Scientific American* (August 1978).

D. C. Johanson and T. D. White, "A Systematic Assessment of Early African Hominids," *Science*, vol. 202, (January 1979), pp. 321–330.

R. E. F. Leakey and A. Walker, "On the Status of Australopithecus afarensis," *Science*, vol. 207 (March 1980), p. 1103.

Richard E. Leakey and Roger Lewin, *Origins*. London: MacDonald & Janes, 1977.

David Pilbeam, *The Ascent of Man*. Macmillan, New York, 1972.

David Pilbeam, "The Descent of Hominoids and Hominids," *Scientific American* (March 1984).

David Pilbeam, "Hominoid Phylogeny and the Hominoid Fossil Record," Harvard University, as presented at an AAAS Symposium, New York, May 26, 1984.

Martin Pickford, "An Account of the New Kenyan Fossil Discoveries," *Interim Evidence*, Newsletter of the Foundation for Research into the Origin of Man, vol. 5 (June 1983).

Hidemi Ishida, Martin Pickford, Hideo Nakaya, and Yoshihiko Nakano, "Fossil Anthropoids from Nachola and Samburu Hills, Samburu District, Northern Kenya," *African Study Monographs* No. 2: Supplementary Issue, Kyoto University, 1984.

Stanley V. Margolis, Peter M. Kroopnick, and William J. Showers, "Paleoceanography: The History of the Oceans Changing Environments," Department of Oceanography, University of Hawaii, Honolulu.

3: The Hard Evidence

Stephen Jay Gould, *The Flamingo's Smile.* New York: W. W. Norton, 1985, pp. 417–437.

L. W. Alvarez, W. Alvarez, F. Asaro, and H. V. Michel, "Extraterrestrial Cause for the Cretaceous-Tertiary Extinction," *Science*, vol. 208 (1980) pp. 1095–1108.

Carl Sagan, "Nuclear War and Climatic Catastrophe: Some Policy Implications," *Foreign Affairs*, Winter 1983/84, pp. 257–292.

Eric Delson, ed., *Ancestors. The Hard Evidence.* New York: Alan R. Liss, Inc., 1985.

Paul Beelitz, "The Ancestors Project," *Curator* 1986.

Phillip V. Tobias, "Dart, Taung and the Missing Link," Johannesburg: Witswatersrand University Press, 1984.

F. H. Brown, I. McDougall, T. Davies, and R. Maier, "An Integrated Plio-Pleistocene Chronology for the Turkana Basin" in *Ancestors*, pp. 82–90.

"Hominid Fossil Found in Kenya," *The New York Times*, April 5, 1984.

"Early Hominid from Baringo, Kenya," *Nature*, vol. 315, no. 6016, May 16, 1985, pp. 222–224.

E. S. Vrba, "Ecological and Adaptive Changes Associated With Early Hominid Evolution," *Ancestors*, pp. 63–71.

Daniel A. Livingstone, "In Praise of Mud," *Duke University Letters*, September 9, 1984.

Daniel Livingstone, Lida Burney, Patricia Bailey, David Burney, Alice Tucker, "Late Quaternary Pollen Diagrams from Eastern Tropical Africa," Department of Zoology, Duke University; as presented at the April 1986 Berkeley Conference in Honor of J. Desmond Clark.

Raymonde Bonnefille, "Past Savanna, Forest Bushland and Hominid Evolution," as presented at the April 1986 Berkeley Conference in Honor of J. Desmond Clark.

Phillip V. Tobias, ed., *Hominid Evolution. Past, Present and Future.* New York: Alan R. Liss, 1985.

4: Handy Man

Jane Goodall, *The Chimpanzees of Gombe.* Cambridge: Belknap/Harvard, 1986.

John Napier, "The Evolution of the Hand," *Scientific American* (December 1962).

G. L. Isaac, Visitor's Guide to the Olorgesailie Prehistoric Site, National Museums of Kenya.

"Who Scalped Bodo and Why," Science News, p. 389, June 12, 1982.

Pat Shipman, "Scavenger Hunt," Natural History (April 1984).

P. R. Jones, "Effects of Raw Material on Biface Manufacture," Science, vol. 204 (1979), pp. 825–826.

"Land Use Studies," Glynn Isaac's Legacy, Part I. 85th annual meeting of the American Anthropological Association, Philadelphia, December 5, 1986.

Transcript of Memorial Tributes to Glynn L. Isaac, Geology Lecture Hall, Harvard University, Cambridge, November 4, 1985, by kind permission of Barbara Isaac.

5: The Hominid Vault

David Lambert and the Diagram Group, The Field Guide to Early Man. Facts on File, 1987.

Alan Walker, Dean Falk, Richard Smith, and Martin Pickford, "The Skull of Proconsul africanus: Reconstruction and Cranial Capacity," Nature, vol. 305, no. 5934, October 6, 1983, pp. 525–527.

Alan Walker and Mark Teaford, "The Hunt for Proconsul," Scientific American (January 1989).

Martin Pickford, "A New Look at Kenyapithecus based on Recent Discoveries in Western Kenya," Journal of Human Evolution, vol. 14 (1985), pp. 113–143.

Martin Pickford, "Miocene Prehuman Fossils in Western Kenya," AnthroQuest, L. S. B. Leakey Foundation News, no. 31 (Spring 1985).

Donald C. Johanson, Tim D. White, and Yves Coppens, "A New Species of the Genus Australopithecus (Primates: Hominidae) From the Pliocene of Eastern Africa," Kirtlandia, Cleveland Museum of Natural History, Kent State University Press, 1978.

William H. Kimbel, Tim D. White, and Donald C. Johanson, "Cranial Morphology of Australopithecus afarensis: Comparative Study Based on a Composite Reconstruction of the Adult Skull," American Journal of Physical Anthropology, vol. 64 (1984), pp. 337–388.

6: Branching Bushes

R. E. F. Leakey and A. Walker, "New Higher Primates from the Early Miocene of Buluk, Kenya," Nature, vol. 318, no. 6042, November 14, 1985, pp. 173–175.

Eric Delson, "The Earliest Sivapithecus?" Nature, vol. 318, no. 6042, November 14, 1985, pp. 107–108.

Stephen Jay Gould, "Empire of the Apes," Natural History (May 1987).

"The Search for Adam and Eve," Newsweek, January 11, 1988, pp. 46–52.

John Noble Wilford "Fossil Findings Fan Debate on Human Origins," *The New York Times*, February 14, 1989.

Roger Lewin, *Bones of Contention*. New York: Simon & Schuster, 1987.

7: Thin Slices of Time

Uwe George, "The Lakes of the Great Rift Valley," *Geo*, vol. 1 (1980), pp. 100–111.

Francis H. Brown, "Dating," *AnthroQuest*, no. 30 (Winter 1984).

Charles Miller, *The Lunatic Express*. Macmillan, New York, 1971.

"A Greater Salt Lake Mightn't Be So Great," *The New York Times*, April 28, 1986.

William Glen, *The Road to Jaramillo, Critical Years of the Revolution in Earth Science*. Calif.: Stanford University Press, 1982.

8: North to Nariokotome

F. H. Brown, R. T. Shuey, and M. K. Croes, "Magnetostratigraphy of the Shungura and Usno Formations, Southwestern Ethiopia: New Data and Comprehensive Reanalysis," *Geophys. J. R. astr. Soc.*, vol. 54 (1978), pp. 519–538.

Francis H. Brown, "Tulu Bor Tuff at Koobi Fora Correlated with the Sidi Hakoma Tuff at Hadar," *Nature*, vol. 300., no. 5893, December 16, 1982, pp. 631–633.

M. H. Day, "Lucy Jilted?" *Nature*, vol. 300, no. 5893, December 16, 1982, p. 574.

John Noble Wilford, "Age of Man's Oldest Ancestor in Doubt," *The New York Times*, December 16, 1982.

Harry V. Merrick and Francis H. Brown, "Obsidian sources and patterns of source utilization in Kenya and northern Tanzania: some initial findings," *The African Archaeological Review*, vol. 2 (1984), pp. 129–152.

H. V. Merrick and F. H. Brown, "Rapid Chemical Characterization of Obsidian Artifacts by Electron Microprobe Analysis," *Archaeometry*, vol. 26, no. 2 (1984), pp. 230–236.

L. S. B. Leakey, *White African*. Cambridge, Mass.: Schenkman Books, 1966.

9: *Homo Erectus*

Frank Brown, John Harris, Richard Leakey, and Alan Walker, "Early *Homo erectus* skeleton from west Lake Turkana, Kenya," *Nature*, vol. 316, no. 6031, August 29, 1985, pp. 788–792.

Stephen Jay Gould, "The Most Compelling Pelvis Since Elvis," *Discover* (December 1985).

Alan Walker, "Finding the Fossil Boy," *Johns Hopkins Magazine* (December 1985).

10: Knuckle-Walkers

H. M. McHenry, "Conference on the Evolution of Human Locomotion," *Interim Evidence*, The Newsletter of the Foundation for Research into the Origin of Man (June 1983).

C. Owen Lovejoy, "Pliocene Hominids from Hadar, Ethiopia," *American Journal of Physical Anthropology* (February 1980), pp. 385–386.

Jack T. Stern and R. L. Susman, "On the locomotion of Hadar hominids," *American Journal of Physical Anthropology* (March 1983), p. 279.

Randall L. Susman, Jack T. Stern, and William L. Jungers, "Locomotor Adaptations in the Hadar Hominids" *Ancestors*, pp. 184–192.

H. M. McHenry, "The first bipeds," *Journal of Human Evolution*, vol. 1 (1986), p. 177.

A. R. E. Sinclair, M. D. Leakey, and M. Norton-Griffiths, "Migration and hominoid bipedalism," *Nature*, vol. 324, 1986, p. 307.

R. L. Hay and M. D. Leakey, "The Fossil Footprints of Laetoli," *Scientific American*, vol. 246, 1982, pp. 50–57.

S. L. Washburn, "Human Evolution," *Perspectives in Biology and Medicine*, The University of Chicago Press, vol. 25, 1982.

Shirley C. Strum, *Almost Human. A Journey into the World of Baboons*. New York: Random House, 1987.

Barbara Smuts, "What Are Friends For?" *Natural History* (February 1987).

Clifford J. Jolly, "The Seed-eater Hypothesis; A New Model of Hominid Differentiation Based on a Baboon Analogy," *Man*, vol. 5, 1970, pp. 5–26.

Sarah Blaffer Hrdy and William Bennett, "Lucy's Husband: What Did He Stand For?" *Harvard* (July–August 1981).

Sarah Blaffer-Hrdy, *The Woman That Never Evolved*. Harvard University Press, 1983.

Donald C. Johanson, Fidelis T. Masao, Gerald G. Eck, Tim D. White, Robert C. Walter, William H. Kimbel, Berhane Asfaw, Paul Manega, Prosper Ndessokia, and Gen Suwa, "New Partial Skeleton of *Homo habilis* from Olduvai Gorge, Tanzania," *Nature*, vol. 327, no. 6119, May 21, 1987, pp. 205–209.

"Lucy Gets a Younger Sister," *Time*, June 1, 1987, p. 63.

11: Shared Characters

Niles Eldredge, *Time Frames, The Rethinking of Darwinian Evolution and the Theory of Punctuated Equilibria*. New York: Simon & Schuster, 1985.

Stephen Jay Gould and Niles Eldredge, "Punctuated Equilibria: The Tempo and Mode of Evolution Reconsidered," *Paleobiology*, vol. 3 (1977), pp. 115–151.

J. E. Cronin, N. T. Boaz, C. B. Stringer, and Y. Rak, "Tempo and Mode in Hominid Evolution," *Nature*, vol. 292, no. 5788, July 9, 1981, pp. 113–122.

Correspondence of Halstead, Gould, and Wood, *Nature*, vol. 288, November 20,

1980, p. 208; vol. 289, December 4, 1980, p. 430; vol. 289, January 1, 1981, p. 8; vol. 289, February 26, 1981, p. 742.

Stephen Jay Gould, "The Clock of Evolution," *Natural History* (April 1985).

Natural History, "Letters to the Editor" (August 1985).

British Museum (Natural History), *Man's Place in Evolution*. Cambridge: Cambridge University Press, 1980.

Owen Lovejoy, from a review of *Ancestors, The Hard Evidence* in *Science*, May 23, 1986, p. 1026.

Stephen L. Zegura, "Hominid Origins: Monophyly, Morphology, and Molecules," Anthropology Department and Genetics Program, University of Arizona, Tucson; as presented at the Symposium on Hominid Evolution, 85th Annual Meeting of American Anthropological Association, Philadelphia, December 7, 1986.

John Reader, *The Rise of Life*. New York: Knopf, 1986.

"The Ape in Your Past," *Discover* (July 1983), pp. 22–40.

Charles G. Sibley and Jon E. Ahlquist, "Reconstructing Bird Phylogeny by Comparing DNA's," *Scientific American* (February 1986).

Morris Goodman, Mark L. Weiss, and John Czelusniak, "Molecular Evolution Above the Species Level: Branching Patterns, Rates, and Mechanisms," *Systematic Zoology*, vol. 31 (1982), pp. 376–399.

Vincent M. Sarich and Allan C. Wilson, "Immunological Time Scale for Hominid Evolution," *Science*, vol. 158, September 14, 1967, pp. 1200–1203.

V. M. Sarich, "Retrospective on Hominoid Macromolecular Systematics," *New Interpretations of Ape and Human Ancestry*, edited by Russell L. Cochon and Robert S. Corruccini. New York: Plenum Publishing Corp., 1983.

Motoo Kimura, *Neutral Theory of Molecular Evolution*. Cambridge: Cambridge University Press, 1985.

Charles G. Sibley and Jon E. Ahlquist, "DNA Hybridization Evidence of Hominoid Phylogeny: Results from an Expanded Data Set," *Journal of Molecular Evolution*, vol. 26 (1987), pp. 99–121.

Roger Lewin, "Conflict Over DNA Clock Results," *Science*, vol. 241, September 30, 1988.

Jon Marks, Carl W. Schmid, and Vincent M. Sarich, "DNA Hybridization as a Guide to Phylogeny: Relations of the Hominoidea," *Journal of Human Evolution*, vol. 17 (1988), pp. 769–786.

Joel Cracraft, "DNA Hybridization and Avian Phylogenetics," *Evolutionary Biology*, vol. 21, Plenum, 1987.

12: Splitters and Lumpers

Andrew Hill, "Ockham Bearded," *New Scientist*, December 6, 1979.

Niles Eldredge, "Creationism Isn't Science," *The New Republic*, vol. 184, pp. 15–17, April 4, 1981.

John E. Cronin and Alan J. Almquist, "Fact, Fancy and Myth on Human Evolution," *Current Anthropology*, vol. 29, (May 1988), no. 3, June 1988, pp. 520–522.

Peter Steinfels, "Struggle in a Church. Southern Baptist Conservative Wing Tries to Isolate Its Doctrinal Enemies," *The New York Times*, June 20, 1988.

"Evolution Theory Stands Tall Without Reservation" in "Letters to the Editor," *The New York Times*, June 29, 1987.

A. Walker, R. E. Leakey, J. M. Harris, and F. H. Brown, "2.5 Myr *Australopithecus boisei* from West of Lake Turkana, Kenya," *Nature*, vol. 322, no. 6079, August 7, 1986, pp. 517–521.

Roger Lewin, "New Fossil Upsets Human Family," *Science*, vol. 233 (1986), pp. 720–721.

Pat Shipman, "Baffling Limb on the Family Tree," *Discover* (September 1986).

Frederick Grine, ed., *Evolutionary History of the Robust Australopithecines*. Chicago: Aldine Publishing Co., 1989.

April 20, 1981, letter to Jack Macrae III, E. P. Dutton Publishers, from Jonathan Ward, Executive Producer, "Universe."

John Noble Wilford, "New Skull Finding Challenges View," *The New York Times*, August 7, 1986.

John Noble Wilford, "A Consensus Emerges That the New Skull Represents a New Species," *The New York Times*, April 14, 1987.

Donald Johanson Lecture to the Annual Meeting of Physical Anthropologists, New York, April 3, 1987.

"The Museum's White Elephant," Kenya *Financial Review*, July 25, 1988.

Ian Tattersall, Eric Delson, and John Van Couvering, eds., *Encyclopedia of Human Evolution and Prehistory*. New York: Garland Publishing, 1988.

A Partial Listing
of Fossil Discoveries
Made by
the Hominid Gang

Kamoya Kimeu	KNM-*WT 15000 "The Turkana Boy" *Homo erectus* skeleton Nariokotome Area III, 1984
	KNM-*ER 1813, skull, Area 123, East Turkana, 1973
	KNM-ER 993, right femur, Area 1, 1971
	KNM-ER 999, left femur, Area 6, 1971
	KNM-ER 1463, right femur, Area 1, 1972
	KNM-ER 1469, part of lower jaw, Area 131, 1972
Mwongela Muoka	KNM-ER 407, skull, Area 10, 1969

Wambua Mangao	KNM-WT 16999, skull, Kalodirr, 1986
	KNM-ER 1477, part of lower jaw, Area 105, 1972
	KNM-ER 2602, cranial fragments, Area 117, 1974
Manudo Muluila	KNM-ER 1482, part of lower jaw, Area 131, 1972
Nzube Mutiwa	KNM-WT 17400, skull, Naiyena Engol, 1986
	KNM-ER 405, upper jaw, Area 105, 1968
	KNM-ER 1464, complete right talus, Area 6, 1972
Harrison Mutua	KNM-ER 732, partial skull, Area 10, 1970
	KNM-ER 739, right humerus, Area 1, 1970
	KNM-ER 820, lower jaw, Area 1, 1971
Bernard Ngeneo	KNM-ER 1470, skull, Area 131, 1972
	KNM-ER 738, partial femur, Area 105, 1970 (featured in foreground on book cover)
	KNM-ER 1590, partial skull, Area 12, 1972
	KNM-ER 818, part of a lower jaw, Area 6, 1971
	KNM-ER 992, lower jaw, Area 3, 1971
K. Kitibi	KNM-ER 810, part of lower jaw, Area 104, 1971
J. Kimengech	KNM-ER 1500, partial hominid skeleton, Area 130, 1972
Kiptalam Cheboi	KNM-TH 13150, part of lower jaw, Tugen Hills, 1984

NOTE: The accession code denotes KNM (for Kenya National Museums), WT (for West Turkana), ER (for East Turkana, formerly East Rudolf), and TH (for Tugen Hills, near Lake Baringo).

Others working alongside the Gang made significant hominid discoveries:

Richard Leakey (skull ER 406) Alan Walker (skull WT 17000) John Harris (ER 1472, right femur, Area 131, 1972) Meave Leakey (ER 803, partial skeleton, Area 8, 1971) and Paul Abell (skull ER 1805, Area 130, 1973)

Index